PENGUIN BOOKS

LOOT!

Eddie Hobbs is probably best-known for his award-winning RTÉ One series, *Show Me The Money*, and for the blockbuster social and economic polemic, *Rip-Off Republic*. But long before his TV work Eddie campaigned on a range of personal finance issues. He is an independent financial consultant by profession and frequent writer and commentator in the Irish media. Eddie is married with four children and lives in County Kildare. His website is www.eddiehobbs.com.

Loot!

The informed guide to your SSIA and other investments

EDDIE HOBBS

PENGUIN BOOKS

PENGUIN BOOKS

Published by the Penguin Group
Penguin Books Ltd, 80 Strand, London WC2R ORL, England
Penguin Group (USA) Inc., 375 Hudson Street, New York, New York 10014, USA
Penguin Group (Canada), 90 Eglinton Avenue East, Suite 700, Toronto, Ontario, Canada M4P 2Y3
(a division of Pearson Penguin Canada Inc.)
Penguin Ireland, 25 St Stephen's Green, Dublin 2, Ireland
(a division of Penguin Books Ltd)
Penguin Group (Australia), 250 Camberwell Road, Camberwell, Victoria 3124, Australia
(a division of Pearson Australia Group Pty Ltd)
Penguin Books India Pvt Ltd, 11 Community Centre, Panchsheel Park, New Delhi – 110 017, India
Penguin Group (NZ), 67 Apollo Drive, Mairangi Bay, Auckland 1310, New Zealand
(a division of Pearson New Zealand Ltd)
Penguin Books (South Africa) (Pty) Ltd, 24 Sturdee Avenue, Rosebank, Johannesburg 2196, South Africa

Penguin Books Ltd, Registered Offices: 80 Strand, London WC2R ORL, England

www.penguin.com

First published by Penguin Ireland 2006
Published in Penguin Books 2007
1

Typeset by Rowland Phototypesetting Ltd, Bury St Edmunds, Suffolk
Printed in England by Clays Ltd, St Ives plc

ISBN 978-1-844-88142-0

Contents

Foreword

When I sat down to pen the introduction to *Loot!* I wondered where to begin the book and my relationship with you, the reader. I thought the best place to start would be with a frank statement: to be honest, and I think most writers would agree, writing specialist books in a market as small as Ireland isn't something you'd do unless you're pretty skint – something else must drive the keyboard. So what can I tell you about the origins of *Loot!*, a book I've been threatening to write for many years?

Back in the bad old days the Life Insurance industry and lenders ganged up in a Faustian pact to make a ton of money by flogging high cost investments with all the transparency of mass concrete to borrowers eager for a smart new way to repay their home mortgages. Commonly called the 'endowment mortgage', this innovation was doomed from the start, having little likelihood of bettering the common repayment mortgage. Of course, no one was too interested in making that observation aloud because everyone was on the pig's back – everyone, that is, except the consumer, who paid through the nose for the excessive costs and hidden sales commissions. It simply wasn't fair.

Around that time I made my first public outing when I wrote a highly critical report of the situation. The report was published in 1993 and greeted with the kind of welcome a sniffer dog could expect on a smuggler's yacht. Subsequently, an industry conference was called in an effort to counter the criticisms being levelled by a media scenting blood. I sneaked in at the back to hear what the reaction would be: for forty minutes I listened as the conference speakers tore strips out of my independent report – to the delight of the sales audience. That's when I popped up at the back, roaming mike in hand, to provoke a debate. After a short technical joust the next speaker from the floor took the mike and turned towards me. What he had to say is one of the main reasons why I wrote *Loot!*

In simple terms, I was charged with treachery, with turning against my own 'community'. I'll never forget it! There was not a dicky bird about the facts, it was simply a tirade about protecting 'the community', which was defined as a coterie of manufacturers, such as life offices and banks, and distributors, like brokers, agents and direct sales forces. The consumer was excluded from this 'happy family', regarded merely as a sales target – in the same way, I suspect, as a man with a dart considers a dartboard a target. For me, that was no way to do business with anyone. From then on I guess I became an outsider, frequently locking horns with industry lobby groups, and later the Government, over the high costs of living in Ireland, especially those being charged by protected markets and contributing to lifestyle debt at sky-high credit rates.

But enough of the past: the important question for you is why you bought the book and what you can reasonably expect from it?

Perhaps you bought this book because, like many people, you regard the whole financial sector, with its archaic language and jargon, as inscrutable and somewhat intimidating, at best, and at its worst like a conspiracy against the uninformed consumer. It's obviously very frustrating because you know you can't go through life without handing over huge dollops of your trust and your hard-earned cash to the financial industry, in return for which you want good returns, good service and value for money – but how do you measure these without insider knowledge? That's the conundrum, isn't it?

Well, together we're going to change all that because *Loot!* will demystify money for you. That's my promise to you. You don't have to spend the rest of your life worried about whether or not you can trust financial firms, instead you can learn what they know, how they make money, and more. Just think about the financial freedom and well-being you'll get from knowing how money really works, from no longer feeling intimidated by fast-talking investment experts, from being able to keep your focus and not be thrown by the latest media headline or sales fashion, from being able to assess products according to their underlying assets and understand their potential, from knowing how you can become financially independent over the course of your working life! What you have to do is to take the book step by step. Put it down if it's getting a bit heavy, write some notes, go back over what you're unclear about and when you're finished and realise that it's all manageable, I hope you'll see *Loot!* as the starting point of a lifelong habit of reading business, investment and economic stories with a new sense of understanding and insight.

Loot! doesn't have all the answers, far from it, but what I can bring you is my experiences from inside and outside the financial industry over nearly three decades. I've done what I can to simplify the world of money, including supplying definitions at the start of each chapter for words that may be unfamiliar. Remember, it's all about knowledge and confidence in your knowledge: you have as much ability to make money as the next person, even if the next person is an investment advisor! It's just a matter of working through the basic information and building on it.

Welcome to *Loot!* and I hope you enjoy the trip!

Eddie Hobbs

PART ONE

Your SSIA

CHAPTER 1

Getting the Loot!

Heartiest congratulations for saving diligently in St Charlie's SSIA scheme for five years, and spare a thought for our erstwhile Minister for Finance as he toils over his new brief in Brussels after Bertie's conversion to socialism! So now it's shortly to be within your grasp, the Holy Grail of investments: a 25% top-up from State coffers and a modest 23% tax on profits and just on the cusp of a general election, too. You couldn't have scripted it!

Just imagine, a staggering 1.2 million savers signed up and stashed away up to €254 per month for sixty months, amounting to a whopping total payout of over €14 billion! That's a lot of bananas, with many savers expecting close to €20,000 and couples close to €40,000 worth of State-sponsored loot. Of course, the SSIA is not the only saving or investments held by many scheme members, but it does mean that the year 2006–2007 will be unique in Irish social history as the year of The Big Review, a time when thousands of Irish families and singles will ponder the Big Question in Life: will I spend it, or invest it? Will I live a little better today, or park it away until tomorrow? And there will be a deluge (that's the old Latin name for a flood) of contradictory advice to contend with, coming from travel agents to credit unions, from car salesmen to auctioneers, all baying for the stash.

This is where a little down-time comes in handy, a little time to take a deep breath, hold your horses and think. You need to think carefully about your nest-egg and the best way to use it. That's what Part 1 is all about: considering your options. But first things first: you need to get your hands on your savings. Here's how to do that.

First, make sure your SSIA provider has your correct address, especially if you've moved house in the past few years. Secondly, ask for a statement and make sure all of your contributions have been invested. Thirdly, you can expect to receive a form from your SSIA provider three months prior to maturity called a **SSIA4 form**.

What you must sign to get your SSIA money at maturity

In order to claim the money you must fill in the SSIA4 form, which is a legal declaration stating that you still qualify for the fund. You probably don't remember by now, but you filled in just such a form at the start of the scheme. (You may not have noticed this in the midst of the goldrush given that many of us left it until the last minute, which explains why 70% of the scheme won't mature until 2007. It might also explain why 80% opted for SSIA deposits over SSIA equity accounts and mostly chose the banks that paid the least amount of interest. But that's another story!)

There has been a bit of fuss around the question of getting the money out, but it's very straightforward. The declaration you will sign upon maturity of your fund simply confirms that you qualify to hold onto all the Government money paid into your account without facing a clawback through a 23% tax charge. This means that the tax charge will apply only to growth and not to capital invested.

That means you must declare that:

- you had only one SSIA at any given time;
- you are the person who owns the money invested;
- you were resident, or ordinarily resident, in the State since the start of the scheme;
- you funded the scheme from your own resources rather than through borrowings;
- you didn't pledge or assign the scheme as security for a loan;
- that everything you've signed off is true and not a fairytale.

Do make sure you get it right because a false declaration is a tax offence that could attract a fine of about €1,900, or up to six months in the slammer! So unless you want your spouse perfecting the art of baking cakes with files in them, take the time to fill out the form fully and correctly.

Just to remind you, when you took out your SSIA scheme you signed a declaration that stated:

- you had only one SSIA account;
- you owned the money going into it;
- you were resident in the State;
- you would subscribe from funds available to you, or to your spouse, from your own resources without recourse to borrowing or the deferral of repayments on existing borrowings;
- you would not assign or pledge your SSIA scheme as security for a loan;
- you would inform the Qualifying Savings Manager (bank, life office or credit union) if your declaration ceased to be materially correct.

Your SSIA provider is obliged to inform the Revenue Commissioners if it has reasonable grounds to suspect that the terms under which your SSIA scheme commenced were not complied with, so don't expect blind eyes turned to accounts opened up for under-18s or for non-residents. Being resident in the State means you live in the Republic of Ireland full-time, which means more than 183 days in a tax year. If you've been resident in Ireland for at least three of the five years, you'll still qualify because you are deemed to be ordinarily resident for a further three years after leaving this beautiful, sunny and dry country for something wetter! Residency rules can be complex so if you're not sure, ring your tax inspector – they just love those calls.

That's it, then. Once you've filled in your declaration form – correctly – the loot is in the bag. Well done! The next thing to do is not to race to the nearest forecourt or travel agency with it all tucked under your arm, but to sit down and examine the question of what you want to do with this money – and, more importantly, what you want this money to do for you.

CHAPTER 2

Blow It! Live Today, Pay Tomorrow

Glossary

- **Working asset:** All of your investing assets, not including your home(s), cars, etc.
- **Equity (in homes):** Your share -what you'd be left with if you sold and paid off the mortgage.
- **Asset cycle:** The natural trends in asset values up and down.
- **Soft landing:** A gentle flattening of returns after rapid growth. Opposite to a hard landing, where values crash and returns are negative.
- **Gearing up:** Borrowing more money so the ratio between the bank debt and your share in an asset is higher.
- **Rental yield:** The rental income divided by the acquisition cost of the property.

Look, it's pretty much written in stone: lots and lots of people can't wait to get their hands on the SSIA loot and blow it on current consumption. Hell, even Governments do the same thing with tax windfalls so we shouldn't be too surprised! I know it doesn't matter a whit that some clown in the media, or on the radio, or in a book like *Loot!* is urging continued investment: the spending boom is still going to happen. It's inevitable. Why do you think car sales rooms the length and breadth of the country are getting makeovers and why new car sales as early as January 2006 have gone through the roof!

Nonetheless, the fact that you've gone to the trouble of buying and reading *Loot!* means you're not totally convinced by the spendies and are searching for arguments to present to your nearest and dearest to avoid blowing the pot, tempting though that is. But one way or another the spend, spend, spend agenda will arise, so we'll look at the most seductive options and you can decide if it's going to be indulgence . . . or celibacy.

Deciding to spend the savings

For those thinking of spending the SSIA pot the first question to ask yourself is: do you need the money over the long term? If you are already buying assets at the proper rate, or you have already accumulated sufficient assets that make you financially independent, then go ahead and blow the money. Enjoy it! Take the world cruise, buy art, jewellery and the best home movie system around – whatever makes you happy.

If, on the other hand, you will need the money later in life, think very carefully before you spend a cent of it because this could be the last-chance saloon to add something valuable to your State pension. Remember, you have a number of options to make the money work in the long term and you have already acquired the savings habit, so it shouldn't be too painful to stick with it.

So, what are the temptations? Here are the pronouncements you'll hear most frequently in relation to the SSIA:

1. 'I'm going to invest in a new car'

Cars are not a working asset and are probably just about the worst 'investment' you can buy with your money. Sure, in a country with a poor public transport system we all need cars to get around, but when you buy a new car bear in mind the substantial loss in the first year, caused largely by Vehicle Registration Tax (VRT) and Value-added Tax (VAT). The effects of both VRT and VAT account for, variously, between 50% and 70% of the pre-tax value of a new car. So, having saved assiduously for five years and taken money *off* the Government for once, by buying a car you're simply handing back a large wad of your hard-saved cash to the Government in tax.

Do you *really* need a new car, or do you just want to be seen in a brand new '06 or '07 because it's good for your self-esteem? Be honest. Of course, if you do genuinely need to change the car, using cash to pay for it is far better than financing the purchase. Why not buy a car that's a year or two old – or cut a good deal on a demo? But, as I said, be honest about it: the national obsession with upgrading cars every couple of years is largely a hangover from the time when cars became bangers quite quickly – and always having a new one was one way to upset the neighbours. That's not reason enough to hand back your SSIA in one go.

2. 'I don't need to reinvest because my home is worth a fortune!'

Rising home property values have created an elephant trap in thinking about money. Subscribing to the notion that long-term investment planning isn't necessary because of the level of equity accumulated in your house value is a dangerous cop-out and leaves you vulnerable to a number of severe threats.

First, all assets are cyclical, including Irish property, and the massive increase in the relative value of the equity you have accumulated in your home, particularly over the past decade, will inevitably be eroded by inflation, more supply and a change in demographics. Don't be fooled by the economists who are linked to auctioneering firms and banks and who predict a rosy future for Irish property values: always look for the hidden agenda in these situations. Property values are likely to decline to more reasonable levels when compared to average incomes.

The fact is that property prices in real money terms, in other words above inflation, cannot continue to rise without a market correction. The bet is that the correction will be soft as supply and demand come into equilibrium. But even if it is a soft landing, over the long term that will not create sufficient wriggle room to base your entire retirement nest-egg on an equity release from your home.

Secondly, the common perception regarding inflated home equity is often bolstered by home equity release marketers who work in an unregulated sector and can hardly be expected to tell it like it is, being more inclined to promote the dream of an idyllic retirement on a Caribbean yacht – all based on an equity release. The initial equity market in Ireland, with three to four offerings, comes in two forms: one for a transfer of a share in your home to a reversion company in return for a lump sum; one based on a lump sum released by a mortgage that is repaid on your death.

The problem is that these schemes are themselves locked into the economic reality of longer life spans. The population has a longer life expectancy thanks to improved personal health management and medical technology. This means that product providers must take account of financing costs in the longer term. Alongside this consideration, scheme providers also have to take their cut. If you qualify for equity release, typically up to 50% of the value of your home will be handed over to the scheme provider in return for a lump sum of 25% of its value. For example, if you have a home that is worth €1m in real money terms, you will surrender 50% of its ownership to the equity provider in return for a lump sum payout of €250,000, the guaranteed income potential from which will be 2%–3% after tax, at best. So much for that option!

This doesn't make such schemes valueless, however – far from it. But they should be viewed as the financial planning of last resort for those who, through whatever circumstances, have failed to accumulate working assets during their working lives.

3. 'I am going to help my kids onto the property ladder'

Now, I'm all for helping kids as much as we possibly can, especially in terms of helping to get their careers going, but one of the faulty lines of thinking I come across regularly is among Irish parents – particularly Irish mothers, it must be said – who are fixated on the idea of helping their children onto the property ladder, even when it adversely affects their own financial well-being. While this parental urge is perfectly understandable, in the vast majority of cases it is also unrealistic and potentially reckless. Rarely do parents consider the priority to first ensure that they themselves don't become financial burdens on their adult children in later life by running out of money before running out of life. It is only after parents have secured their own position that they should even consider surrendering assets prematurely to adult children.

Quite often parents take the view that their adult children will look after them in old age should they themselves run into financial difficulties. This assumption carries a number of risks. First, little Johnny and little Mary can change and reorder their priorities in later life. Secondly, little Johnny and little Mary may never have the financial strength to support themselves and elderly parents. Thirdly, parents often take such decisions before the arrival of the in-laws! What happens if your daughter-in-law or son-in-law has parents whose financial needs are greater than yours? One of the significant problems facing middle America is the burden placed on forty-year-olds and fifty-year-olds who are trying to put their own children through college while helping elderly parents who have run out of money. Furthermore, what happens if little Johnny gets divorced and loses half of his assets, including the stuff you gave him?

The rule must therefore be: before deciding to pass assets prematurely to an adult child, consider seriously whether your generosity comes with an enormous price tag, namely your financial dependence on your children later in their lives.

There is another side to this particular coin, and that is those parents who cannot afford to help their children get onto the property ladder but facilitate them by allowing them to continue living at home, even when they have good jobs with decent incomes. This dilemma can cause long-term and potentially fatal damage to the financial strength of parents. Rarely have I found adult children contributing to the household at an economic rate. Typically, in a complex nexus between Mums and live-in adult children over the age of twenty-four, tiny contributions are made to the household, like €100 per week, where the economic cost of running the household is at least twice that. This common situation results in a haemorrhage of money from parents who have little of it to adult children who should know better.

Sure, there are genuine cases where adult children have to live at home because, for whatever reason, they simply cannot cope under their own steam independently, but in an increasing number of families it's a simple case of adult children finding they are just too cosy and well cared for at home.

The rule must therefore be: out the door by twenty-four. If you brought up your children well and invested in their education, you have more than fulfilled your duties as a parent. Do not make the ultimate sacrifice of your long-term financial stability by destroying your savings to finance a second home – without a rental income.

If, despite all warnings, you do decide to put your toe into this pond, then at the very least look for a share in your child's property, which can be bought out later when, as is likely, the property is sold for another home. That way it's a viable investment with a possible benefit for you.

4. 'I will spend first and save later'

Economically speaking, there are two types of money-owner: those who spend first and save later, and those who save first and spend later. If you prioritise spending first, the chances are that at the end of the month, or at the end of the year, you will have spent everything. That's because spending fills a vacuum.

Time and again I hear people say, 'That's all very fine, but I can't afford to save.' Sure, that may be true if you're on the average industrial wage or less and trying to raise a family in an expensive country, but for most it's just a cop-out. The bottomline is that all too often we give priority to immediate gratification – the next makeover, the newest gadget, or a weekend away. This is Id-spending, and well you know it!

One of the best ways of countering this destructive spending pattern is to set up a savings programme that deducts a stipulated amount directly from your salary, *before* it reaches your bank account. Remember, if you have been contributing to a SSIA, you have already proven to yourself that you *can* save. This should provide the impetus to maintain the habit.

There are plenty of salary deduction arrangements available, particularly for retirement funds. Under the PRSA initiative overseen by the Pensions Board, every employer in the country who does not already operate a pension scheme is mandated under law to provide salary deduction facilities for PRSA investment, the contributions to which are written-off against your income tax. If you're in a reasonable income category, there are no excuses for not saving. If you are not saving, it simply means that you have decided, you have *chosen*, to give priority to living today and letting tomorrow look after itself. That's a choice you'll have to live with for a long time.

5. 'I know investment is a good option, but I don't believe in taking investment risk'

This is the favourite slogan of people who hoard money in cash deposit, usually at lousy market rates. They cherish and extol the most recent media headline that reinforces their Doomsday beliefs. Nearly everybody knows somebody who blew a fortune by gambling: mention the word 'risk' and all sorts of negative images are brought to mind.

No wonder some people believe 'risk' means the risk of losing all your money. The notion of a meltdown in capital values gets mixed up with volatility. Volatility refers to temporary downturns and upturns in value, which are as natural in asset values as snow and sunshine are in weather. People who put all of their money in the bank do so because they believe it's safe; what they are actually afraid of is a financial default that could wipe out their money. Banks themselves exist entirely on confidence and never have enough money to meet all deposit demands. Most banks are publicly quoted companies, therefore the value of their shares is an important barometer of their strength. So if there were, say, a collapse of 1929 proportions, what do you think will happen to bank stocks and how do you think depositors would react if they thought their money was at risk? You got it, banks can collapse too!

So, here's the financial collapse strategy for the Armageddonists:

- pull all of your money out of banks;
- go armed to collect it yourself;
- have your bank manager's home telephone number handy just in case he tries to make a run for it;
- try and pass your useless share certificates to somebody else by convincing them that the market will bounce back;
- get down to the petrol station before the big queues start and make sure you get plenty of fuel – fast;
- next, go to the shops and stock up on food – tinned food is probably best;
- turn on your radio to find out where the traffic is massing to avoid snarl-ups;
- close all windows and doors so that your neighbours won't know how well-stocked you are;
- start reading farming and DIY journals: remember, you are working on the assumption that all goods and services will no longer be available, which means you will have to grow your own food and repair your house from the scrap metal lying around the garden;
- keep your prayer book handy, but if you're an atheist, put your head between your knees . . .

6. 'I am going to spend it on an investment property'

Unless you have other liquid funds available from cash deposits, such as from savings policies, etc., it is likely that your SSIA maturity would require you to gear up strongly in order to buy into the property market. After paying for entry costs, such as stamp duty, legal fees and engineer's report, and arranging banking finance, the net amount left to act as equity in your property investment will be significantly reduced.

The trick to investment property is to organise it so that the rental income covers the cost of the mortgage. But with relatively low rents now available in the Irish market and when rental yields can be as low as 3% and less, you would need to look abroad to buy a decent investment property that will be self-financing. In spite of the current trend in buying overseas investment property, this step shouldn't be taken lightly. It could have very significant long-term consequences, both positive and negative. Before taking such a decision, refer to chapters 9, 10 and 11.

7. 'I'm going to finally build that extension/convert the attic'

This is really a question of family priorities. Trading up the property ladder to get desperately needed extra space is not very attractive, particularly if it comes with substantial extra borrowing costs that could prove a heavy financial burden. That's why many families consider extending their current home, or converting the attic in order to create more space for growing kids. This isn't a matter of building up working assets because your home isn't a working asset, but rather is a practical and commonsense step.

If your family is tripping over one another and living in cluttered, overstuffed rooms, then diverting your SSIA maturity to enlarge your home makes a lot of sense – but this applies if, and only if, borrowing the money by adding it to your mortgage does not threaten your ability to meet your lifestyle costs without resorting to lifestyle debt, such as credit cards. Later, when the kids have grown up and your mortgage is your own again, you can always trade down to a smaller property and free up the equity as a working asset.

In the end, what to do with the SSIA stash might come down to a battle of wills and the strength of argument in debates between spouses and partners arising from different calls on the money. In order to assess your options realistically, you need to be aware of the benefits and ins-and-outs of continued investment, which we'll look at in the next chapter.

CHAPTER 3

Plan B: Investing the Loot

Glossary

- **ECB base rate:** European Central Bank lending rate that sets the floor interest rates for the banking market.
- **DIRT:** Deposit Income Retention Tax paid on Deposit Account interest at source at 20%.
- **Lifestyle debt:** Borrowings for lifestyle and not for assets like property, usually stored in credit cards, term loans and overdrafts.
- **Money Advice and Budgeting Service (MABS):** Government grant-aided network of free advisory centres that coach citizens with debt difficulties.
- **Cannibalise a debt:** Upping monthly repayments into a standard mortgage so that more and more monthly repayments cut into the outstanding balance, clearing it much earlier.

The maturity of the SSIA scheme heralds the beginning of endless dinner discussions on a common set of vexing puzzles. The maturities alone will bring up to €40,000 into many households, but for most even that will not be enough to solve the conflicting dilemmas facing many families. That means hard choices between current spending and debts, between medium-term cash calls, like children's education, and long-term retirement planning. It's enough to give any family a headache! However, the real biggie for many of us will be the mortgage question.

Should we use the loot to clear off our mortgage debt?

At first reading this seems like an attractive thing to do. After all, there is nothing like shedding a bit of weight off the home mortgage and freeing up some monthly cash flow. But is it financially correct?

The most common type of mortgage finance is the traditional **repayment mortgage**, also called the **annuity mortgage**. Rising off a low of 2%, by March 2006 the European Central Bank (ECB) base rate stood at 2.5%, and thanks to the external intervention into the Irish market by Bank of Scotland in August 1999 mortgage margins (i.e., the gross profit added by lenders) have typically been squeezed to between 0.8% and 1.5% above the base rate. Accordingly, for most borrowers this positioned variable mortgage rates at just over 3.3%–4%. These rates are likely to increase if, as is expected, the ECB base rate lifts to as high as 3.5% in the near future, adding another 1% and pushing variable rates to between 4.3% and 5%. Don't assume that rising interest rates will peak the ECB rate at a 3.5% base because the ECB rate could go higher if European inflation exceeds expectations.

When you take a cash lump sum and reduce your variable rate mortgage, thereby avoiding a cost at the borrowing rate, it is equivalent to investing the money, tax-free, at this rate. This is a better rate than leaving the money in cash deposit and paying DIRT, and comes with the added benefit of reducing your monthly repayments.

However, the question of whether or not you should sink your SSIA maturity in your home mortgage really comes down to the relative strain placed on your monthly income by those mortgage repayments. As a general rule, if your mortgage repayments are eating up more than 40% of your net monthly income, then this option is worth considering. As interest rates rise, more borrowers will find themselves diverting larger chunks of cash into jumbo mortgages taken out when interest rates stood at historical lows. As a result, stretching out mortgage terms and reducing the debt by cash injections will become more common practice.

What about clearing other debts?

The viral effect of development land values, which accounts for up to 60% of the cost of a new home, has pushed many Irish borrowers beyond prudent borrowing limits. Squeezed, on the one hand, by mortgage repayments in excess of 40% of income and, on the other, by making ends meet, Irish households – including many who have been saving in the SSIA scheme – have resorted to plugging shortfalls with lifestyle debt, such as credit cards. This means examining your debt position is not as simple as targeting your mortgage.

If you have been borrowing on one side of your balance sheet from credit cards, credit union loans, etc., over the past five years in order to make ends meet, then effectively you have been borrowing to invest in your SSIA (even though directly linked borrowing is specifically prohibited under the favourable tax rules of the scheme). It makes no sense to service debts at rates of interest hugely in excess of what you'll get on deposit once the scheme ends. When this crossover is reached, clear your borrowings with the SSIA money.

If you fit this category, write down all of your debt, but don't start with your biggest loan, as might seem the obvious thing to do – instead, put the most expensive debt repayment at the top of the page. Remember, your borrowing rate is likely to range from 9% for term loans to as high as 18% on credit cards, and even as high as 40% from certain catalogue retailers.

Once you have prioritised your debt based on the most expensive rate you are paying, you will probably find that debt number one is your credit card rate (unless you have been extravagantly availing of money-lender facilities, or buying through catalogue companies). The next thing to do is to consider how you can move the most expensive debt from the top of the page to less expensive lifestyle debt (not your mortgage) at the bottom, for example, moving it from your local credit union or retail bank.

When this is done you should use your SSIA maturity to eliminate all lifestyle debt, beginning with the most expensive. Pay off these debts and redirect the old loan payments to buying assets. Remember, it makes no sense to reinvest your SSIA maturity in working assets if, on the other side of your balance sheet, your earned income is being used to finance borrowing at rates of interest likely to be double or treble the rate of return you can expect on assets. So pay it off and start again with a *carte blanche*.

When clearing any debt, always check first to see if there are any penalties for doing so. This is especially the case for fixed rate mortgages, hire purchase agreements and leases.

If you find digging your way out of a debt hole a real challenge, even as your SSIA matures, help is at hand: pick up a copy of my first book, *Short Hands, Long Pockets*, which comes with software to help you bring down your spending while you eliminate your borrowings. If the problem is particularly serious and you feel that taking the DIY approach will prove too difficult, contact your local Money Advice and Budgeting Service (MABS) for free advice and assistance.

Cannibalising Your Mortgage

Where you are not carrying lifestyle debt but are concerned about the scale of your mortgage, then it is correct to use the SSIA maturity to bring down your homeloan debt so that it is not absorbing more than 40% of your net income. The problem is that above this ratio it is difficult to fund a lifestyle while repaying a mortgage. When you reduce your mortgage debt in this way, your mortgage repayments also fall proportionately. This provides you with an option, but not a compulsion, to cannibalise your mortgage debt by instructing your lender to maintain your mortgage repayments at the old level.

Example

You have an outstanding homeloan mortgage balance of €200,000 with 25 years left to run. At an interest rate of, say, 4%, this costs €1,047 per month. Two SSIAs mature and both are used to reduce the mortgage balance to €160,000. Ordinarily, repayments would be reset to about €838 per month after this lump payment.

If repayments are kept to the present level, however, then the mortgage debt would begin to cannibalise and should be cleared over 17.7 years, shaving over seven years off the mortgage term. If the 'old' SSIA monthly saving rate of €508 is added to the 'old' mortgage repayment you can expect to collect your deeds after 10.5 years.

Many fixed rate mortgages (although not all) come with the disadvantage that repayment penalties are levied if you attempt to make capital repayments either as a lump sum or in the form of accelerated monthly repayments to cannibalise the debt. You'll need to check the terms of your mortgage loan to ascertain your position in relation to such repayments.

Where your home mortgage is not a burden on your monthly income and at a time of relatively low interest rates, it makes more sense to put your capital to work elsewhere at a rate that should out-perform the mortgage rate. Generally, over the long term, investment across equities (shares) and property should outperform this rate by a comfortable margin. In practice, most Irish balance sheets are geared in this manner, i.e. repaying mortgage debt and at the same time putting money to work in investment property and through retirement schemes. It makes sense to continue this as a long-term habit, except in circumstances where there is a very sharp rise in interest rates. Given the weakness of the German and French economies, in particular, that possibility looks highly unlikely at present. So if your mortgage is not a burden, continue to clear it with income and invest your capital elsewhere.

Should I invest in an education fund for the children?

College fees are only part of the cost of sending a child to college: accommodation, travel, books and expenses can create a substantial financial burden for parents. For those who cannot meet these costs from earned income, the likelihood is that they will find themselves having to borrow later in life. The more children you have, the greater the financial burden their education will bring – but the SSIA maturity can provide a solution.

Ring-fencing your SSIA maturity and continuing the savings habit monthly could provide a sufficient capital pool to deal with education costs. Where the costs are imminent, such as within the next five years or so, you should restrict your savings to high interest cash deposits to avoid the volatility inherent in investment in risky assets. Where the costs are a little further down the line, particularly if you have very young children, it can make sense to invest monthly in funds that invest in real assets, such as property and equities, and which are available from most life companies.

The chart on page 21 illustrates the level of education capital that could be accumulated in real money terms where an SSIA maturity of €20,000 becomes available and where there are continued contributions of €254 per month, escalating in line with inflation. Where there are two maximum SSIAs in a household the results can be doubled.

Should I double the Government money by buying assets through retirement funds?

Generally, this is a very good idea if there is tax relief space to do so. Over the past five years you have been getting a credit of 25% on your contribution from the Government. If you are a top rate

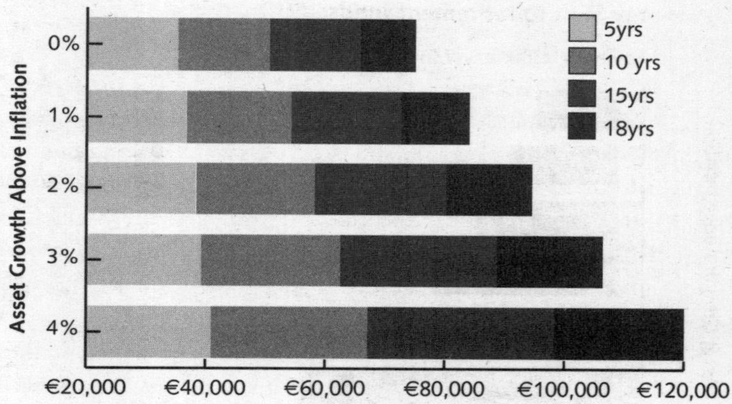

Based on an SSIA maturity of €20,000 and continued contributions of €254 per month escalating with long-term inflation of 3% pa. All values in present day terms and rounded for clarity.

tax-payer, a saving of €254 per month is equivalent to pumping at least €440 per month into a retirement fund while claiming full tax relief on the contribution. That's an annual saving of €5,280 into retirement funds. For the lower rate tax-payer a monthly SSIA contribution of €254 is equivalent to about €320pm into a retirement fund, or €3,840 yearly. (In practice, not only do you get income tax relief on your contribution but you also get relief from PRSI and the health levy.)

The charts on page 22 show the amount of capital that can be accumulated in a retirement fund at these two rates of saving over the long term.

Many tax-payers do not use up their yearly allowance for investment through retirement funds, leaving plenty of room to gross up the SSIA monthly contribution into a bigger contribution before tax relief, with no impact on lifestyle spending. There is a separate chapter on investing through retirement funds (see Chapter 16), so here I'll just give a brief synopsis of the tax allowance:

Redirecting €254 net per month from my SSIA to retirement funds:

Lower Rate Tax-payer (now €320 per month)

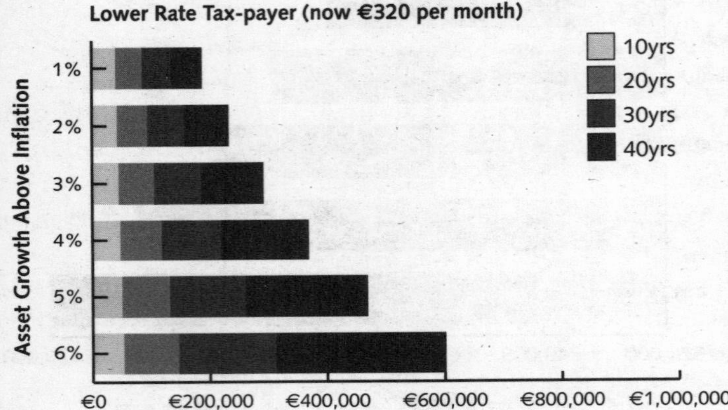

Top Rate Tax-payer (now €440 per month)

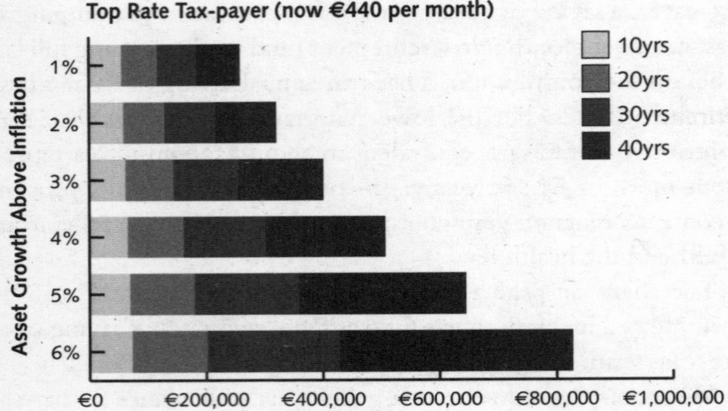

Based on savings in retirement funds escalating savings at long-term inflation of 3% pa.
Figures rounded for clarity. All values in present day terms.

- You are in employment without access to a pension scheme; you can invest in a PRSA, writing off the first 15% of your earned income up to age 29, 20% between 30 to 39, 25% between 40 to 49, 30% between 50 to 54, 35% between 55 to 59 and 40% for 60-plus. These allowances apply to your first €254,000 of earned income and this cap will be increased each year to take account of inflation.
- If you are self-employed you have the exact same allowances, except they relate to your net relevant earnings, which is broadly equivalent to your taxable net profits (check this with your tax advisor if you are unsure). You have the choice of investing either in a PRSA or in a personal pension.
- If you are a member of a company pension scheme, then whether or not you are contributing you might be entitled to invest up to the same ceilings in a parallel investment account known as an Additional Voluntary Contribution (AVC), less any contribution you are making to the main staff pension scheme. This also relates to you if you are a proprietary director of a limited company. Check first with your pension consultant to ensure that you can fund into an AVC without hitting pensions ceilings.
- Low rate tax-payers earning less than €50,000 can grab another €1 from the Government for every €3 transferred directly from their SSIA maturity into a retirement fund. This once-off incentive is limited to €2,500 of Government cash and requires a matching contribution of €7,500 from the SSIA maturity. The normal exit tax on SSIA profit of 23% is binned on the amount thus transferred.

For the revolutionary changes introduced by the former Minister for Finance, Charlie McCreevy, in the Finance Act 1999 and 2000, which makes these investments much more flexible and attractive, see Chapter 16 on retirement funds.

I am going to manage my own money

Taking a DIY approach to managing your own money makes a bundle of sense for those who are good at it. For proprietary directors of limited companies, for example, this can come in the form of self-administered pension schemes where running your own share portfolio is facilitated. But for every one person who tells me that this is his/her philosophy, there are dozens who are using it as an excuse to do nothing, instead simply hoarding money in cash and waiting for the killer investment to pop along. Back in the dot.com boom hundreds of thousands of amateur day-traders took to stock trading, subsequently losing a fortune in the downturn by ditching first principles and over-concentrating on the wrong stocks in the wrong sectors. Remember, it's easy to make money in a rising market – it's a tide that lifts all boats.

I regularly hear people saying that it's all a scam, that passing over your money to professional asset managers is a recipe for high charges and lousy performance. Maybe so, but that depends on which asset manager you choose, which time period you were invested and whether you contributed by bailing out of investments at the wrong time. If the alternative to investment is to do nothing effective yourself, then tirades against the industry are merely a cop-out. People who are serious about investing and making money know their limitations and weaknesses as well as they know their strengths.

Making the decision to invest the savings

Many households have invested in the SSIA at the maximum rate of €508 per month for two adults. In some cases accounts were opened for adult children as well, creating a potential bonanza of €20,000 per maximum SSIA account in the household. It's not just about the amount of money becoming available, however. The real value of the SSIA is that it has fostered a **national savings habit.**

For many savers the contribution has been taken out of after-tax earned income, money which would otherwise have been spent on lifestyle. The maximum individual saving rate of €254 per month translates into an after-tax saving of over €3,000 per annum for five years. This savings habit is now embedded in lifestyles throughout the country – people don't even notice the monthly contribution leaving their accounts. In the meantime rising incomes have made the savings rate much more bearable. In order to gain real long-term value from your SSIA the best option is to continue at this rate of savings, or higher, over the years ahead.

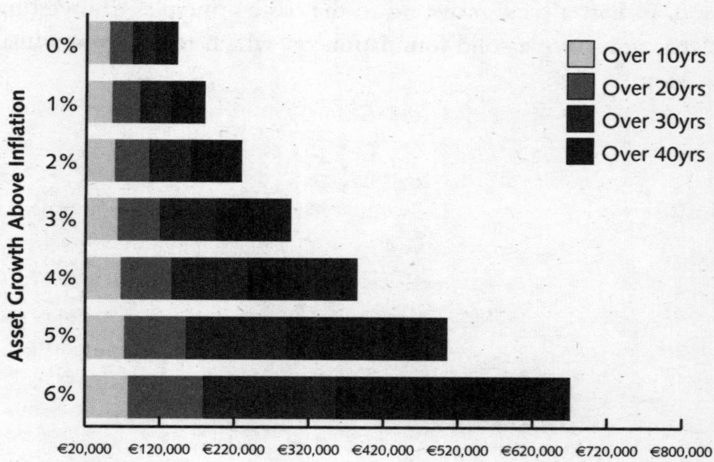

Based on €20,000 SSIA maturity and savings continued at €254 per month escalating with long-term inflation of 3%pa. Figures rounded for clarity.

The longer the investment period, the greater the difference in final results between squirreling money away in cash deposits, which will at best match the inflation rate and give a zero real rate of return, and investment in the two wealth generators, property and equities, which have the capacity to perform above 4% per annum over inflation. This is the key element of successful investing: time. Get-rich-quick schemes have tantalised investors for generations, but anyone who has given in to that particular temptation will warn you to steer clear. Instead see investing as a long-term activity: time is the money-maker's friend!

So we've opened the great SSIA debate. Balancing conflicting calls on your money won't be easy and the decision to prioritise one choice over another is rarely one-dimensional and based purely on the maths – especially when kids are involved. However, the argument, and ensuing decision, is best had where *all* the options are considered. At least then you can look back knowing you didn't make hasty and ill-informed decisions.

If the investment/savings argument is starting to sway you, that's good. In Part 2 we'll move on to the basic principles of investing so that you have a solid foundation on which to base your final decision.

PART TWO

Getting the Basic Principles Right

CHAPTER 4

Ditching the Myths About Investing

Glossary

- **Asset allocation:** The strategic or overarching decision about how you spread your money across the major asset classes, property, equities, bonds and cash.
- **Inflation:** the rate at which the general price of goods and services rises each year.

Whether or not we like to admit it, practically all of our investment decisions are influenced by emotion. Sometimes that's not a bad thing, but oftentimes our emotions fly in the face of reasoned thinking and logic, costing us valuable opportunities to do a lot better with our money. Consider, for example, that eight out of ten SSIA savers sought refuge in cash deposit accounts because the stock market had fallen dramatically in the period prior to the commencement of the scheme: this was an emotional response by many who would otherwise have chosen equities. The fall in equities actually represented a golden opportunity for bottom-buying shares at cheap prices, a situation that was to last well into 2003, but only two in ten people read it so. This canny 20% are likely to grow their money much more by maturity than cash deposit savers, furthermore they will also benefit over the long term because they've learned to resist emotional thinking when it comes to investment decisions.

Faced with the inscrutability of the finance industry, you may have gathered a set of beliefs that draws on your own experiences, on conversations with peers and with your parents – who are, of course, never short of advice or correction! These beliefs can be hard to ditch and can inform many decisions simply because they reinforce familiar, existing beliefs, which makes them the easiest route to choose in emotional terms. But if we're honest, lots of the methods we employ to solve problems don't stand up to scrutiny.

That's why we need to look at the popular myths and ask ourselves how true, or false, they are. I'll put my own credentials on the table now! In my own life, and despite knowing I should avoid the temptation to bypass first principles, like taking the time to do the research, I've bought into complete lemons and lost a bundle – and even, on one memorable occasion, the lot. So don't beat up on yourself too hard if you've followed some of these myths in the past and gotten burned: see them as learning experiences – that's the excuse I used! Don't let it put you off investing your time, energy and money in small businesses – that's different, but expect failures en route to successes because that is simply the nature of higher risk investments.

Myth 1: *Everybody* is investing in it, so it must be good

I only wish it were true because then all we'd have to do to get good returns would be simply to follow the crowd. Unfortunately, when everybody is bailing into an asset type like equities or property, the asset in question is probably close to the end of its run. You see, everything is cyclical: values can't rise forever and declines are inevitable as rain. Investment decisions are often taken in a lemming-like fashion, especially when the big numbers of new entrants arrive into a sector dazzled by past performance data and glowing media reports. The word goes around: it's a sure thing, no research or analysis needed! In this way, time and time again, soft money arrives just in time for the classic downturn. These fair-weather investors suffer heavy short-term losses and being impatient to make a fast buck and lacking long-term focus, they sell at the bottom to cut their loses. By doing so, they reinforce the cynical belief that it was all a stitch-up anyway.

As the new millennium dawned in 2000 the media was full of stories about people making vast riches from technology companies. There was a new economy, an on-line economy, and it was bypassing the old one. We were told that we were entering a new era and that old economy stocks, like utility companies and heavy industry, were *passé*. Cast-iron tips on the next sure thing abounded. There were oodles of fast-buck schemes and money began to flood into the latest stock, with little or no research.

The Irish State sold off its State Telecom company, Eircom, amidst a wave of national euphoria. It was the politician's dream: the quoted share for the common man. Banks got in on the act by pushing loans so people could get even more of 'the sure thing'. It just had to be right – the Government itself was backing it solidly and effusively. In the money-making melee that ensued most people ignored the warning about stock select risk, about putting all your eggs in one basket – until it was too late. Eircom's share price, along with the telecom sector and the entire technology sector, collapsed and public scepticism about the shares market being a big scam was heavily reinforced.

The irony was that it had all happened before. In the late 1970s rumours abounded of oil finds off the Irish coast. Investors rushed into banks to borrow money to buy exploration shares; some even queued at Cork Airport to interview riggers departing from helicopters. Alas, there was more oil to be found under the sump of an old Morris Minor. The investors lost a bundle.

Today, there's a new 'sure thing' as hundreds of millions of Euro are on the move to overseas property, despite warnings of property bubbles in many markets. 'You can't beat bricks and mortar' is the catch cry, invoking the myth that property is a one-way bet. Thus the pattern repeats itself.

Myth 2: You too can get rich quickly!

Ever since we sat around the fire and told each other tall tales there has been a desire to find the pot of gold at the end of the rainbow, to rub the magic lamp, to get to the Nirvana of investments. This desire is stoked by spell-binding stories about the few people who did hit the jackpot and made billions *en route*. But what is so often overlooked is the likelihood that these were people of exceptional ability, or were just plain lucky and therefore owned the right business in the right place at the right time. Some of those tantalising fortunes may also have been made by breaking the law, by using insider information, by bribing, or by buying rezoning decisions. Most property developers have, of course, made their fortunes legitimately, albeit usually by applying exceptional skills for the business and by taking risks that would hospitalise most investors. Some have done so by failing, or by going bust and starting all over again from nothing – these possess natural entrepreneurial intelligence in abundance and can't understand why we just can't see things quite the way they do!

These are great stories, but for most investors building working assets is done over many years and ideally through a spread rather than a concentration of investment. It's a plodding journey, not a ride in a Ferrari. Comparing yourself to professional investors or gifted individuals is entirely unfair, but nonetheless occurs frequently. I regularly meet the brightest of the bright from the professions to owners of small- and medium-sized companies who regale me with their stories of the guy in their class who found the magic lamp. Does anyone really believe that you can work sixty or seventy hours a week and also expect to manage a thriving international property portfolio, be a whiz at trading shares, or build a vast business from shoestrings? Well, maybe you are one of the privileged few and your lamp is just around the next corner – but most of us are better dreaming these things at night, followed by a strong coffee and practical investment by day.

If that sounds familiar, maybe you need to stop comparing your balance sheet to that of someone who is vastly richer than you: not only is it financially incorrect but it will lead only to frustration and stress – the constant nagging feeling that you're missing out on some kind of coded knowledge. There is an entire publishing industry dedicated to books about the money-makers and the secrets of their success, many of which are impractical and some of which are mere vanity exercises, written by complex individuals desperate to distil their personalities, skills and experiences into simplistic sound bites.

You need to recognise and accept that there will always be someone a step ahead, someone luckier, smarter and richer. But that doesn't mean you're worse off. It's a mistake to think that success is measured in purely monetary terms, in assets gathered: that's a way of seeing the world that can only serve to sour your sense of well-being. True success is best defined by philosophers and religious leaders; it's sure not measured by the size of a balance sheet – and you can chalk that down!

Myth 3: It's a fact – it said so in the papers

There are some insightful and hard-hitting personal finance journalists who write well-argued columns in the Irish media, but they are thin on the ground. If you are expecting to develop a clear investment strategy that fits your circumstances while perusing a personal finance column over coffee and croissants, you are expecting a lot. We're talking Holy Grail levels of expectation here! Personal finance isn't yet regarded as one of the best gigs in journalism; therefore it doesn't attract the same resources as the big sellers: politics, business and sport. Generally, newspapers pay about €500 for 600–1,000 words and no one is going to burn the midnight oil for €500! As a result, some of what's written on personal finance is inadequately researched, rehashed, or simply trite. The most turgid stuff is unashamed space-filler, involving comments from industry talking heads speaking in corporate tongues and pushing the latest sales agenda.

Worst of all, though, is the advertorial, the gushing page-killer paraded as some kind of quasi-journalism. Frankly, this sort of waffle embarrasses old hacks, who put up with it only because it helps pay the bills and bolster profit margins in Ireland's small, fiercely competitive market place. Always ask yourself: if a scheme is so good – whether it's a trophy property abroad or some kind of gravity-defying equity investment that promises guarantees – why would a firm with a strong existing client base want to pay hefty fees to market it to new clients? And who pays the costs ultimately?

The financial industry is hooked on fashion-based sales because these cost far less to promote and, after all, why swim against the tide? Knowing that many investors would like to have their cake and eat it too, many promotions appeal to the lowest common denominator by under-reporting risks, hyping guarantees, hiding true costs and overstating investment expectations. It's a universal game that's played time and time again with great success, and it's easy to see why. Consider, for example, the chances for an equity promotion the day after the US-led invasion of Iraq, which came during one of the deepest troughs in share prices. It didn't happen. Even though conditions were ideal, with hugely undervalued shares and some shares paying dividends almost double cash deposits, the industry chose instead to promote expensive, guaranteed products with limited benefits, because that's what sold.

In 2005 and into 2006 the market has been flooded with overseas property schemes and new buyers are signing up in increasingly larger numbers. This is happening despite a prolonged upturn in property prices in many markets for several years and warnings about overvaluation from some Central Banks. Product promoters know this and privately reckon the end of the current cycle is nigh, but if it sells, hell, push it unequivocally.

Myth 4: I have invested in a pension

Everyday I hear people say things like, 'I invested in a pension', or 'I invested in a savings policy', or 'I invested in a retirement trust'. When I ask what asset they chose, in other words, what was their fund choice, few can tell me. To put it simply, this is like shopping in Dunnes Stores and remembering only the wrappers, with no earthly idea as to their contents. I know it sounds nuts – after all, if you bought a property or put money in the credit union you'd know what you'd bought or saved – but with alarming frequency I encounter investors who can't even recall the name of the asset manager into which their thousands are poured annually. Honestly, I've had countless conversations with investors who ask me to name all the life offices in Ireland so that they can hopefully recognise theirs – even when it's listed on their monthly bank statements! Typically, all that they can recall is how much it 'cost', which is hardly ever seen as a 'contribution' to an asset. I've asked large audiences of well-paid supervisors and managers in Ireland's leading industries which assets they chose to buy through their staff pension schemes – into which typical contributions exceed 10% of their total remuneration – few could answer. Mostly, the question is greeted with deafening silence!

Consider for a moment how you think about property. When you discuss your house, for example, you rarely ever refer to the cost, instead referring to its current value. You know something about local market conditions, rents and possible outlook. Now consider how you think about your business. No doubt you know roughly how much it's worth as a going concern. You know about your car, your cash deposits, your An Post bonds and your shares, but when it comes to stuff administered by life and pension companies, well, it's a rather big blank.

How terminology is used is a key to our thinking, with the most common myth being that we invest in wrappers rather than in the underlying asset. This is the prevailing belief, even though one of the most powerful influences in building your financial strength is your decision regarding which asset to choose. This decision is commonly referred to as 'asset allocation', which means choosing between the major asset classes, that is property, equities (shares), bonds and cash deposits.

Let's get one thing straight here and now: there is no such thing as investing in a pension, or in a savings policy, or in a self-administered retirement trust. These are just wrappers – they are ways of administrating investments, or, if you prefer, types of bookkeeping, which is why they appear at the very end of *Loot!*, after all the stuff on assets. The only differences between these wrappers are the tax rules and costs they apply to the assets they hold.

So you must promise that you will never again, from this time forward, refer to investing 'in a pension'. You must instead think about investing in property, or equities, or whatever asset class you choose through the long-term tax shelter commonly called a pension. Remember, the tax rules that apply to a wrapper are common to all: the critical differentiator is the asset to which you are exposed through the wrapper. This can range from cash deposits to Chinese equities, with vast differences in long-term returns.

The asset allocation decision has a far more powerful influence on long-term results than the quality of the asset management itself. Now there's a thought the next time you meet someone who hasn't a clue which asset he has invested in, but just remembers that he chose his asset manager because it had no.1 performance figures. There's no such thing as being number one, just 365 opportunities a year to choose a past start date over which time your fund did better than the rest. That way, you can dupe investors into thinking that you have a magic formula in a market where there isn't a comprehensive standard that regulates how past performance data is presented.

So now that some of the myths are out of the way, let's get on to the new rules of the investment game. The world, and the economy, is constantly changing and you need to be aware of this to safeguard your investments and to make informed investment decisions. In this new socio-economic terrain there are challenging lines of thinking for us to explore.

CHAPTER 5

New World, New Rules

Glossary

- **National Pensions Reserve Fund:** An investment fund owned by the State and invested long term to pay future Old Age Pensions.

In talks I've given all over the country, one thing always draws gasps from audiences: the realisation of just how much is needed, in working assets, to fund a pretty modest long-term lifestyle once you have finished working for a living. Nevertheless, decisions are made everyday to buy another new gadget, or another new outfit, putting today's pleasure over tomorrow's necessity. So, before you choose between spending your SSIA or investing it and then what to invest it in, consider how the world has changed and what this means for you and your loot. This will give you the 'why' of financial planning and long-term investment!

Chances are, your parents and grandparents never heard of the term 'financial planning'. That's hardly surprising. In times past middle Ireland had little possibility of building balance sheets, or becoming financially independent – you know, that fairytale point where your working assets (that is, all of your investible assets, but not including your home, car, etc.) are capable of permanently replacing the cost of your lifestyle. Back then, that notion was neither a real possibility nor a real problem. High unemployment and mass emigration, set against a backdrop of continuous economic failure, meant that most people were just making ends meet – often just barely.

The employment deal was also fundamentally different. It was common to stick with the one employment for the entire length of one's career, putting in forty years' service and earning a pension that could be beefed up with the State old age pension. And, of course, there were no envious glances at the Joneses because most people were in the same boat – without life jackets . . . and it was leaking.

There was also a fundamental difference in attitudes to retirement. There was no economic necessity to build up a strong balance sheet for later in life because average mortality looked after that problem: typically, men and women died on average seven to nine years after retirement. All that has changed, of course. At the start of the twentieth century the average life expectancy was 47 years. At the start of the twenty-first century it is accelerating into the 80s, and the graph continues to head skyward. Right across all the developed nations of the world, we are living an awful lot longer. In Japan, for example, there are over 25,000 centenarians. Some commentators believe that the human race will reach very long life lengths, such as 150 years of age, over the next 100 years.

So, what's the problem? Simple – people want to retire earlier, and are living longer. These days it is perfectly possible to have a retirement that lasts thirty to forty years – an idea that would no doubt have shocked our forebears. This new state of affairs has a profound meaning for financial planning: the ratio of working years to non-working years used to be 5:1, now it's closer to 1:1.

In supporting State pensions, Ireland is positioned well ahead of the posse because we have such a young population, with a mean age of 32 as compared to the European mean age of 42. Based on current trends, however, the ratio of workers to retirees, currently standing at 6:1, is on course to change to 2:1, at present delayed only by the influx of young immigrants. The Irish Government has reacted to this by setting up a National Pensions Reserve Fund, which each year receives an injection of about 1% of GNP. The plan is that as the population greys, the cost of future pensions will be financed from invested assets and not from current tax revenues, which is the practice at present.

This is a good idea: it puts real assets, like equities, government bonds, property and money market instruments, behind the payment of future old age pensions. But even having taken this far-sighted step, the facts are that State support will just about cover one-third of the average industrial wage. This means that State pensions for a single person stand at a little over €10,000 per annum – about enough to cover three months of moderate lifestyle spending. The rest is up to each of us, and with longer and longer life lengths the amount of working assets you will have to accumulate to plug your long-term savings gap is on the rise. Past generations could comfortably top up State pensions by €20,000 a year for less than €200,000 in working assets, and live quite comfortably to average mortality. But that's changing rapidly to nearly three times the old levels, which is a bit of a shock when you're faced with them for the first time, especially if you are intent on blowing your SSIA, like the rest of your income, on having a good time now.

Three things you can do if you run out of money before running out of life

1. Go into cryogenic suspension for nine months of the year. This will require you to use the State pension to support a good lifestyle, ideally during the summer months, while you hibernate through autumn, winter and spring. You'll need to keep a close eye on developing technologies and lobby the Government for State support for nationwide cryogenic facilities.
2. Start writing letters to relatives. Rather than wait for the last moment, you should let your relatives know now that you will be running out of money so that it doesn't come as too much of a surprise. In particular, target those relatives that have lots of loot. Start practising imaginative, innovative letter writing because you will be writing lots of them, and people might tire of standard stuff.
3. Hop on a plane to Switzerland, where they allow euthanasia. Alternatively, start an Irish People for Euthanasia action group now to avoid flight and accommodation costs in later years.

Wouldn't it all be so simple if, at the end of our birth certificates, there was fine print giving the precise date of death. That would make financial planning a doddle! After running out of our own cash, we could borrow as much as possible, exhausting applications to every bank, building society and credit union in the country and then die screaming with laughter at the look on our bank manager's face as he monitors our declining pulse. Yes, that would be nice, but, of course, the problem is that we don't know in advance how long we need our money to last.

While the Society of Actuaries currently predicts that average life expectancies look likely to extend into the mid-80s, these are only averages. What happens if they're wrong in your case? You could always write a letter of complaint to the Society of Actuaries, or you wait for the cheque from the President when you hit age 100. There's another possibility – you could wait for the transfer of assets to take place from your old folks. Well, it *might* work, that is, if they have loads of loot and plenty to finance a long retirement and you don't really mind waiting until you are in your fifties or sixties to find out. Picture yourself trying to pick up chicks in your Masserati when you're sixty, check the family genes and ask yourself if that would really rock for you! But what if your parents are not filthy rich, if they get divorced and remarry, if they take an equity release on their home, or just blow a huge hole in the pot paying for exorbitant health and nursing care costs: what then?

The rising life expectancy is a problem for just about everybody, including the Irish Government, which is already beginning to look at encouraging longer working lives. Hell, you can keep going for ever – maybe get a part-time job serving hamburgers in your eighties and nineties, in spite of the sciatica!

Why do we aim to retire at 65?

On the question of retirement age, have you ever wondered why sixty-five is the definitive age of rest? It is so embedded in our thinking that we rarely question it, but where did it actually come from? The answer is: Germany. Chancellor Bismarck set the German state pension at 65 because – wait for it! – that age was several years beyond the average life expectancy of Germans in the nineteenth century. That's a piece of financial chicanery even our own Finance ministers would be proud of! Since then, and despite extending life expectancies, it has been copperfastened into popular thinking and set indisputably as 'normal' retirement age.

So, age sixty-five is the year we settle down to a steady life, when we quietly wind down and become ultra-cautious investors, watching every cent? This notion is so instilled in financial planning that many pension schemes are accounted by software programmes that commence a phased movement to low return and cautious investments as your clock ticks towards age sixty-five – even after the advent of open-ended Approved Retirement Funds that carry forward your investment for life!

Does it really make sense that you should become a cautious investor, bailing out of high performing properties and equities, simply because of an age barrier set by a German chancellor over 130 years ago? Where's the law enforcing that? Some of the best investors I've run across are in their seventies and eighties and would leave younger investors with half their experience in their slipstream! Besides, contrary to popular wisdom, if you want to support your non-working years comfortably, you will need to stick with 'risky' investments throughout your life and not ditch good lifelong investment habits because of a cunning decision in the nineteenth century.

Inflation

Past generations were successful through not taking investment risk and keeping money in a good, safe place, like in the bank, or under the bed. This was understandable at a time when banks went bust, when there was no deposit or protection scheme, when options were limited and inflation wasn't recognised as a problem.

Those who lived in the 1700s and 1800s would not have been

conscious of inflation at all. By modern standards, there was none. Inflation only became a menace after the Second World War. Cash deposits, the long-favoured investment of past generations, can be devastated by inflation. This lesson was harshly learned during the inflation burst of the early 1970s, which was triggered by the oil crisis. It wiped out the financial strength of many people who had over-invested in cash deposits, although it also came with the happy side effect of trashing the relative value of mortgages.

Modern economic management is designed to keep inflation subdued and to avoid economic cycles that flip-flop from boom to bust. This requires the Central Banks to raise interest rates in advance of inflationary pressures within the economy. But consider inflation as a constant menace, much like a posse that pursues your assets throughout your life, always attempting to narrow the gap by eroding the real value of money.

How much working assets do I need, then?

How much you need to build onto your balance sheet by retirement age really depends on where you're starting from and how long you've got before R-day. Bearing in mind increasing life expectancies, on page 43 I have outlined, in today's money terms, the values required in working assets to sustain different levels of income.

The power of the three

There are three factors that influence how much working assets you will accumulate during your lifetime:

- how much you contribute each year to buying new assets;
- what long-term rate of return you earn on your assets after management charges, tax and inflation;
- how long you invest.

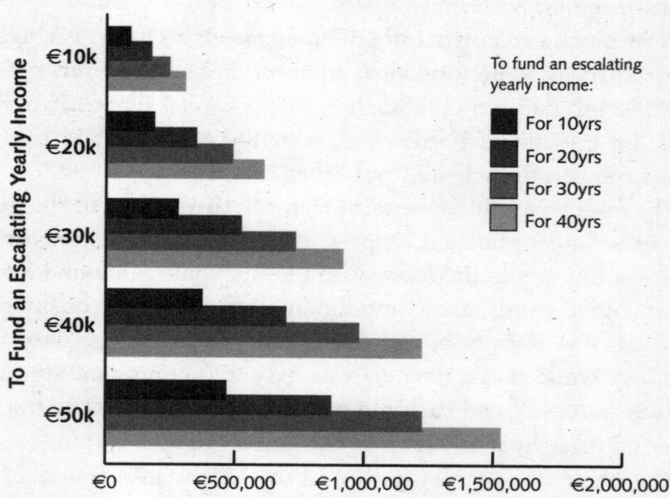

The financial institutions competing for a share of your money spend vast sums of money promoting **asset performance**. These campaigns naturally give the impression that the most powerful of the three factors is asset performance. It's not. Apart from the canniest or most fortunate investors, the long-term behaviour of assets will work out within pretty predictable ranges, with some spectacular investment successes and losses *en route*. Claims about getting very high real rates of return above inflation are merely that, just claims. Extremely high rates of return come only at extremely high rates of risk – rates most of us aren't stupid enough to take. However, by placing most of the emphasis on geared investment in property (using borrowings) and in equities, you do have a chance to out-perform management charges, tax and inflation over the long term by a reasonable margin, that is in the range of 3%–6%. This is by no means certain – remember the outcome of investment is uncertain and there can be huge variations around long-term forecasts.

How much you **contribute** to buying assets each year is a bigger factor than asset performance, in most instances. Your annual contribution rate is a combination of the capital repayments you make on investment borrowings, your SSIA savings and contributions to pension schemes and other investments.

The most powerful of the three factors is **time**. It has the biggest, and most underestimated, impact. Albert Einstein reckoned that the most important discovery wasn't $E=mc^2$ but compound interest, in other words, the compounding effect of time on money values. If you want to be financially independent at age sixty and you start work at age twenty, you have 480 compounding time periods (months), and each month delayed is permanently lost. A sobering thought at any hour of the day or night!

The chart on page 43 gave you an insight into the level of working assets required to sustain escalating incomes over short- to long-term time periods. The graph on page 45 shows you how much you can hope to accumulate taking, as a base-line, a yearly contribution to assets of €10,000, escalating in line with inflation. So, what lessons can we glean from this graph?

- *Lesson 1:* Time and its compounding effect have a dramatic impact on the amount you can accumulate in working assets. So the earlier you start, the greater the chance you have of becoming financially independent.
- *Lesson 2*: Wasted years, particularly in your twenties and thirties when priority is often given to other matters (like enjoying yourself), can be measured.
- *Lesson 3*: The asset values you accumulate over a short period, say, ten years, varies little between 1% pa and 6% pa, but as time goes by the gap widens. This tells us two things: first, if you leave it too late and have just a short number of years left to retirement age, the relative reward you get by taking exposure to risky investments is greatly diminished; second, the converse

How much will I accumulate in working assets at €10,000pa?

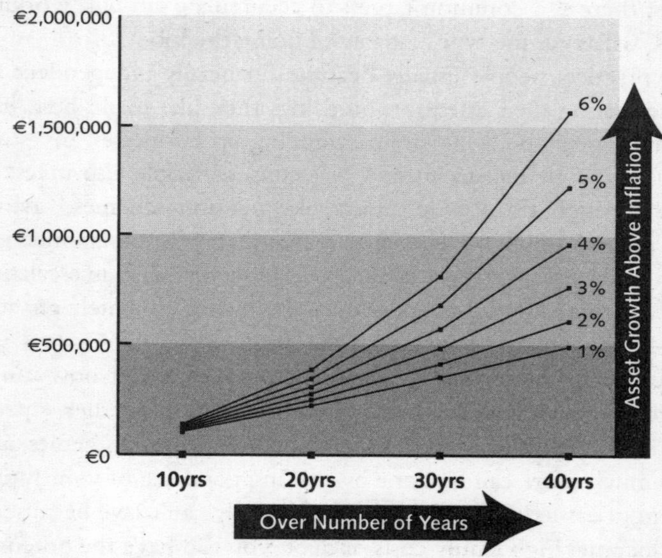

Based on contributing €10,000pa escalating in line with inflation of 3%pa.
Figures rounded for clarity. All values in present day terms.

applies, that is the longer you have until retirement age, the higher the degrees of investment risk you should consider.

Unfortunately, it's all too common to find younger investors parked in overly conservative investments, wasting the ideal years when strong levels of investment risk are likely to yield substantial rewards. This usually happens because younger investors are sold guaranteed and conservative investments. Why? Because that's what everybody is investing in and it's the quickest way to make commissions.

There isn't a panacea, or an ideal route. In theory, the best approach is to become financially independent over the course of your working career by getting the highest rate of return on your investments at the lowest rate of risk. Ideally this should happen across a spectrum of uncorrelated assets, so that you are never overexposed to any one asset. Although there isn't a common route, there is a common target: to accumulate enough working assets, whatever the type, capable of doing the job

In practice, people usually become financially independent by concentrating their attention on things they like to do best, like building up property portfolios, building up businesses, investing in shares, or trading in art and collectables. People also invest in assets through financial products like pension schemes, savings policies and funds, or by being a member of a superannuation pension scheme that rewards each year of service with an escalating future income known as a pension and which is ultimately guaranteed by the employer, including the State.

You might be pleasantly surprised to discover just how much progress you have made when everything is added together, especially the enormous help from superannuation pension schemes, and how much more can be done by making good use of your future stream of earned income. Unless you simply can't save because of low income, high family costs or debt, you too have the potential to become financially independent by the time you finish work. You can certainly ensure that you're not solely dependent on the State old age pension.

Think long-term and pick assets accordingly

The trick to long-term investment is to think long-term and not to get distracted by current events. The media magnifies both the upside and downside of events that affect assets, especially investment in equities (shares), but in practice large up-swings and down-swings in current values should be viewed as investment opportunities and part and parcel of the volatility of investing in equities. Equally, any near-term fall in property values should be seen for its very long-term effect, which, fingers crossed, is likely to be a temporary blip on the long-term chart.

A 40-year-old investing today should consider investment that is likely to be held for the next fifty years – full life length – and not something for the next few years just because that's what it says in the brochure. As a general rule, it is the time that you spend in an investment rather than the timing that influences the rewards.

Remember, as we've noted before, when the SSIA opened in 2001–2002 it coincided with the beginning of a substantial fall in equity markets. This current event gave fright to many savers – a fear not assuaged by Doomsday reports in the media – and led 80% to opt for cash deposits. Investors, on the other hand, who were thinking long term, saw the decline in equity markets in a completely different light. To them it was a bottom-feeding opportunity as monthly contributions, boosted by the Government's 25%, would buy shares through equity funds at depressed prices. The inevitable stock market recovery has now positioned those investors – despite some media predictions to the contrary – ahead of cash depositors, most of whom will never invest in equities if they continue to follow easy sales pitches.

Over the long term the rate of return from continued equity investment is likely to out-perform cash deposits by at least 4% per annum and more, leading to massive long-term differences between Ireland's population of SSIA depositors and SSIA investors. My guess is that a disproportionate amount of SSIA savers will leak their money into lifestyle spending because, shorn of the Government inflow, values will stagnate and depositors will find better things to do. Investors, on the other hand, are more likely to stay invested through thick and thin, even if redeploying to alternatives like property.

And the lesson for the day? If you want to be financially independent for all of your life, you have to take responsibility for managing your money properly – regardless of whether that strikes you as a drearily boring prospect. One simple decision – to put your SSIA in cash deposits – has cost you money. And why? If you had a definite target for the SSIA after five years, which meant you couldn't take the long-term view, then saving in deposits was the right thing to do – but that hardly accounts for nearly one million decisions not to choose investments! Maybe it was because you didn't really research the options and made a quick decision based on convenience and vague fears. I know that sounds harsh, but it's essential that you understand that every financial decision comes with repercussions – and that you can, to a large extent, control those repercussions with a bit of sensible planning. You have the ability and the wherewithal to make a success of your financial planning – what's more, you deserve it!

CHAPTER 6

The Ups and Downs of Asset Behaviour

Glossary

- **Consumer Price Index:** A method of measuring inflation or deflation by tracking the price of a basket of goods and services.
- **Hedge:** A method of reducing the risk of financial loss on an investment.
- **Capital gains tax:** Tax levied on profits from asset sales.
- **Credit rating agency:** Independent firm that measures the financial stability of a company and the risk of default.
- **Bear market:** Asset prices are falling, or expected to fall.
- **Bull market:** Asset prices are rising, or expected to rise.
- **Optimisation theory:** The ideal mix of assets to get the desired return at the lowest risk.
- **Liquid:** Easy to transform into cash.
- **Illiquid:** Difficult to transform into cash.
- **Liquidity crunch:** When a liquid market suddenly becomes illiquid, trapping sellers.
- **Weight of money:** Impact of wave of capital moving in or out of a market.
- **Contagion effect:** Impact on neighbouring or interlinked markets from events in another market.

- **Annuity rates:** The rate at which retirement capital is changed to a lifelong pension income.
- **Economic overheating:** When an economy is growing too strongly.
- **OECD:** Organisation of Economic Co-Operation & Development.
- **Gross roll-up:** Tax model where tax is not deducted at source on assets but on exit when cash is withdrawn from a fund.
- **Double taxation agreement:** Tax treaties between countries to avoid the impact of paying tax twice on the same activity.
- **S&P 500:** Index tracking the prices of 500 US plcs.
- **Gearing:** Ratio of debt to owners funds.

The best approach to investment planning is, as the old adage says, not to have all your eggs in one basket, to chase after the highest rate of return at the lowest rate of risk, to understand how the stuff actually works, to buy well at the right time and to hold good properties and equities through thick and thin. Knowing what to reasonably expect from different assets and the type of factors that affect them is the foundation of good long-term strategies. Not knowing is a fast route to frustration and anger, as each in turn will inevitably let you down at some stage. A lack of understanding of how assets behave when under certain stresses, like interest rate rises or negative sentiment, can also lead to poor decision-making.

First off, there are four major asset classes: cash deposits, bonds, property and equities (shares), each of which is treated separately in *Loot*! But there also are others creeping into mixes to enhance diversification of investment portfolios, including commodities like oil, steel and base metals and especially gold, which rises in value during times of uncertainty and rocketing oil prices. There has also been marked growth in hedge funds which concentrate on different sectors, using borrowings and derivatives to drive up returns and attempt to protect against large losses. The behaviour of the asset classes is affected by various forces, including the way in which Central Banks implement interest rate policy. What they have in common is that they can each experience violent swings up and down, particularly equities (shares) and commodities, but also property – a fact that's frequently overlooked.

Black Monday, mid-October 1987, is etched into the memories of a generation of flip-flop investors who waited until the very end of bull market in shares, which had lasted most of the 1980s, before committing their cash. During this time property was a dog and equities were all the rage. These late arrivals awoke on Black Monday to startling front-page headlines of huge single-day stock market falls. Within hours the ground-floor lobbies of most Irish Life Offices were crammed with investors yelling for their cash and baying at overwhelmed reception staff. In practice, the stock market hadn't actually collapsed and results for the calendar year 1987 were, in fact, positive. Eventually, after a recovery, the next generation of flip-flop investors tip-toed back, just in time for the Gulf War five years later, when the market fell heavily again.

Yep, sometimes you just can't win in markets – and you sure can't if you don't bother to understand them and view risky assets, like property and equities, as short-term investments: they are not. For example, when the inevitable shake-out in overvalued property markets arrives, short-term speculators hoping to make a quick buck on asset growth will take a real hiding. Long-term investors who bought into a solid rental stream will tough it out – and be better off for it.

The Investment Pyramid

A reasonable framework to help fathom where assets stand in relation to one other is to compartmentalise them into an Investment Pyramid that ranges them from 'safe' to 'investment high risk' (see page 53). Bear in mind that foreign currency exposure pushes some assets up the Pyramid, depending on the currency zone in which you reside. So, for example, Eurozone citizens get extremely low default risk with, say, UK Government Bonds but experience volatile values because of movement between Sterling and Euro.

In practice, the pyramid is really an over-simplification of the diverse and complex world of asset choice; the relative positioning of each could be debated into eternity. Nonetheless, much like a food pyramid, the Investment Pyramid does help put things into a digestible framework. And don't forget, there's a Masonic pyramid dominating the most frequently used money in the world: the dollar bill!

How the heck do they create money?

The European Central Banks, just like the Bank of England and the US Federal Reserve, can influence the **volume and price** of money available in the economy. The chief weapon of the Central Banks is to increase or decrease interest rates. By increasing interest rates they can make markets illiquid, thereby drying up the supply of money. By reducing interest rates they create more liquidity, thus increasing the supply of money. But how is money created?

Let's say a bank has €1,000 on deposit. Typically, it will hold €100 and lend the remaining €900. This will be pushed out through avenues such as overdrafts, credit cards, car loans, mortgages, etc. Let's say this €900 is then used to buy a holiday. The travel agent deposits the €900 back into the bank. The bank holds onto a small bit again and puts out the rest through overdrafts, credit cards, mortgages and car loans. This process is repeated over and over, and so the money is multiplied.

There are various ways of measuring money supply. These differentiate between narrow measurements, such as those that look at the number of coins in circulation, to broader measurements that capture credit cards and overdrafts. When a Central

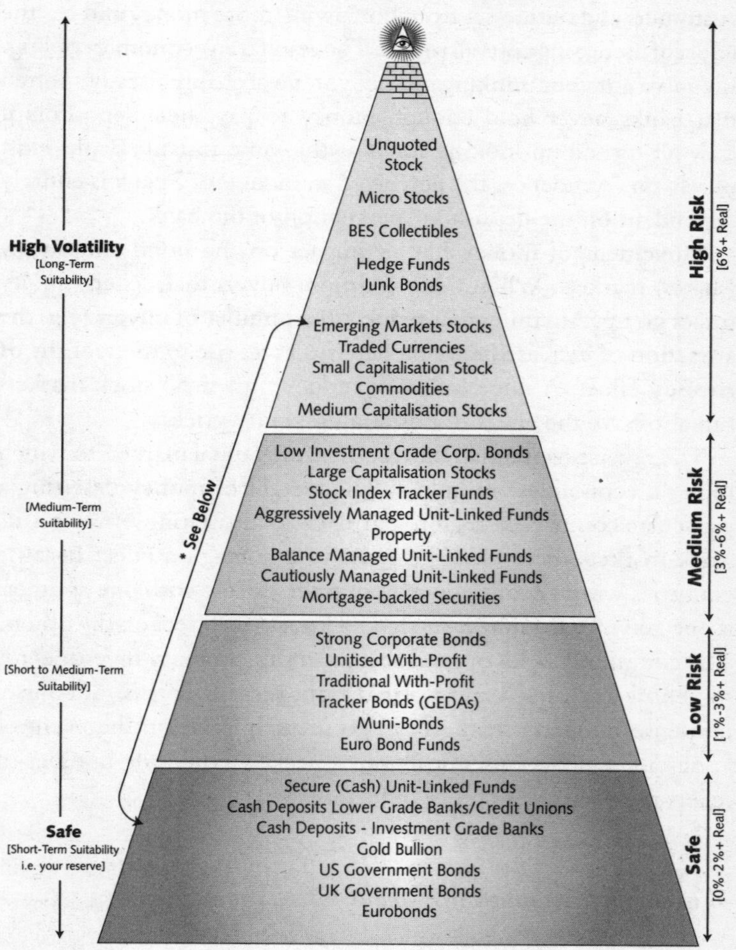

* Collective investments such as Unit Linked Funds, Open-Ended Investment Companies (OEICs), Unit Trusts and Exchange Traded Funds (ETFs) provide packaged products that invest in different parts of the pyramid.

Bank believes that an economy is likely to overheat, it increases the rate of interest it charges to retail banks. They in turn pass on the increase in their product pricing. This discourages individual customers and businesses from borrowing more money and has the effect of increasing costs all round. The result is an economic cooling. If you've got your thinking cap on, you've probably already spotted that banks never hold enough money to pay their depositors if they all turned up looking for it at the same instant. Banks exist purely on confidence: the perceived soundness of a bank is entirely dependent on the depositors' perception of the bank.

Movement of money has an impact on the bond and equity (shares) markets. When there are more buyers than sellers, equity prices go up. Anything that reduces the number of buyers (e.g. the attraction of increased rates on deposit) gives rise to the **weight of money** effect. A huge influx of money into small stock markets can also have the effect of pushing up equity prices.

The reverse happens in the free-flowing capital markets to which modern economies are linked. The weight of money deserting a particular country or region can have a devastating effect on its stock markets. It can also give rise to a contagion effect because countries within economic regions trade closely with one another: if one gets into trouble, it can have a knock-on effect on the others. The commonly held, optimistic notion that property investment is somehow decoupled and isolated from these events is, of course, nonsense: property markets can go severely south in the event of a substantial economic restriction, especially when the number of sellers rises and the number of buyers falls.

Why is there so much fuss about interest rates?

Central Banks apply rising interest rates to head off any perceived threat of inflation, to cool down borrowing and to avoid economic overheating. Sharp rises in interest rates are usually temporary, but the cost of borrowing capital affects just about everything and is certainly not limited to your mortgage or credit card.

Rising interest rates decrease the capital value of bonds and can have a negative effect on equity markets, depending on the size of the increase. It can also affect the property market if borrowing costs increase, thus reducing demand. Interest rate decreases can also cause pain to people whose income is based on high interest rates, and can have a devastating effect on pension rates, also known as annuity rates, which is the rate at which assets in pension funds commute to pension income.

The effects of liquidity on assets

If you need money fast, property is not the most liquid asset to choose. This is an important consideration when investing in funds that specialise in property, small stock markets or lesser-known bonds – or just about anything for which there is a limited market.

There's nothing quite like a run on property, which occurs when more and more owners decide to sell, taking the view that the market is about to fall. This becomes a self-fulfilling prophesy as the number of sellers quickly exceeds the number of buyers, who in turn decide to hold off, expecting further falls, and so the market becomes more illiquid still, further extending sales time. Eventually buyers come back in and the bottom is reached.

Small stock markets suffer more from higher liquidity risks than large ones because their prices are influenced by the weight of money moving in and out. When the money tightens in small markets, it may be difficult to match buyers with sellers, making deals illiquid and hitting prices. In very large markets, such as those of the US and the UK, a liquidity crunch is likely to affect very small companies only.

Can markets go mad?

At the end of the day markets are made up of people, therefore despite the vast sums paid in education and investment software, waves of emotion regularly flood markets. Nobody has yet managed to define **sentiment,** but sentiment can drive stock markets up and down. These movements are based on one simple criterion: are investors feeling cheerful, or gloomy?

'Irrational exuberance' is the label used to describe a relaxed attitude to sky-high share price valuations, which was a general feature of the 1990s technology-led bull market. The collapse in equities following the subsequent technology bubble burst – which started in 2000 and persisted into 2003 – marked the deepest bear market since the 1930s and once again redefined attitudes towards equities.

The result has been a substantial shift towards property worldwide. This huge increase in demand, coupled with limited supply of available properties, has pushed up property prices in many areas to levels that appear overvalued.

Can politicians affect markets, too?

Basically, politicians can mess up just about anything! **Political risk** refers to the potential change in economic policy likely to arise as a result of a change of government or policy. If a new political party or coalition is expected to be tough on business, or to raise taxes, this expectation will depress stock markets and vice versa. **Geopolitical risk** refers to the effect of political power-play on the global market. For example, there has been an increase in geopolitical risk following the US-led invasion of Iraq. This action has arguably increased the risk of a dirty bomb event or, worse still, a nuclear terrorism event in the USA. It has also increased tension between the USA and the newly emerging big boy in the playground, China, which may have unwelcome consequences in the future.

Isn't the trick with investment to avoid investment risk?

No. Investment risk is good. If people and companies didn't risk capital, nothing would ever happen on the stock markets. It's the old chestnut: you have to speculate to accumulate. Unless you win the lottery or benefit from a huge inheritance, it is an economic fact that you won't become financially independent without taking investment risk. What's important to remember is that taking risk does not mean taking unacceptable risks. The best approach is to spread your assets across high risk, medium risk and low risk investment. This method incurs far less risk than concentrating your investment at one particular point. That boils down to four investment risk options:

- Low risk, low return
- High risk, high return
- High risk, low return
- Low risk, high return

So, which of those four basic outcomes is the best? You've got it, low risk, high return. Consider two funds that produce similar cash results over a five-year investment period – which one was the best? Well, I can tell you that it's not a draw. The best fund is the one that did the business by taking less risk, thereby exposing you to less volatility in value – and less sleep loss! I regularly hear people incorrectly comparing different asset performances by judging them purely on absolute returns. An investor might say, 'Hey, I made 50% on my money by flipping an apartment off the plans in Shanghai while European Government bonds just did 5%, so Shanghai is better!' That's plain illogical: it isn't the performance you get from an asset, it's the performance after adjusting for the risk you took.

You don't need a degree in standard deviation analysis to figure out that loading everything into a high risk, high return investment contains the seeds of destruction. Of course, that doesn't mean that you shouldn't have *some* high risk investment: loading everything into low risk investment means you will never get anywhere. The trick is getting the right balance. If you want a real risk to keep you awake at night consider how your assets quietly devalue as you sleep!

The silent killer: inflation risk

When you open your wallet this year and pull out some Euro notes, you don't think about the fact that when you did the same thing last year, or the year before, the notes were worth more. The effect on prices of rising inflation is practically invisible, but it happens all the time and is a sucker punch for assets, which can't counteract its corrosive effect.

Inflation risk can be regarded as the opposite of investment risk. It does far greater damage to investments with low investment risk, such as cash deposits and bonds, than it does to property and equities. For this reason equity investment is an **inflation hedge**. When money decreases in value, businesses counteract by increasing the nominal price of their goods and services, which in turn filters through to stock market values. This means that although equities pose a higher investment risk than cash deposits and bonds, they contain a lot less inflation risk. Inflation decreases the real cost of outstanding mortgage debt and rents are typically adjusted upwards to counteract loss in money value, so property is a good inflation hedge too.

The risk of over-concentration, aka, putting all the eggs in one basket

Across the technology sector highly paid and educated technologists and electrical engineers wiped millions off their balance sheets by over-concentration in one asset – the shares of their employers. Before the technology share price collapse lots of staff wouldn't trigger share options at prices vastly cheaper than market prices because they didn't want to pay Capital Gains Tax (CGT), even though CGT was at an historic low of 20% of profit, plus they were seduced by the notion that the price would hit a new high, like $100. Instead, share prices plunged well below staff option levels and became worthless. It's a simple, important lesson: putting all of your eggs in one basket is never a good idea (unless you are ideally positioned, such as owning and running the asset, and even then you should diversify).

This is equally true of strategies that involve keeping most of your money in one cash deposit, bond, stock, or property. Diversifying across assets reduces your risk, but not necessarily your returns.

Can prices fall? Deflation risk

Deflation means that prices fall in value, which is already happening in the USA and other countries as their manufacturing base for white goods and the like is undercut by competition from much cheaper manufacturers in China. Thankfully, this fall has been offset by rising prices in other sectors, like services, but widespread deflation has happened before. It occurred during the US depression of the 1930s, and again in Japan after its economy went into reverse for much of the 1990s.

Deflation occurs when there is a severe economic downturn, which has the effect of reducing the value of property, equities and just about all goods and services. Since governments have almost a limitless ability to raise money through taxes, government bonds are regarded as a hedge against deflation. Strong sovereign governments are unlikely to default on their bonds. Gold is a hedge against inflation. Government bonds are normally viewed as a hedge against deflation. Both are creeping onto balance sheets around the world because of concerns about the weakness of the dollar. We will examine these threats in more detail in the next chapter. For now, it is enough to note that deflation exists as a risk to investments, so you need to be aware of global events and how they might impact on one another.

Can I avoid currency risk?

Currency risk is all around you and no, you can't avoid it. It would be nice to live in a world free of currency risks, but unfortunately this is impossible due to the globalisation and integration of world markets. (Next time you are filling the car with petrol, think of it as pumping a dollar/Euro exchange risk directly into the tank, and onto your credit card statement.)

As an investor, you inherit currency risk from the companies you invest in, which sell their goods and services in international markets. Because they run businesses in different parts of the world with different currencies, their balance sheets and cash flows contain large degrees of currency risk. Don't be misled by the fact that the balance sheet published by one of your investment companies is presented in dollars, sterling or in Euro. For very large companies, these are simply photographs of the value of the business taken through one particular currency lens.

The other common investment that is open to currency risk is property. When you buy property in countries outside the Eurozone, or not pegged to the Euro, you take on board a large dollop of currency risk. For example, if you buy a pad in Florida for €300,000 and it rises in value to €330,000, but the dollar falls against the Euro by over 9%, your gain is automatically wiped out.

Can I lose all my money? Default risk

Yes, you can lose all your money if the product provider or company holding your money goes bust. Depositor and investor protection schemes are a feature of modern investment, but in many cases they will pay only a fraction of the sums invested if such sums are large. Credit rating agencies such as **Moodys,**

Standard & Poors and Fitch, provide benchmarks ranging from AAA to D. If a financial firm has a poor credit rating, it will offer a higher yield in order to attract investors and vice versa. This is what differentiates top corporate bonds from junk bonds: Junk bonds pay out more, but carry greater default risk

Credit ratings are also provided for Government bonds; US Government bonds will attract the highest credit rating. The US Government has never defaulted on paying its debts, but sometimes Governments play tricks, like deliberately letting their currencies devalue in order to lessen their total debt repayments.

As a matter of good practice, or because of regulations, certain types of asset manager do not hold the assets they manage. Instead these are ring-fenced using custodian banks unconnected to the asset managers. This was illustrated in one of the most famous investment debacles of recent times, when Nick Leeson cost Barings Bank vast sums of money through derivative speculation. Investors in Baring Asset Management were protected from the losses, but depositors in Barings Bank were exposed. (Leeson is now General Manager of Galway United, where losses won't quite make the same headlines or cause the same amount of fretting!)

What can I expect from the major assets?

The outcome of investments, even over the very long term, is uncertain but assumptions are made all the time for planning reasons. Concerned with meeting future income promises or liabilities, these are the type of numbers actuaries use in assuming long-term asset growth for pension schemes above inflation. Of course, nobody knows what the future will bring and all forecasts are wrong – it's just a question of degree. While actuaries might suggest that these assumptions, which don't include the effect of taxes and expenses, are pretty repetitive in historical long-term data, it's important to remember that they are *averages* and actual results will vary a lot depending on the choppiness or volatility of an asset. Short-term asset performance, on the other hand, can be hugely different, often confounding forecasts. The capital risk and the volatility of your assets will vary enormously between guaranteed assets, like cash deposits and Government bonds, and 'risky' assets, like geared property and equities.

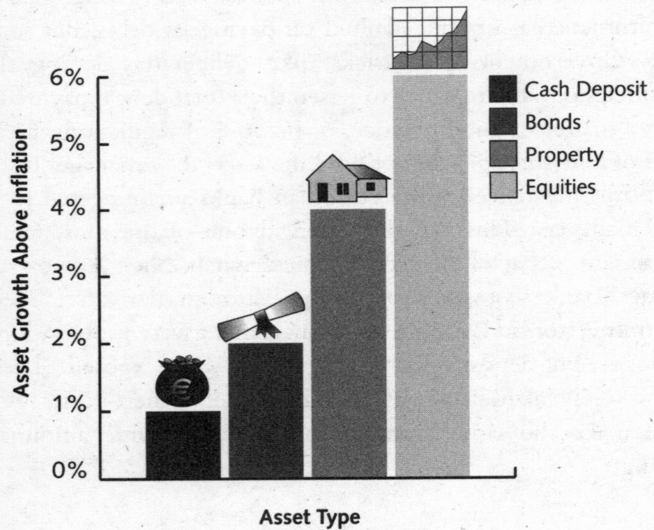

The averages for equities and property are averages based on a wide variety of experience of different types of equity and different types of property over a long period of time. When the focus is on a small number of shares, or a number of private properties, the real rate of return above inflation can be a lot higher than long-term averages, or lower – depending on your skill, or luck.

If you've ever felt that your sleeping tablets were not working, it might be because you decided to delve into a little actuarial 'literature'. Actuaries use estimates to do certain calculations, such as when, for example, you change jobs. In such a case, an actuary would calculate the cash value of the pension you built up with your former employer so you can move your pension entitlement to a retirement bond, or bring it with you to the pension scheme of your new employer.

In actuarial literature you will find 'estimated' long-term rates of return used by actuaries for various purposes. Depending on where you look in the literature, you might be able to come up with assumptions about long-term asset growth ***before inflation is deducted, i.e. nominal returns.***

Annual Long-Term Rate of Return on Various Asset Types

Asset Type	Annual Rate of Return
Cash Deposits	3.00%
Bonds	4.50%
Property	6.25%
Equities	7.25%

On their own averages are misleading, however, telling you little about the risk of not getting the average return. Think of it like this: suppose I were to offer you a grand to walk across a river with an average depth of one metre – you'd be very suspicious, wouldn't you? *A grand?* What's the catch? So, what question would you ask me before deciding to accept? Obviously you'd ask me about the variation in depth: are there places where the depth of the river is 5 metres and places where the depth is 20 centimetres? If there are places where the depth is 5 meters, you might not accept the challenge. If, however, the variation in depth is no more than 5 centimetres, you would probably accept the challenge.

So the next time you see a table that reports average returns like the assumptions used by the life insurance industry, you'll know there is a missing ingredient – the variation around the average!

Here is my adjusted version of the table given above, showing the variation around the average value for investments over a very short period, i.e. one year. It tells a different story, especially the danger of using long-term averages for short-term objectives:

Annual Long-Term Rate of Return on Various Asset Types

Asset Type	Annual Rate of Return	Likely Variation Around the Average Rate of Return over One Year
Cash Deposits	3.00%	0% to 6%
Bonds	4.50%	−11.5% to 20.5%
Property	6.25%	−13.75% to 26.25%
Equities	7.25%	−28.74% to 43.25%

So the lesson is that while long-term averages can provide some pointers, choppier assets with higher volatility can produce results well below and above the average, especially over very short periods like one year, but they are still worth investing in strongly if you want to grow your balance sheet at good rates above inflation. The trick is to do so with your eyes open, understanding how assets can behave.

It's reckoned that, in practice, about two-thirds of Irish balance sheets are in property, which is hardly surprising given its huge leap in value over the past decade as Ireland has been transformed from an economic backwater into a competitive economy. Because it is illiquid, property isn't favoured as heavily by large institutional funds that invest across all asset classes. For example, the chart on page 65 shows what USA, UK and Japanese pension funds hold. These are the world's giant funds.

There are lots of textbooks crammed with portfolio optimisation theories purporting to guess the best mix, but in practice much is dependent on where you start from, switching costs and taxes. Irish balance sheets would look a lot different than those shown above, and even within these vast fund sectors asset exposure is heavily influenced by local events and practice. So we see that, in the teeth of historic deflation, Japanese investors are heavier into bonds and far less enamoured with their own stock market, as compared to, say, the Americans. It would be nice if you could reallocate your balance sheet at the stroke of a pen, but you can't, and even if you could, there would still be the thorny issue of tax and costs.

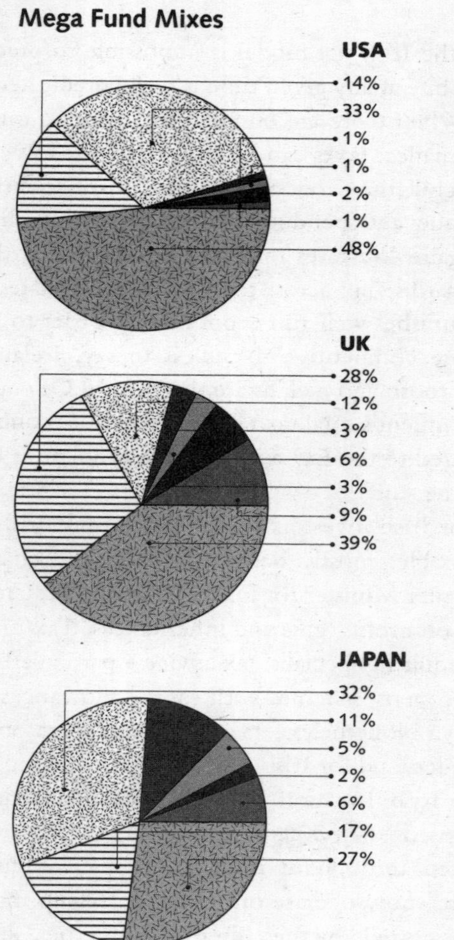

Source: UBS Global Asset Management – Pension Fund Indicators 2004

Understanding tax

The future shape of the Irish tax model is impossible to predict. The extent of the tax bite at any given time is really predicated on the local economy. When there are bumper tax revenues on the back of strong performance, taxes can be kept relatively low. But come an economic chill the Government may want to bridge deficits between revenues and spending without borrowing, therefore taxes can rise again. Pressures may also be brought to bear from Europe to standardise tax across the EU member states – a nutty proposal that punishes well-run economies in order to help laggards become more competitive. Needless to say, Ireland is fighting this proposal tooth and nail, as are the British. Of course, while the Irish Government's total tax take as a share of economic activity is low compared to the EU averages, the problem is how efficiently we spend the stuff!

The good news for Irish investors is that the current Irish tax model is very favourable, mostly because of dramatic changes introduced by the former Minister for Finance Charlie McCreevy TD, who halved tax on profits, gifts and inheritances. Tax can be a complicated area, requiring specialist tax advice – particularly for investment in local property schemes with capital allowances and for overseas property. Nonetheless, tax is generally reasonably straightforward to understand for Irish investors. One helpful tool is the website of the Irish Taxation Institute, where current tax rates are well summarised – www.taxireland.ie.

Collective investment through funds, such as unit-linked funds, OEICs and unit trusts, now operate on the gross roll-up model. This means that the assets held by these funds in properties, shares, bonds, cash deposits and other assets are not liable to Irish tax on income and capital gains created within the fund from rents and dividends, or on profits made by the fund from trading. It is only when cash is physically taken out of a gross roll-up fund that you are liable for tax at 23%, which is deducted by domestic asset managers, such as life insurance companies. Where you invest in a fund managed by an asset manager outside of Ireland but within the OECD, a similar tax applies to your profit under self-assessment rules.

Income tax has been steadily declining in Ireland with a strong economic performance and bumper tax revenues. The top rate of tax before PRSI and levies is currently 42%, with the lower rate standing at 20% – although PRSI and health contributions can add on another 6%, up to certain limits, on earned income. Income such as rents and dividends is subject to tax at the marginal rate, but interest on borrowing for investment in property can generally be used as an offset. There is a range of special tax incentive schemes that have been employed by the Irish Government over the years to encourage investment in particular sectors, and the tax rules differ across these various schemes. Your particular questions should be referred to your tax advisor, who can supply you with the information relevant to your particular situation.

Halving CGT to 20% is perhaps the most important tax change to have occurred over the past ten years. Capital Gains Tax is the rate of tax applying to profits made from selling shares or property. By halving the rate, the Government encouraged higher activity in trading assets, thus increasing the level of inflows from CGT to the Revenue Commissioners. The top rate of Capital Acquisitions Tax (CAT) on inheritances and gifts was also halved to 20%, while threshold limits above which the tax applies were increased and linked to the consumer price index.

Another significant change introduced by the Government was the implementation of Approved Retirement Funds (ARFs) (see Chapter 16). These are vehicles that continue to carry forward the capital accumulated in pension schemes for the self-employed, proprietary directors, PRSAs and those saving through AVCs. These investors are no longer compelled to surrender the vast bulk of capital they accumulate in return for a taxable pension income for life. From 2006, an accumulation tax and limits will apply to ARFs.

But tax is still a drag!

Tax creates a drag effect on asset growth whether you pay it on deposits yearly, like DIRT, or at the back end, but obviously the lower the rate, the better. The pension model (covered in Chapter 16) is an efficient way to delay tax payment on chunks of your income for many years, and following the revolutionary changes implemented in the Finance Act 1999, it has percolated to the top of the agenda for action.

When you invest abroad in foreign property, you need to consider the tax effects carefully. Begin by looking at the availability, or otherwise, of a Double Taxation Agreement between Ireland and the country in which you are investing. You would be wise to take specialist tax advice even where a Double Taxation Agreement exists, in order to mitigate the effect of being taxed twice. This is because not all countries have tax models as favourable as Ireland's, therefore there can be significant long-term effects, particularly from inheritance tax, CGT, community taxes, stamp duties and tax on rent. It's never a good idea to embark on a substantial investment without understanding the basics of how the relevant taxes are going to create a drag effect on your return. The bottomline is: always, always be aware of tax and how it will affect your investment options.

Other costs

You also need to bear in mind the other costs that will affect your returns. This applies to property, in particular, where you need to be mindful of stamp duty, entry costs, maintenance costs and exit costs, all of which will reduce your return. The costs affecting collective investments, such as unit-linked funds and syndicated property schemes, is an area all in itself and is therefore given its own chapter: Chapter 15, Investing Through Funds.

Can I learn anything from what's happened in the past?

While the past cannot be used as a guarantee of what will happen in the future, it does provide some grit on the icy road of your expectations of your asset performance. Investment performance has been recorded for UK assets as far back as 1700, giving us a wide area of study. For example, stg£1 invested in bonds in 1700 would have grown, by 2000, to over stg£630,000, but if that same pound had been invested in shares, it would have grown to over stg£51m!

Across the ocean in the USA, the S&P 500, which tracks the value of five hundred US companies, opened in 1926. Over the next seven decades the market made money in 60% of the months, 70% of the years and 100% of the time for every fifteen-year rolling time period. There were also significant falls during this period, corresponding to major world events:

- 1940, −9.76%: Germany invades France.
- 1941, −11.59%: Japan attacks Pearl Harbor.
- 1962, −8.73%: Cuban Missile Crisis.
- 1966, −10.06%: Vietnam War.
- 1973, −14.66%: Middle East oil crisis.
- 1974, −26.47%: Heavy recession in USA and Europe.

The S&P 500 shows that these falls were balanced by up-swings, which again related to global events:

- 1945, +36.44%: Second World War ends.
- 1975, +37%: US & Europe recession worsens.
- 1976, +23.84%: Price of Gold Dives.
- 1991, +30.55%: Gulf War.
- 1995, +37.43%: Oklahoma Bombing.

You might well be wondering, where is the 1987 stock market crash? It wasn't actually a crash. The result for the full calendar year in 1987 was positive for the main markets in the US and London. The market corrected itself. It was overvalued. It did not crash. The dot.com bubble did lead to a collapse of technology share prices and dragged the entire market down between 2000 and 2003, with very significant falls in Europe and the US, as high as 60% from peak to trough. But the strong stock market bounce-back over the following two years recovered most of these losses.

Below is the year-by-year performance of the FTSE 100 in the London stock market, and the ISEQ in the Irish Stock Market, which underlines the fact that sticking with the ups and downs over the long haul is the right approach:

	London	Dublin
1987	+2.01%	−6.40%
1988	+4.71%	+37.81%
1989	+35.09%	+27.37%
1990	−11.53%	−31.53%
1991	+16.32%	+14.85%
1992	+14.18%	−11.08%
1993	+20.09%	+53.90%
1994	−10.32%	−2.02%
1995	+20.35%	+20.62%
1996	+11.63%	+22.09%
1997	+24.69%	+48.73%
1998	+14.55%	+23.24%
1999	+17.81%	+0.43%
2000	−10.21%	+14.05%
2001	−16.15%	−0.27%
2002	−24.48%	−30.00%
2003	+13.62%	+23.17%
2004	+7.54%	+25.95%
2005	+16.71%	+18.82%

Source: Bloomberg

Despite the juicy long-term returns from stock markets like Dublin and London, the impact of the most recent equity decline has meant investor wariness of equities, which has pushed billions into property markets on both sides of the Atlantic, increasing demand and pushing up prices. In Ireland the recent economic boom has further pushed up property prices because of an under-supply of housing stock and a large inflow of immigration at a time of historically low interest rates. Property is self-evidently a less volatile asset than equities, but it is also illiquid and much slower to respond after sharp declines.

Property wasn't always sexy

Property investment is a good diversifier from equities because the correlation between these two behemoths isn't strong, which means while one is lagging, the other may be powering ahead. In the heat of any bull market, whether in property or in equities, it's important to keep your head and continue to diversify, even though the emotional urge is to bet on a longer and longer bull run – rarely a good idea!

Reliable Irish property performance data doesn't go back too far, but the table below shows the average performance each year for unit-linked funds sold in Ireland that largely specialised in Irish commercial and retail property since 1980. These funds are taxed at source each year, under the old tax model. In many years during the 1980s and early 1990s these property funds performed worse than deposits and inflation. The impact of Ireland's economic transformation is clearly visible in later years, but this too is reflected in the ISEQ, as you will see from the last table.

Year	Unit-linked Property Funds
1980	22.19%
1981	15.80%
1982	7.46%
1983	6.07%
1984	−0.74%
1985	−0.29%
1986	1.24%

Year	Irish Commercial Property
1987	7.36%
1988	12.13%
1989	18.82%
1990	3.89%
1991	−9.82%
1992	−6.72%
1993	7.30%
1994	11.03%
1995	10.55%
1996	11.75%
1997	17.23%
1998	27.16%
1999	24.02%
2000	18.61%
2001	0.25%
2002	2.95%
2003	10.65%
2004	11.86%
2005	14.7%

Source: Standard & Poors Fund Services

Gearing property works best in the good times but . . .

When property is geared using a combination of a bank loan and your own equity, any increase in the capital value of the property passes onto your balance sheet, not onto the bank's. Equally, when the property falls in value your balance sheet takes the hit, not the bank's. The return to the bank is the profit margin it is making on the mortgage, regardless of whether the property market is rising, falling or crabbing sideways. Gearing magnifies both the upside and downside of property prices on your balance sheet, which is why it is important to approach property investment carefully – and why I have devoted three chapters to our favourite national topic. See Chapters 9, 10 and 11 for a full discussion of property investments.

What's the best mix?

There is little evidence of professional or individual investors applying complex portfolio optimisation theories in day-to-day practice. Most individual investors use commonsense rules of thumb when making investment decisions, matched by their current tolerance for taking investment risk and taking into account tax and switching costs that discourage frequent remixing of balance sheets.

One workable rule suggests that you set the percentage you ought to have in real assets, i.e. in property and equities, by deducting your age from 100, or from 120 if you want to be more aggressive. The remainder of this subtraction is what you ought to have invested in bonds and cash deposits. For example, a 40-year-old deducts 40 from 120, giving 80, so that means our 40-year-old ought to have 80% in real assets (property and equities) and 20% in paper assets (bonds and cash deposits).

Commonsense quickly establishes that loading all of your assets into the cash deposits at the bottom of the Investment Pyramid (see page 53) is nuts. Equally, loading most of your assets into one small stock or one investment property greatly increases the threat to your overall balance sheet in the event of a crash in the value of the stock, or significant problems in the local property market. There's no hard and fast rule for this. Some financial commentators err on the side of reducing the level of equity exposure, principally because it's more comfortable. On the other hand, respected commentators and lifelong professional fund managers, like Peter Lynch of Fidelity, are so won over by equities they don't rate investing in bonds at all. While US investors might love their shares lots of Irish wealth has been made by astute investment in property by people that wouldn't be seen dead with a share certificate. You'll need to examine the options and see which best fits your balance sheet, your tolerance for taking investment risk and your goals, but don't forget the central message in *Loot!* – it's better to build a diversified mix of uncorrelated assets than putting too many of your eggs in one basket, no matter how enticing that may be.

What's better: buy well and hold, or bail in and out?

Many professionals, especially those selling asset management services, propose that the best solution is regular active switching of your assets to take account of cyclical changes in economic circumstances. This approach has two practical problems: first, switching costs, commissions and taxes; second, the risk of getting the timing wrong. You might be lucky and get the exit timing right, but then you're faced with having to get it right twice because you'll need to get back in again!

The best approach is to buy good assets and stay with them through thick and thin. That is more likely to lead to better and safer long-term results than hopping in and out of assets that are constantly blown this way and that by the latest news. A little bit of reallocation from time to time will certainly help, but over-active management runs the risk of getting timing wrong – and paying for it. The challenge is to allocate towards assets when they are out of favour, which normally means they offer good buying opportunities.

What makes sense?

That depends. For everyone, it makes a lot of commonsense to hold a liquid reserve in cash deposit so that you are solvent for at least six months in the event of your income drying up. We'll call this your solvency, and it's purpose is twofold: first, it means you can call on it to meet unexpected draws on your income; secondly, it sets a limit to how much you're prepared to let wither on cash deposit long term.

Where you need the cash over the short term, like in a few years to buy a house or pay for a wedding, you can't risk the volatility of assets that can fall in value – to do so wouldn't be investing but gambling. In this case you should stick with cash deposits and short-dated Eurobond funds.

Where you need to generate a recurring income to support retirement, you should concentrate on income-producing assets, like property and high dividend shares, and on bonds, both Government bonds and investment grade corporate bonds.

If, on the other hand, you are in for the long haul and are chasing asset growth to build your balance sheet and are therefore prepared to weather the volatility of growth assets, it makes sense to position much of your balance sheet in the medium risk part of the Investment Pyramid. This means putting your money in geared property and large shares where you have a chance to out-perform inflation by 4% pa or more. It also makes sense to have an allocation in the high risk part of the Investment Pyramid, gaining exposure to medium and small stocks and to fast-growing areas, such as China and the South East Asia region.

Investment in alternatives like commodities, traded currencies and in gold can also feature in a long-term, diversified mix. All of these assets are available to Irish investors either directly or through funds, whether traded on exchanges as ETFs (Exchange Traded Funds), held by OEICs (Open-Ended Investment Companies), or issued as unit-linked policies by life offices. (These various structures for holding assets are discussed in Chapter 15.) ETFs and OEICs are available through stockbrokers and specialist investment intermediaries.

The case for a fifth asset class: commodities, traded currencies, gold, antiques and collectibles

The classic objective of diversifying an investment portfolio is to chase a target rate of return from an asset mix while pushing down the risk. Increasingly, investment in commodities such as oil, gas, steel, cement, gold, uranium and base metals like nickel, copper, etc., is featuring in asset mixes. However, as a general rule of thumb, diversification into a fifth asset class probably shouldn't exceed 15% of total investment.

Traded currencies are also an alternative diversifier and are entirely uncorrelated to the main asset classes because returns are typically based on trading between the Euro, dollar and yen. Specialist currency managers are available to Irish investors, including through unit-linked funds.

An asset class that's been out of favour since the 1970s, the case for commodities is growing because of a structural shift in demand for commodities. In the last century **commodity bull markets**, where prices are strongly rising, averaged eighteen years in length, so it would be unwise to bypass what's happening now. There is every sign of continued rising demand for commodities, especially from China, which is the dominant force in the market along with India, Brazil and Russia. Demand is rising to levels that can't be met by supply – a recipe for rising prices as competition for the world's scarce natural resources grows. In 2003, for example, China alone consumed half of the world's supply of cement and one-third of its steel supply. So while commodities are a very volatile asset class, if the world has entered a commodity bull market its length should eventually compensate for the choppiness of the ride.

Of course, you don't have to load up your garage with uranium, copper bars or gold bullion to invest across commodities. Funds are available that hold a broad mix of commodities, although you can expect to find increasingly higher allocations towards gold. During times of stress, instability and a loss of confidence in currencies, gold tends to do well, making it a good asset through which to diversify investment risk. Gold is unusual because it is both a commodity and a monetary asset that traditionally supported currencies. If gold sounds like the asset class for you, you can invest in gold bullion through Exchange Traded Funds quoted in London and the market is highly liquid.

Investing in antiques and collectibles makes a bunch of sense if you've built up a high level of knowledge and expertise. It also brings an element of pleasure that, let's face it, you can't get from bricks and mortar or paper assets. However, antiques and collectibles carry their own unique risks. These, to a great extent, relate to each individual antique or collectible, and to the laws of supply and demand relating to its sector.

The value of collectibles appears to have an inflation link. Money moves into high valuable collectibles and antiques at a time when there is a loss of confidence in money value. Whatever type of antique or collectible you specialise in, whether it is impressionist paintings or antique vases, factor in the costs of **insurance**, **security** and the **length of time** it may take you to find a buyer (**liquidity**).

The market for collectibles and antiques is a fertile ground for con artists, who will attempt to pass off copies as the authentic item, so you'll need a thorough knowledge of your subject and of your suppliers before you speculate. Warnings aside, the market for collectibles rarely ceases to amaze, with **attic finds** such as comics, old dolls, toys, autographs, books, photographs and wines frequently attracting premium prices due to their rarity.

If you are interested in learning more about collectibles and antiques, find out where your local **auction rooms** are and begin to visit them to build up your knowledge. Check if any **courses** are available that would provide you with a detailed understanding of decorative arts, antiques and collectibles. You may even earn a diploma – you only go through life once and this may be just the thing for you!

A closer look at the eggs in the basket

Harry Markowitz won a Nobel Prize in 1990 for taking a much closer look at the 'eggs in the basket' concept. Put simply, Harry said it was not the *number* of eggs you had in the basket, it was the number of eggs that *behaved differently* in different market conditions which made your basket of eggs deliver you more return for less risk – or made your basket of investments more diversified.

It's loopy to have all your assets tied up in property, even if it's spread across the globe. If there is a global rise in interest rates, for example, it's going to hit property across the board. The highly borrowed recent entrants to the market will not have enough cash flow to fund the higher interest bill because rents will not rise in line with interest rates – at least in the short term – so selling will be the only option and that will push property prices down: a classic rout in a market.

Similarly, there is no point having your investment basket stuffed exclusively with equities. You might think that you are getting diversification – *'I've thousands of companies in my share portfolio'* – but you are not because you are invested in a single asset class, namely equities. Think about it: given the globalization of equity markets, when the major global equity markets start to fall sharply, almost all of the world equity markets fall in value.

There is no 'all-weather' asset class

There is no magic asset that only ever goes up in value – more's the pity! The reality is that each and every asset class runs through cycles. Take equities as an example: a bull run, such as we had in equities from 1995 to 2000, is followed inevitably by a bear market, which we saw from 2000 to 2003. In 2004 and 2005 most equity markets rebounded sharply in what now looks like the beginning of another bull run. The cycle is the same in property: the early to mid-1980s were an extremely depressed period for Irish residential property, but look what has happened since! The cycles in property tend to last longer because property prices are less transparent and slower to adjust than equity prices. Bonds have similar cycles, as do commodities. What goes up, must come down, etc. etc.

So, how can you get the biggest return possible for the least amount of risk?

Put simply, the only thing you can do to get as much return as possible for as little risk as possible is to combine assets that don't have their good and bad times at the same time. This means building a balance sheet on a range of assets that tend to compensate each other in terms of performance. In other words, their investment cycles are generally not completely in step.

You can lower the risk in a mix of assets by just dumping everything into the bank in cash deposits, but while this will eliminate the choppiness in your balance sheet, it will also screw up any hope of strong returns above inflation. Be careful of diversification illusions. It's very common for advisors to spread your money across a range of similar investments according to whatever is the current rage, like property, or so-called managed funds. This may give the appearance of diversification because a range of fund managers is being used, but if you look behind these, you'll find similar assets.

Big falls need even bigger recoveries

If you overload into one asset type, you'll go through periods of excessive return only to face periods of deep troughs. Remember, if an asset like property falls 30% in value, it has to go up 42% just to get back to the value from which it fell. At, say, 10% per annum, a bounce-back of 42% will take close to four years.

The golden rule – diversify, diversify, diversify

Choose assets that don't tend to have their good and bad times together. If property makes up a large part of your balance sheet, don't buy any more for the moment and invest in assets that have had a good track record of performing well during times when property fell in value and which give you at least as good a return as property. In this case, equities would fit the bill. Don't just invest in one equity, however. Don't buy all technology shares or all banking shares. Instead, buy shares in each industrial sector. Don't confine yourself to just one market – like the Irish stock market – but spread your investment in equities across several markets. Another don't: don't stop diversification at the front gates of property and equities – invest in Government and Corporate bonds of different strength and duration. In particular, look at diversification into commodities and traded currencies, which are uncorrelated to the major asset classes.

The proof in the pudding

Let's avoid the technical jargon of correlation and look for evidence of risk reduction in a very simple manner. Here's what happened over nearly five years to January 2006 from investment in two common-or-garden variety managed funds, which use a mix made up mainly of equities, property, bonds and cash. The two funds behaved very similarly: each month 'A' was up, 'B' was up 58% of the time; each was down together 40% of the time. In fact, in no month that 'A' was down was 'B' up and, in the reverse case, 'A' was up only 2% of the time when 'B' was down.

Month by Month Analysis	Fund A UP	Fund A DOWN
Fund B UP	58%	0%
Fund B DOWN	2%	40%

Managed funds in Ireland largely maintain pretty common asset mixes, usually dominated by equities and bonds, so other asset classes would act as a diversifier; for example, property is a good diversifier to equities. In this example we consider what happened where two uncorrelated investments were made, one involving Managed Fund 'B' and the other involving something completely different – a diversifier, like a traded currency fund, for example. While past performance isn't a reliable guide to the future, it's clear that this mix behaves very differently. In 22% of the months that 'B' was down, the diversifier, i.e. the currency fund, compensated by being up. In 27% of the months the currency fund was down, 'B' the managed fund was up. They were both up together 31% of the period, and down together 20% of the period.

Month by Month Analysis	Currency Fund UP	Currency Fund DOWN
Managed B UP	31%	27%
Managed B DOWN	22%	20%

So, how does that filter through to performance when, say, the mix starting out was three-quarters invested in the managed fund and one-quarter in the diversifier, i.e. the traded currency fund, compared to being fully invested in the managed fund only?

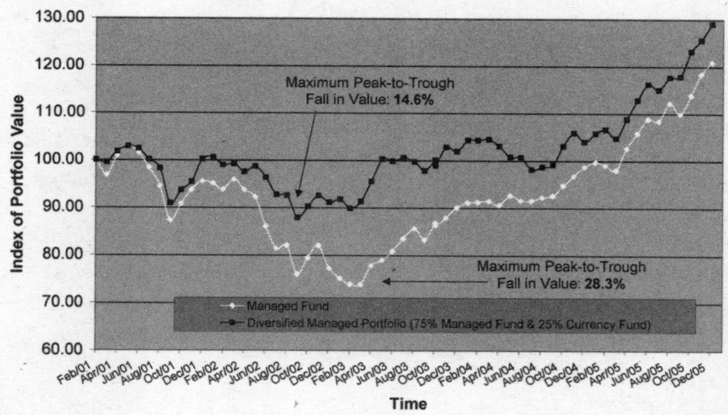

Source: Alder Capital

For most of the time 'B', the managed fund, was below its opening value. From its peak, the managed fund fell over 28%, yet the diversified mix fell 14.6% from its peak. At the end of the period the diversified mix was 6.7% ahead of the value of the managed fund. Looks like Harry Markowitz was on to something! While this is just one example and past risk reduction and return enhancement like this may not be a reliable guide to the future, it does help tell the story at the heart of *Loot!*, which is that despite current fashions, all assets are cyclical, therefore over-concentrating in any particular asset class comes at higher risk. Diversifying can help reduce the overall risk in your balance sheet without necessarily reducing the return, but it will require you to avoid the temptation of following the crowd and, literally, betting the house on the latest hot asset.

CHAPTER 7

A Word of Warning on Near-Term Possibilities

Glossary

- **ETF:** Exchange Traded Fund quoted as tradable instrument in stock market.

Sometimes I wonder how doctors and solicitors can get out of bed in the morning, knowing, as they do, all the ways you can get seriously sick or get sued in a normal working day. In the investment world lots of folk are afraid ever to make a decision, petrified of losing their money unless it remains in cash at the bank, where they can visit it and hug it like a comfort blanket. Time and again these ossified billions are left stewing, with lousy real rates of return, while investment opportunities are lost. It's better to be in markets, taking the volatility and sticking with it through thick and thin, than hiding in a bank afraid to do anything. Even if there is a substantial correction in the world economy, it's impractical to think about switching out – after all, most of us are up to our necks in illiquid property.

Doom and gloom prophets have been with us since the dawn of time, and they'll always be there, forecasting catastrophe, but the truth is that for every bull market, there's a bear, and for every optimist, a pessimist. This doesn't mean, however, that expert analysis on the potential for a major structural shift in the world economy can be ignored. Lessons taught by history and set against the backdrop of current economic events are worth a pause for thought, particularly for those with more vulnerable balance sheets than others.

There is probably nothing as upsetting as the thought that the guy next door is growing his wealth faster than yours. This paranoia can propel normally cautious and careful investors into taking high risk decisions that could quickly unwrap in the event of a sharp correction. Some Irish investors have unacceptably high gearing in balance sheets as mini property empires have gradually become the norm. But the availability of interest-only finance for those on modest incomes, in many cases secured against the family home, isn't a one-way ticket. Circumstances can change. If your overall level of borrowing exceeds 50% of your assets, you are taking a big bet on two things:

1. There is no property bubble and valuations are reasonably set against economic circumstances.
2. You are in an employment, or in a sector that is feather-bedded against any structural shift in the increasingly globalised and interconnected world economy.

Before you embark on any further gearing, you should carefully assess the risks involved. That's what this chapter is about – it's a little gloomy, but we're going to look at the global economic situation and the various quarters that pose threats to your swag bag.

A snapshot of the world today

The world population is growing quickly and, according to the UN, is expected to reach 9.4bn by 2050. This has serious repercussions as population increases fuel the appetite for raw materials, causing scarcity and rising prices. This applies particularly in relation to energy, a situation exacerbated by the fact that 65% of oil reserves are located in the troubled Middle East region.

The reason for the prolific population increase is our increased life expectancy. Back in AD 1000 life expectancy was just eighteen years, now there is a population of 50,000 Americans who are over the age of 100. The 'grey population', as our oldsters are affectionately known, is expected to reach 2bn by 2050 according to some forecasts, which represents a threefold increase from the present level. The developed world is greying at a faster rate, with a substantial fall between the number of workers and those retired from work. As a result, old age pensions are placing a strain on developed economies. In Germany, for example, pensions currently account for 15% of GDP.

More people also means more inequality. There is an ever-widening gap between those who live comfortably and those who just subsist; 80% of the world's population lives in developing countries. Even within developed countries, such as the United States, wealth is skewed: 1% of the population controls one-third of the national wealth, and the top 1% of US shareholders hold 50% of the values of all stocks, while one-eighth of Americans live below the poverty line, with annual incomes of less than $20,000. Although the developed nations of the world represent just one-fifth of the global population, they account for 86% of private consumption.

The removal of international trade barriers has created an increasingly globalised economy, throwing into sharp relief the difference in labour costs between rich and poor countries. We are already witnessing widespread movement of labour-intensive industries from rich to poor countries.

Global economic risks

The single greatest risk is a sharp correction in the worldwide economy triggered by the twin effect of the softness of the US economy and the potential structural shift that could occur as wealth moves East. The dollar has been the traditional reserve currency, but the US has accumulated an enormous budget and trade deficit. The trade deficit – created by an excess of imports over exports – is shifting dollars out of the US, principally to China and South East Asia, where vast dollar reserves are being accumulated. Meanwhile, the US Government continues to swell money supply and ramp up US Government debt, much of which is purchased by foreigners, thus creating further dollar outflows.

These twin deficits along with the substantial debt accumulated by US consumers, businesses and financial institutions must eventually be repaid. If the US were a limited company or a person, then, technically, it would be declared bankrupt. As it is, it is supported largely by confidence in the dollar as the favoured world reserve currency. But confidence in the dollar may not continue forever, and in the event that the US resorts to protecting its traditional industrial base from the threat of foreign imports by raising trade barriers, the strategic response from developing nations with vast dollar reserves may be to switch to the Euro as the new world reserve currency. Meanwhile, in order to lessen the real value of the debts outstanding, the US Government may be forced to let the dollar devalue sharply. The resulting shock to the world-wide economy could trigger a sharp and prolonged recession, followed by significant falls in property and shares values.

This is one prediction. Other analysts differ in their outlook, anticipating that the US will gradually ease its way out of its debt without triggering these responses and reckoning that a falling dollar would trigger large-scale buying of US assets from big funds underweight in US positions. But in the event that the doomsayers get it right, it's important to understand how to protect your balance sheet so that it can weather any significant downturn and, in particular, why over-extending your position by being too highly geared might lead to your balance sheet being destroyed by events entirely beyond your control.

So what are the stress points?

The developed world, particularly the US, has become heavily debt-reliant as Governments continue to spend beyond their means by financing deficits. The OECD reckons that by 2008 the total amount of Government debts accumulated by OECD members will account for 86% of their total GDP. Already the debt mountain has accumulated to about $16 trillion, half of which is held by the US Government and issued in the form of Government bonds held by pension funds, life offices, unit trusts and foreign Governments. Interest rates are once again on the rise, increasing the debt repayment burden for Governments. The continuation of debt-based spending is largely dependent on confidence amongst investors, consumers and companies who invest in further economic growth. The threat of deflation – which is already happening in core areas in the US, such as manufactured goods – has been offset by inflation, particularly in services like insurance, banking, etc., and in commodity prices like oil. But the elasticity of spending on the back of increased debt can't continue forever and a readjustment is therefore likely.

China's emergence as a major economic power with a vast pool of cheap labour poses a threat to the US economy that may be met by protectionist barriers, like its recent imposition of tariffs on steel and Chinese-made television sets. If, as some believe, there is excess global capacity through an over-supply of most products, then deflation could replace inflation as the major threat to the worldwide economy in the early part of the twenty-first century, a century that is likely to be dominated by China's emergence as a major world economic power.

China's GDP has been growing at around 10% per year, leading to a huge boom in exports and consequently creating a massive trade deficit with the rest of the world, a quarter of it with the US. China already produces half of the world's cameras, one-third of its air conditioners and television sets and one-fifth of its fridges. Falling prices have already affected these sectors, mainly because of Chinese imports. The reason is easy to see: in 2002 factory wages in the US were $17.00 per hour; in China they were $0.40 per hour. Having grabbed a vast share of worldwide household goods, China is poised to move up the value chain into the high-tech sectors. Its vast labour pool of 800 million workers is producing IT engineers for foreign firms, who then relocate to China with wages of $15,000 a year – some fifteen times the average national wage in China, but a tiny fraction of equivalent costs in developed countries. Furthermore, the Chinese Government does not have to worry about paying old age pensions – there is none. It's a situation that contrasts sharply to that pertaining in the developed world, with is greying populations. It's not all one-way traffic, however, and China is hugely dependent on the USA. A sharp decline in the US economy, leading to a fall in Chinese exports, could have very serious implications for internal Chinese stability, arresting the huge move in population from poor rural areas to wealthier urban areas and potentially triggering unrest on a vast scale.

Other geopolitical risks to be aware of

Well, if the level of debt held by the developed world, the potential for trade wars, manufacturing and technological transfers, and the emergence of low-cost labour juggernauts like China weren't enough to give you some sleepless nights, the geopolitical map is not exactly a sea of calm either. US foreign policy has become increasingly unilateralist in recent times. It's now become clear that the US-led invasion of Iraq had nothing to do with weapons of mass destruction and everything to do with securing US oil supplies. The resulting increase in global terrorism and insurgency was an inevitable backlash and acts of terrorism will continue to pose a serious threat so long as the US persists with its current foreign policy. While acts of terrorism will not, on their own, trigger a worldwide economic correction (except, that is, in circumstances where terrorist cells use so-called dirty bombs, or in a nightmare situation, a nuclear device), they will accelerate the pace of any recession. These threats are also posed from other quarters of US foreign policy, with growing tensions between the US and China and a fragility of relations between the US and Iran, North Korea, Sudan and Syria, all identified by the current US administration in its 'axis of evil'.

And finally . . . the threat of bubbles

The history of bubbles in economic events has been well documented. Irrational exuberance is nothing new – we've seen entire populations abandoning reason to hop on board the latest get-rich-quick scheme. Examples of such events range from the tulip mania that gripped Holland in the 1630s, the 1720s South Sea bubble in Britain, the property and share bubble in the US in the 1920s that triggered the Great Depression and the dot.com collapse in 2000 after the bubble in Internet stocks throughout the 1990s. Bubbles are typically characterised by strong growth in property or share prices, followed by dramatic growth leading to sky-high valuations. The US depression of the 1930s was triggered by this pattern following the introduction of electricity, gas and water supplies, to which crazy valuations were applied. Before the dot.com collapse valuations on technology stocks in the so-called 'new economy' reached insane levels, as did property in Japan before being hit by deflation and a whopping 60% fall in property prices. Closer to home, Irish residential property at the outset of 2006, and projected to grow another 10%, looks increasingly like it's in a classic bubble.

In Ireland, private sector credit has continued to explode upwards at rates close to 30% year-on-year growth. At levels unprecedented in Irish economic history the total level exceeded €260 billion in 2006 – nearly twice Ireland's GNP. Eventually this debt must be repaid, and with interest rates rising the cost of servicing debt may sharply reign in consumer spending and impact on the construction sector, which accounts for one-fifth of Government Revenue and 13% of the workforce. As an investor, you can't prevent a bubble burst, but you can respond sensibly when all around you are losing their money!

After all that, how can you protect your investments?

A fundamental correction in the worldwide economy is not a new prediction, nor is it a certainty. Throughout the course of history there have always been significant threats to economic well-being, but it would be an unwise investor who would blissfully ignore past trends. In the event that there is a correction, however, it will not happen overnight. The warning signs should be well signalled in advance. So, how can you protect yourself?

1. Reduce your debt

Lifestyle debt, such as credit cards, term loans and other forms of short-term financing, should be eliminated through the sale of liquid assets, such as cash deposits, saving policies and shares. Ideally, your overall level of investment mortgage debt should not account for more than 50% of your investment property values.

2. Switch your debt to dollars

In the event of a correction and the beginning of a freefall in the dollar, one way of reducing your relative debt burden would be to talk to your bank about switching from Euro mortgages to dollar mortgages and, if the bank isn't forthcoming on the subject, move to other lenders, if necessary.

3. Sell properties

In the event that your balance sheet is over-geared, it would be wise to read any coming correction as leading to a fall, followed by a prolonged period of flat property prices. Depending on the degree of risk associated with your property, its tenants, lease lengths and location, you would be wise to consider taking your profit and reducing your property exposure to very strong properties and leases only. Don't leave this move too late as in the event of the start of a fall in property prices, the lead time to liquidating property will lengthen as prices fall.

4. Shift your financial investments

Investments in pension schemes, collective investments, such as unit-linked funds, and private stock portfolios, particularly those exposed to higher risk equities, should be shifted temporarily to Government bond funds and gold funds. Any investments held in US dollar assets should be switched to Euro-based assets as anticipation increases that Euro will become the world reserve currency.

5. Diversify into precious metals

Commodities such as gold, silver and diamonds are the typical reserve during times of very significant economic uncertainty. Until the early 1970s gold was the reserve asset supporting the dollar, and gold typically increases exponentially in line with a fall in confidence in currencies. This means that in a deflationary cycle, gold is likely to increase significantly in value. If you want to invest in gold bullion, you can do so through Exchange Traded Funds quoted in London.

6. Other practical steps

On the basis that your income is likely to be uncertain for some time, revert to the traditional family budget to avoid over-spending. Keep your spending to necessary expenditure only and avoid optional spending on lavish items. Remember, you are trying to avoid building up debt.

7. Be careful with cash deposits

It's been many years since bank defaults were major news, but a very severe correction could threaten the stability of banks with low investment grade and over-exposed to property lending. Shift those deposits you have with weaker financial institutions, including some local credit unions, which may face instability due to localised job losses, and spread your deposits across banks that have received the highest credit rating from rating agencies such as Standard & Poor's, Moody's and Fitch. These ratings can be monitored on websites such as www.standardandpoors.com. In the Irish market the bank with the highest credit rating is Rabobank, which has an AAA rating.

8. Avoid stock select risk

If a large part of your balance sheet is dependent on the performance of one stock – whether by choice or because you work for a public limited company that rewards staff by issuing shares – you may be particularly exposed. It makes sense to undertake a phased sale of share options on a methodical basis so that you don't have too many of your eggs in one basket and are not over-reliant on the performance of any one. Don't let CGT on profits deter you from following the strategy of diversifying your balance sheet.

That's enough of that. We'll leave our gloomy discourse there and head to pastures new. But don't fret about it too much: if there is a long economic winter in store, at least you'll have plenty of company, you know, sitting around the fire while the former multi-millionaire next door gets his turn to go off for more turf on Ned the donkey. Every cloud has a silver lining!

CHAPTER 8

Choosing a Good Investment Advisor

Glossary

- **Multi-Agency Intermediary:** An Investment Intermediary that gives advice on the products of the firms for which it acts as agent.
- **Section 10 Advisor:** Investment Intermediary regulated under S.10 of the Investment Intermediaries Act 1995 and required to give broad-based investment advice – not just advice on products from firms with which it has terms of business.

Loot! is designed to help you to steer your way through investments from an informed position, but you can't isolate yourself entirely from advice because, quite simply, you can't be an expert in everything. When you do seek advice, however, it's important to be able to measure the quality of the advice available to you, and the motive of the advisor. First off, there are three basic types of advisor:

1. A **bad advisor** usually trips up, at which point their poor quality becomes apparent. The problem is that bad advisors can get away with it for a long time, expertly disguising just how bad they are. If continually followed, their advice is a bit like weeping gelignite – and the results can be just as dramatic.
2. A **good advisor** is worth his or her weight in gold. Don't be afraid to pay a little bit more: if the advice is good, it can

dramatically improve your long-term position. Remember, advisors are in business to make a profit from giving you advice. If you are driven by bargain basement fees or commissions, don't expect to retain a good advisor.

3. Then there's the **just-about-competent advisor,** who's probably the worst of the bunch. His/her advice is never really bad enough for you to actually sever the relationship, but it's never really good enough to really help grow your financial strength robustly. You become trapped in a relationship of niceties and gritted teeth – and your portfolio stagnates.

How can you tell an advisor is good?

A number of characteristics differentiate good advisors from bad and just-about-competent advisors. The quality of the advice will be a function of the quality of the research undertaken by the advisor on your affairs and his/her ability to communicate with you. There is no such thing as 'best' advice, rather it's a case of what is the most appropriate advice for you in your particular situation. If your advisor has not undertaken a detailed assessment of your position, then, just like a doctor, how can you be sure that the diagnosis is correct? So, the first characteristic to look for is a preliminary and thorough assessment of your affairs.

Second, is there transparency in your dealings with one another? Regardless of the form of remuneration structure they use, good advisors will always adopt a code of transparency on all earnings made by them when you follow their advice.

When assessing a potential advisor, ask the following questions:

- How long has the advisor been in business, what experience does he/she have and what educational qualifications does he/she hold?
- What is his/her reputation, both within the industry and amongst clients? What types of client are advised and are client referrals available to you?

- Are the advisor's recommendations benchmarked against other types of recommendation, or are they always provided to you in isolation from others?
- Does he/she take time to explain recommendations to you carefully, or do you find he/she uses jargon in order to wear you down?
- Who will deal with you on a day-to-day basis and what is the ratio of administration to advisory staff? What quality of service can you expect? Are phone calls returned quickly? If your advisor's office is untidy and disorganized, how can you expect their financial planning to be any different?
- Does he/she have an unblemished professional record? Has he/she been sued in the past for negligent advice, or sanctioned by a regulator?
- What kind of remuneration structure is provided and does he/she automatically disclose all commission earnings to you at point of sale, as a matter of business practice?
- Is he/she authentically independent, or tied to one, or a small number, of financial manufacturers? Does he/she push products he/she has designed in conjunction with financial manufacturers?
- Does he/she seek discretion over, or access to, any part of the management of your money?

What is the advisor's motive?

The answer to this question is a key clue to whether your advisor is a good advisor. Legislators have found it difficult to define 'independent advice', but it's easier to understand what's not independent advice, in other words, what constitutes dependent advice. You receive dependent advice when the advisor is acting as the agent of another party. You can only be certain that advice is impartial if the advisor is acting as *your* agent. At best, this is when you pay a fee for the advice provided and there is no conflict of interest, or when commissions are discussed and negotiated openly before you act.

How are advisors paid?

Financial advisors are in business to make a profit. This is how it should be. It is up to you to decide whether or not the profit they will make from you is **appropriate** for the advice and service provided. There's no such thing as free advice, of course. When an advisory firm takes account of fixed costs, like communications, rent, electricity, etc., and variable costs, such as travel, meetings and reporting, it typically needs to recover at least €200 per hour or more. If it appears 'free', you can be sure that you are paying through commissions.

There is a number of different types of remuneration structure used by advisors and each has its own advantages and disadvantages:

1. Commission only

The commission-only advisor does not charge you a fee for undertaking analysis and recommendations on your behalf. The advisor is instead paid a commission from the product providers to whom he/she introduces you. There is nothing wrong with the commission approach. It is the common currency through which many financial products and services are distributed worldwide. But a difficulty arises with commission when it is non-transparent. Quite frankly, this is the worst type of advice. When an advisor is being paid by a concealed commission, he/she cannot be acting as your agent. They are acting as the agent of the product provider. Nonetheless, commission-only advisors provide a vital service to those who don't want to pay fees (and that's most consumers), provided the commission is fully disclosed.

2. Fee-only advisors

There has been an increase in fee-only advice at the high net worth end of the market. These advisors will charge you a fee for analysing your position and producing a report. They will also tell you which products to buy and why, but they will not arrange for the purchase of those products. Fee-only advisors produce authentic, independent advice, free from conflicts of interest, but the service suffers from two drawbacks. First, any firm not in receipt of commission income must compensate for that loss by charging high fees. Secondly, the financial planning service will not have momentum.

Momentum is extremely important. It is human nature to procrastinate, which means that frequently the good advice provided in expensive reports is not acted upon by the recipient. When the recommendations are followed, you will still incur entry costs and annual management costs for the products and services recommended. As a result, you may pay twice – a fee for producing the analysis and transaction fees for following the advice. If you know yourself to be a procrastinator, get this advisor to diary follow-up action to push you along.

3. Fees and commission

About 70% of US fee-based advisors use a combination of fees and commission. This remuneration model has quickly spread across the Atlantic and is becoming increasingly common in Ireland. The commission flow keeps fee costs down and provided the commission income is disclosed, this type of remuneration has merit.

Advisors will usually charge a moderate fee for undertaking analysis and reporting to you. They will then earn commissions on the implementation of the recommendations made. This type of advice can contain commission bias, but **if commissions are disclosed,** you will be in a position to measure the balance in the advice provided. Remember, one of the characteristics of a good advisor is willingness to discuss commission openly, without being prompted by you to do so. A good fee and commission advisor will have no difficulty in standing over the level of commission income earned for the service and the quality of advice provided.

4. Fee offset

A variation on the fee and commission advisor is fee offset. This model operates by charging you fees, broadly equivalent to what a fee-only advisor would charge you, but crediting any commission income earned against the fee. This compels the disclosure of commission in an automated way. Usually you will be provided with regular statements, which will credit the commission income against the fees accrued to date.

5. Salaried advice

Salaried advisors are typically employees of financial services groups. Rather than charging you fees, or being paid commission, they receive a salary, plus bonuses, from their employer. While their advice is free from distortions, it remains captive or dependent advice because a salaried advisor will only recommend those products and services provided by his/her employer. Buying all of your products and services from one financial services group may be convenient, but it breaks some of the golden rules of financial planning, namely:

- Diversification – not putting all of your eggs into one basket.
- Default risk.
- Fund manager risk, i.e. being locked into one fund group and that group experiences a sustained period of under-performance.

All financial groups have individual strengths and weaknesses. An insurance group, for example, might have a good track record in equities but be poor in property schemes. Remaining a captive client to a financial group only makes sense if the group is genuinely strong right across the board for investment *and* highly competitive on costs.

The 'Never, Nevers' of investing and investment advice

1. **Never, never deal with a faceless voice over the telephone** who uses high-powered sales tactics to sell you stocks or bonds from companies you have never heard of, particularly if those firms are not based in Ireland. This is a favoured tactic for fraudsters. At best, these firms are unlikely to be covered by investor compensation arrangements.
2. **Never, never buy a financial product or service when your instincts are telling you something negative about the seller.** The shoddy advisor typically covers poor quality with ostentatious display. Look for a lot of gold, large bangles, rings, expensive cars and suits. For the lousy advisor or confidence trickster, these are tools of the trade – distractions designed to keep your focus away from the core issues. In nearly all such cases you will encounter expensive offices, crystal chandeliers and high-powered client entertainment. All of this costs money – and the clients are paying for it. The better types of advisor are usually low-key and rely on the merit of their advice rather than gaudy distractions.
3. **Never, never write a cheque made personally payable to your financial advisor for an investment.** The only cheque you should write in this way is for a fee. Always ensure that your cheques are made payable to the insurance company, or to the collective investment provider with whom your investment is being placed, except where an intermediary firm has an Authorised Cash Handler licence. Ensure that any credit transfers of money from your accounts are going into a designated client account held by the financial institution with whom you are placing your business. Always make sure that you check first that the account into which you are transferring your money is authentic.
4. **Never, never lend money to your financial advisor** in order to complete a deal. Transferring money in the form

of a temporary loan, in return for which large monies are promised, is a classic tactic of the fraudster.

5. **Never, never give your advisor power of attorney or discretion over the management of your money** under any circumstances. These types of powers allow your advisor to undertake transactions without your knowledge, or consent. If these transactions pay the advisor a commission, he/she might encourage multiple transactions in order to build up commission income.
6. **Never, never sign a blank form** presented to you by your financial advisor in order to facilitate a transaction or make things more convenient. Ensure that any area on any form you sign that contains a large blank section has heavy lines drawn through it so it cannot be doctored later in order to change the meaning of the form and therefore the agreement.
7. **Never, never agree to invest your money on the basis of guarantees that are clearly substantially in excess of the norm.** When a guarantee looks unbelievable, it is exactly that: unbelievable, not to be believed. Sky's-the-limit guarantees and 'sure bets' are traps for the unwary, set by fraudsters who know only too well that greed is the Achilles' heel of clear thinking.

Is there any independent body protecting my interests and rights?

Investment advice is regulated in Ireland by the **Irish Financial Services Regulatory Authority** (IFSRA), or the **Financial Regulator** for short, although holes do exist in the system: property advice, home equity release schemes, certain pension schemes and certain types of sub-prime (high interest) lender are not covered. IFSRA, which is a hugely important force in the modernization of the Irish market, measures the behaviour and advice quality of banks, building societies, stockbrokers, life offices and intermediaries against primary legislation covering these sectors and against special codes of conduct. While this is a great help in eliminating anti-consumer practices, it doesn't shield you from poor advice.

In the independent intermediary sector there are several types of licence:

- Multi-Agency Intermediaries can only advise you on the products sold by the product providers for whom they act as agent. This advice is therefore restricted and basic.
- Authorised Advisors and Section 10 Advisors are required to give broader financial advice that is better matched to holistic financial planning.
- Cash Handlers can be either of the above and have special authorisation to receive client funds into accounts they control. It is illegal for other intermediaries to do this.

IFSRA's codes of conduct require firms to present you, the customer, with a Terms of Business prior to engagement. Make sure you read this document line by line – it will tell you much about the firm and what it charges.

There is a second watchdog at work, too. The Pensions Board regulates Occupational Pension Schemes, PRSAs and Pensioneer Trustees, but not other aspects of the pensions market. There is confusion in the market by having two regulators, namely IFSRA and the Pensions Board. So, which do you go to if you have a complaint? You should take it, in the first instance, to the authorised firm and then notify the Regulator if you are unhappy with the response you receive. Disputed complaints may be taken for arbitration to the Office of the Financial Services Ombudsman, after first exhausting the complaints procedure available in the firm with which you are in dispute. The office's findings are binding on the regulated firm but not on the complainant, who can proceed with litigation, if required.

Stockbrokers

Another breed of investment advisor you may wish to consult or engage is the stockbroker, that much-maligned creature. For advice on seeking out and instructing a stockbroker, read Chapter 13, Equities for the Direct Investor.

PART THREE

The Wealth Generators

CHAPTER 9

Fancy Yourself as a Property Tycoon?

Glossary

- **EPRA:** European Public Real Estate Association Index, comprising of the shares of 30 European Property plcs.
- **Opportunity cost:** the economic benefit that could be gained from an alternative use of the same resource.

In Ireland, to bring a noisy dinner party to a complete halt, all you have to do is turn the conversation to the subject that provokes unbridled lust in Irish people – investment property. Sharp and sustained rises in property values, a growing population and historically low interest rates have combined to create lots of wealth. And how we love to drool over our *crème brûlée,* lost in the spellbinding alchemy of how small sums of money grew into vast fortunes. Your fellow diners will be bathed in the glow of property ownership, lost in a reverie about all their lovely dosh. But dare to mention that property is just like any other asset class and therefore can be affected negatively and cause substantial loss and misery for those badly exposed, and you'll be sent out with the dog!

If you are considering using your SSIA and other resources to start an investment property portfolio, consider the timing carefully. Some market observers believe Irish property may be entering a bubble in 2006, and many overseas markets pose other risks. This shouldn't stop you in your tracks, but before you bail in at least know what to expect. Remember, a property price correction isn't the end of the world, especially if you've invested in properties with strong tenants, like blue chip firms. On the other hand, if your exposure is to highly geared residential units with tenants in at-risk industries, you could face some real problems paying mortgages without rents to support you. Investment property is a great asset for the long haul, but you need to determine if it's right for you as a person and whether adding more investment property to property you already hold is better than diversifying into other assets.

So, what's at the heart of the property story?

The nub of the property formula is straightforward:

Capital Appreciation + Rental income > Net Cost of Borrowing, entry costs, stamp duty, maintenance costs, exit costs and taxes.

It is the gearing, or leveraging, effect of property that drives the formula, the essence of which is to ensure that net rents (i.e., after costs) exceed the cost of borrowing. Under Irish tax law, the fact that the interest costs of borrowing money from the bank are offset against rents helps enormously.

Cash is a scarce resource – especially difficult to generate after paying income tax, PRSI and health levies and meeting lifestyle costs. The least amount of your own cash (equity) that you can pump into direct property investment and the more of the bank's money that you can use, the higher the level of gearing you create. While the old adage that property is about location, location, location is generally true, on its own it is misleading.

Location, location – and rent!

The most important feature is the **net rental yield**, which is the amount of income the property will create after costs, including taxes, divided by the total acquisition costs. For example, net rents of €6,000 on a property costing €100,000 (say property value €92,000 and costs €8,000) is a net rental yield of 6%. Ideally, if the net rental yield exceeds the cost of borrowing and you have good tenants with good leases in good locations, you are on very good ground indeed.

The higher the net rental yield, the higher the level of gearing and the less of your own scarce resource, i.e. cash, you have to inject into a property investment. This frees up your scarce resource for other opportunities and hopefully, in time, capital appreciation will give you greater scope to buy more property with less cash down. Capital appreciation is the by-product of getting the rent versus costs/borrowing/taxes formula correct. If you invest purely for capital appreciation you are engaged in speculation, not investment.

In the current Irish property market, buying investment property is difficult due to high values, with rental yields in the market typically at 3% or less. This explains why Irish investors are taking to other markets in their droves, seeking deals where loan:value or debt:equity ratios can be higher because net rental yields are higher. Of course, as a sports-mad nation we also love the excitement of the hunt, the wheeling and dealing that's part of the game when we invest directly. But not only is this entirely impractical for very busy people, there is no guarantee that you will out-perform either the market average return for the sector or the alternative ways of investing in property.

Four ways you can invest in property

If property investment sets your heart aflutter, then there are four basic ways you can do it. Obviously **investing directly** is a big ticket item, requiring the investment of time, research and energy plus lots of your own cash. A large part of your balance sheet will be concentrated in a small number of properties. This can either be a good thing or a bad thing, depending on how the properties perform, but the notion that it is indisputably the best way to invest is incorrect. The other routes are via **geared property syndicates, property plcs** or through **open-ended unit-linked funds** administered by life offices, and each has its own pros and cons.

Geared syndicated property

Property syndicates were traditionally the market for ultra-high net worth investors, who pooled resources and acquired trophy properties in exotic locations; we read about these guys in the headlines. Recently, the development of a mass affluent market in Ireland has stimulated scheme designers to construct geared syndicated property schemes with much lower ticket investment, sometimes as low as €30,000. Typically, but not exclusively, these are held, for tax and administration reasons, as close-ended unit-linked funds and target a trophy property, or portfolio of properties, in locations like Britain, the USA, Holland and France.

Equity is introduced to the fund in the form of hard cash from a large number of investors and gearing is provided by banks, which lend to the fund on a non-recourse basis. This means security is limited to the assets of the fund and there is no recourse to the investors in the fund, whose balance sheets are ring-fenced from the fortunes of the fund. Depending on the net rental yield, which usually ranges 5%–7%, gearing would be in the region of 50%–70%.

Let's take a simple example:

> A prospectus is issued to buy the headquarters of a financial institution in Britain with a guaranteed lease from the blue-chip tenant for 10 years. Stg£10m is raised as cash from investors: this is the fund's equity. The fund borrows a further stg£20m, providing for a gearing of 67%, or two-thirds. The rental income from the tenant covers the cost of borrowing, which is fixed for the period of the investment, expected to be 6–8 years.
>
> The investment is issued to Irish investors in the form of units in a unit-linked fund administered by a life office, as units in a unit trust, or as shares in a private limited company or an unquoted plc. The intention, which will be outlined in the prospectus, is to hold the property over this period and then sell it, changing the fund entirely to cash. In the meantime, rental income provides a small surplus above the cost of borrowing and costs.

Geared syndicated property schemes such as this allow investors to build up a portfolio of diversified property investments over many years by carefully selecting from the product offerings on the market. There are dangers, but they apply equally to any other property investment, most particularly rip-off prices and swollen margins. Good schemes, however, are likely to provide better value to investors than direct investment by lowering risk. Remember, few direct investors will be able to capture blue-chip tenants in long leases and are more likely to be exposed to vacancy risk. Neither is there any guarantee that smaller ticket direct investment will provide higher capital appreciation. There is normally an audit trail in larger syndicates that you will not have when investing on your own directly. This offers piece of mind that a professional has at least run the figures on the potential from the investment. Just remember, this isn't a guarantee of success – bean-counters don't always make the best property investors – but it can be a safeguard if it's not the type of thing you can do on your own.

Property plcs

Publicly quoted property plcs are available in the European and British stock markets, where shares can be acquired in companies involved in large-scale development and management of properties covering the wide spectrum of development land, commercial and retail, industrial and large residential units. A mix of property plcs can be acquired by investing in Exchange Traded Funds which specialise in this sector. The property business requires quoted companies to be heavily geared using a combination of cash held by the plc and borrowings from banks. Much like any other part of the stock market, there will be stars and laggards, well-managed businesses and poorly managed businesses.

In reasonable market conditions property plcs generally reflect market conditions but remember, it's not like investing directly in property assets – you're investing in stocks. Unlike direct investment in property and geared syndicated property schemes, your money is not locked into an illiquid investment. If you want to sell a direct property, there will be delay in reverting it to cash due to the time required for marketing, negotiations and everything that goes with a property sales cycle. Equally, geared syndicated property schemes are illiquid and generally you are locked into them for the investment term.

Investment in property plcs, by contrast, means you hold a liquid asset, i.e. shares that can be liquidated quickly in the market. You can invest in property plcs for very small sums and build up a portfolio of shares over many years either through your own research, if you have the skill, or by taking the advice of a good stockbroker. For example, launched in May 2000, the EPRA Eurozone Property Index is a publicly quoted Exchange Traded Fund that can be acquired through stockbrokers or through unit-linked funds available from certain Irish life offices (at an additional intermediation charge). This type of index spreads your investment across 30 large European property plcs and trading in countries like Holland, France, Germany and Spain.

Open-ended unit-linked property funds

Irish life offices have had open-ended unit-linked property funds available to investors for decades, typically concentrating on Irish and British commercial and retail property. These funds come with and without gearing and remain open-ended, allowing investors to come and go. But when there are more fund sellers than buyers, as has happened on a number of occasions in the past, fund trading can be suspended or exit penalties levied so that the fund has a chance to sell some property assets to meet the high number of encashment requests.

Which way to choose?

There is nothing written in stone to say that investing directly in property yourself will out-perform professionally managed, pooled property schemes or property plcs. As we noted earlier, each approach has its pros and cons, so it really comes down to whether or not you are fitted for the direct game. By going direct you will bypass the intermediation costs associated with pooled property schemes, but you won't avoid costs or market risks and you don't have a guarantee that you will out-perform average market performance. Going it alone can also mean you are more exposed to downturns in the market, especially if you invest in residential property and the potential pool of tenants dries up or defaults when economic activity declines.

Well then, am I a good fit for direct investment?

Before you hop on a plane and head off into the great blue yonder to make your fortune from direct investment in property, consider the following questions carefully:

- **Does property get your juices flowing?**
  Is it the type of investment you would really enjoy handling – dealing with negotiation, risks, vacancies, advertising and everything else that goes with the process? It's very, very hands-on. Some people are just made for it, but for others it's a shortcut to migraine, worry and grey hair – life's too short when there are other options.

- **Do you have sufficient time and is it economically viable?**
  Bear in mind that direct investment in property will require a lot of your time, probably much more than you think. Your time comes at a cost. If you're going to spend a lot of time abroad dealing with property, what personal aspects will you be compromising and what business opportunities will you be losing at home? This is called the **opportunity cost** of investment. The idea is to ensure that each hour you spend is spent doing the most efficient thing to grow your assets. If you are in a flexible employment that allows you plenty of time off, this is probably not an issue. But if you are a busy professional, owner of a SME or self-employed, you need to be certain that the time you take away from your business will create added value. Calculate the opportunity cost and decide if pooled property schemes and property plcs would be a better alternative.

- **Do you like problem solving?**
  You better, because researching, negotiating and dealing with legalities, taxation and tenancy issues will require concentration and problem-solving abilities.

- **Is more property a good fit for your current balance sheet?**
  When you take a helicopter view of your financial strength, are you already heavily exposed to property as an asset class? Would adding more over-expose you, perhaps accounting for, say, over three-quarters of your balance sheet? Financially, would it be more correct to diversify into uncorrelated assets, such as equities and commodities, even if it is new ground for you?

- **Honestly, are you cut out to be a landlord?**
  This is a multi-layered question because being a landlord is not simply a matter of collecting direct debits in your bank account. You need to understand the extent of the undertaking before answering this one, so read on!

Am I a landlord?

At some point you will have to decide whether you are going to manage the property yourself or hire a professional property management company, which will typically charge a percentage of the rental income for all the operations of the property, including selecting tenants, collecting rent, marketing, maintenance and book-keeping. Management fees will vary widely, but in the residential market you can expect to pay up to 10%–15% of your rental income, subject to certain minimums, and even as high as 20%–30% in some resort locations. Generally, management fees will be moderately lower for modern properties that require less maintenance than for older properties, which have the potential for higher call-outs for management companies. Stand-alone properties with swimming pools may attract higher rent, but they also attract much higher management and maintenance charges.

If you decide to let a management company take the strain, when choosing which company to go with bear in mind that the flat fee arrangement may not provide sufficient encouragement for a company to ensure that all rents are collected and kept at local market levels. You can give a better incentive by paying a percentage of your rental income, but of course this will also put a hole into your rental income.

So, we're back to our original question: should you do it yourself? Answer the questions below honestly to first find out if you *can* do it yourself:

- If the property is far away, will the landlord role be complicated by language barriers and local market culture?

- Do you like dealing with people? Being a landlord requires you to be firm but fair, able to be patient and understanding when things go wrong. If you are the type of person who flies off the handle easily, don't expect to change when things go wrong with your property.
- Are you comfortable with paperwork, doing tax returns and maintaining records?
- How are you at DIY? Typically, small things are best repaired yourself.
- Is there a network of professional tradespeople you can rely upon when something goes seriously wrong?
- Do you mind been woken at unusual, off-work hours? When tenants have a problem, they will call – regardless of the time of day or night, the time difference, or whether the baby is crying.
- Are you a good negotiator, committed to putting in the time and effort to get the right price?

As you can see, managing tenants isn't as easy as it might seem. Remember, too, not only will you have to deal with tenants, you will also be dealing with utility companies, suppliers, neighbours, and local municipal employees. A successful landlord is someone who is professional, patient, a good problem-solver and a good negotiator. If you are the type of person who is a soft touch, is short-tempered and impatient, the best advice is: don't take the DIY approach; hire a professional manager.

If I decide to be a landlord, what will I have to do?

There is a range of activities a landlord needs to be responsible for in order to get the best from the property:

- You will need to **advertise** to let people know that you have a vacant property. The best ad is a property that looks well maintained, with fresh paint and cared-for grounds. Check advertising and marketing costs for typical rental properties in the area.

- **Showing** your property is time-consuming and you need to exercise great patience with tyre-kickers. Showings should be by appointment, allowing you to screen out the unwanted. Nonetheless, you must be prepared to show the property in the evenings and on weekends. Set up an appointment diary and make sure that anybody who calls understands fully the agreement on offer, and particularly the rent.
- Be prepared to **deal with questions** relating to rights, such as tenant rights, environmental issues and disability rights. You will need to research these issues as they pertain in the country where the property is situated. Ignorance of these would be a poor starting point and would send the wrong signal to potential tenants.
- Where you are taking over a property with existing tenants be **diplomatic and professional** in your first meeting. Prepare to deal with the basic questions a sitting tenant will have, such as: 'Is the rent going up?' 'What is the status of my deposit?' 'Are your policies new and what plans do you have with regards to the condition of the property?' It's a good idea to pre-prepare a summary for tenants, delineating how rent is collected, contact information and what to do when maintenance is required. As a landlord, you don't have the right to walk into your property unannounced, so ensure you have procedures in place to deal with setting up a convenient appointment time.
- If you are going to look for **rental increases** within the terms of the rental agreement, do so diplomatically. This is always a difficult issue, but can be softened if you can establish and prove that the rent currently being paid is below the market rate in the local area for equivalent properties. Be careful of rent ceilings, which can apply in some rent-dominated countries and which prevent you raising rents beyond certain preset limits. Remember, if interest rates rise on your mortgage and you're stuck under a rent ceiling, you'll have to bridge the gap from your own earned income.
- Where you are looking for new tenants, don't do so willy-nilly: first, establish the profile of the type of tenant you want. Use a

systematic process of **evaluating tenant applications** so that you don't get a real beauty who is bouncing around from one property to another, a smooth-talker who is highly unreliable. The best tenants pay their rent on time, are financially strong, treat your property well and won't cause a headache for the neighbours.

- Look for ways of improving both the **external and internal appearance** of your property, such as well-tended lawns, good landscaping on the outside and thoughtful planning on the inside. This really can make all the difference. Remember, the basics influence people: is the property clean, particularly the toilet, closets and storage areas? Do all the lights, plumbing, appliances and air conditioning work? Are there modern wiring and smoke detectors? Has the interior been well maintained without lines, scratches and smudges on walls? Make sure you put the best possible insurance cover in place – not just to protect your property from fire, floods, burglary and vandalism but also to cover your liability exposure should there be any injuries on your property arising from dangerous conditions.
- **Keep good records**, particularly if you have more than one investment property. Good file-keeping is a skill in itself. You will need a basic documents file to store title deeds, loan documents and correspondence with the municipality, etc. A separate file should be kept for your income and expenses, which will be particularly important when undertaking tax returns.
- Where you have separate properties, keep separate **maintenance files** on each one, otherwise everything will get mixed up. Finally, you will need to maintain a tenant file, keeping accurate and up-to-date records of rents paid, agreements and correspondence.
- Where you are handling a large property portfolio it makes sense to invest in a professional property **management software** programme, such as Tenant Pro 5.0 for Windows or Expert Landlord Lite from Expertlandlord.com.

Getting ready to go – building a network

One of the mistakes commonly made by property investors is to put the cart before the horse and select the investment property before building up a network. The first step is to decide you are going to invest in property. The second step is to establish your network. A good network will save you a fortune and ensure you have proper professional supports in place to deal with the multiple issues that will arise when buying investment property. Although it might seem like a slog, the best thing to do is build the team first, before going to the market to select your investment property.

Your network will comprise: a solicitor, a tax advisor, a lending institution and an independent surveyor.

1. A good **knowledgeable solicitor** with an impeccable local record is an absolute must if you are going to avoid many of the pitfalls hidden in legal documentation. A good solicitor will make you aware of vitally important information often hidden in fine print, or obfuscated by selling agents. If you are investing overseas, ensure the solicitor is fluent in both the local language and in English, is experienced in dealing with foreign investors and is properly authorised and licensed by the local authorities. Make sure you ask for references and be especially wary of choosing a solicitor recommended by the selling agent, Remember, whenever the Irish arrive, the sale of property becomes big business and close links can develop between solicitors, agents and developers – too close!
2. If you are raising capital against Irish property to finance an overseas purchase, **organise your finance,** in writing, with an Irish bank or through an Irish mortgage broker. It's amazing how many investors forget to do this and pay a deposit on a property, then arrive back, wild-eyed, desperately looking for the finance to complete the purchase. If your finance is pre-prepared, it puts you in a much stronger negotiating position and tells you in advance how far you can stretch things.

3. An informed and **knowledgeable tax advisor** is another absolute must, particularly when investing in overseas property. Your tax advisor will be in a position to check out the effects of double taxation agreements between Ireland and the country in which you are investing, and the potential impact of double taxation. This is a skilled job, requiring the ability to examine and assess the integration of Irish tax and foreign tax on rental income, the gains or losses you stand to make, as well as the inheritance tax implications down the road. Your Irish taxation advisor may not be expert on the intricacies of taxation in the foreign country, but he or she should certainly be in a position to understand the basic tax situation. On the ground in the foreign country you should also seek taxation advice to validate the views of your Irish taxation advisors and to put both advisors in touch with one other.
4. Don't forget to investigate the property using the services of a professional and **independent surveyor** – that is, not the one recommended by the selling agent. Good local surveyors will know and understand a lot more about the local property than you and spending a small bit of money on a decent report could save you from buying a money-pit.

Raising capital and banking finance

After you take account of equity investment, stamp duty and other costs, typically you will need to stump up 20% of the value of the property if you want the mortgage finance secured against the property in isolation from other properties you own. To achieve this, consider creating the cash by **selling other liquid assets**, including the cash value of savings policies and your SSIA, and calling in any outstanding **debtors**, such as loans to family members. Where you have a **minority shareholding** in a small and sluggish private company, consider offering your shareholding to other shareholders to raise the cash to finance your investment property.

Given the wide gap between older Irish mortgages and the current value of Irish property, there is the temptation to take out a **second mortgage** with your existing lender and use it to finance a new property purchase. This is an option if the overall level of mortgage debt does not create a financial burden on you. The first test of this burden is to consider the impact on your financial position if no rental income arises from the new property investment, or there is a prolonged vacancy period, for example, one year. If you pass the one-year test, you have sufficient solvency to opt for this approach.

The second test is to ask yourself what would be the impact on your position in the event of a **sharp decline in property prices** in both properties versus the total level of mortgage debt you are considering. In the event of, for example, a reversal of 30%, is there still plenty of space between the readjusted property values on your balance sheet and your mortgages? If there is, then you are on reasonably steady ground.

Getting a mortgage

Right, we've decided to plunge into property investment and we've set up our network. We've examined our financial position and we can't do it all alone. The next step is to get the mortgage sorted.

The introduction of Bank of Scotland into the Irish mortgage market in August 1999 has completely changed the landscape for mortgage finance. The Irish market is now competitive and provides a range of options to borrowers. So, who should you choose? When your aim is to build up a property portfolio, some banks are better than others for your needs. You will need a bank that specialises in property investment. Generally, these lenders are not the mass-market lenders but specialists who concentrate principally on this part of the market. As a result they understand things more easily and move more quickly than a mass-market building society or bank, which is usually a little more sluggish when considering mortgage finance. You don't have to pay a higher premium to get mortgage finance from faster companies with better services, but even if you do, it's not necessarily a deal breaker.

A specialist mortgage broker can be of considerable assistance, particularly if its services are transparent, it has a track record in raising a lot of finance in this market and has terms of business with all mortgage lenders. In particular, when dealing with a mortgage broker, look for written disclosure of broking commissions so that you know precisely what the mortgage broker will make when the deal is placed.

When you are trying to raise mortgage finance, it's all about the presentation. Your mortgage is **an asset** in the balance sheet of a lender – don't ever let them forget it! You're doing them a favour by offering them your loan asset. Prepare a written presentation of the proposal, beginning with background, personal information, occupation, age, address, contact details, etc. Lenders on the lookout for first-class mortgage assets, where you can demand the tightest possible margins, i.e. as low as possible, are always on the lookout for the three Cs:

- ***Collateral* – what security will be provided and how is the bank exposed to a fall in the property market?** This is why banks typically restrict loans:values or debt:equity ratios to no more than 90%. But remember, the amount of the banking finance should be matched to the net rental income, otherwise borrowing costs will exceed income and you will be subsidising it from your own earned income, which is not a good idea.
- ***Character* – what is your track record in repaying existing mortgage finance?** The lender will look for statements on your existing mortgages, possibly your banking statements, to ensure that you are telling the truth with regards to your overall level of debt and lifestyle costs and that you do indeed have an unblemished service history on existing mortgages. Your credit history is registered at the Irish Credit Bureau (Tel: 01 260 0388), so check your records for accuracy.
- ***Capacity*** – this is the acid test, **do you have sufficiently strong**

cash flows to make mortgage repayments? Borrowers often assume that the bank is fixated on collateral: it's not. It's mostly fixated on capacity. Banks love to see strong cash flows. The last thing a bank wants is to take a legal action to recover their mortgage by selling a property. It costs them a fortune, erodes their profits, affects their public profile and takes many years.

Put all the facts together in one strong presentation. Begin by describing the proposition, the property, the tenants, the potential rental income, the economic story behind why that property in that location makes sense and the network behind you. This is convincing stuff for a lender and shows you have done your homework and are therefore serious about the investment.

Summarise your financial position with a **Statement of Affairs**. This is a balance sheet or asset and liability summary that tells the lender a lot about your overall gearing ratio and whether or not the new deal represents too high a risk. Support your Statement of Affairs with your most recent set of financial accounts or tax returns to validate your income to the lender.

Finally, **name your price**. Never wait for a lender to make an offer – tell the lender what you want. Remember, your mortgage is an asset to the lender, you are doing the lender a favour. If you are strong on all three Cs, you should be looking for the tightest possible margin above the cost of funds.

For variable rate mortgages the cost of funds can be taken as a slight fraction above the European Base Rate. This is the cost of finance to a bank in the wholesale market. For a first-class loan asset you should be looking for a margin above the cost of funds of no more than 1%–1.5%. Bankers will seek a higher margin in order to compensate for any perceived higher risk.

You will also need to offer assigned life insurance cover so that the mortgage will be cleared in the event of your premature death. Although this may not be a stipulation in the loan agreement, it is wise to put one in place so there can't be a forced liquidation of the property in the event of the death of the principle income-earner. You should also consider the potential impact on your position in the event of long-term ill-health. Remember, if you get sick and your future earned income stream is cut off, then the potential mortgage repayments are at risk as you use up the rent to pay for lifestyle. Ideally, you should ensure that up to 75% of your earned income is replaced using tax-relievable Income Replacement Insurance Cover. Ask your insurance advisor for details of this cover.

The interests of the lender will also need to be noted in the general insurance cover put in place for an Irish property. If the finance is being raised against an Irish property but is being used to buy a foreign property, make sure you have adequate general insurance cover, including public liability. Remember, cutting corners on insurance runs the risk of running foul of Murphy's Law!

Should I choose a fixed or variable rate mortgage?

The typical interest rate curve produces fixed rates that are more expensive than variable rates, i.e. there is an expectation of rising interest rates. Fixing mortgage rates makes a lot of sense for investment property. Ideally, you should be looking for a net rental yield a percent or two above the cost of a fixed mortgage. This is an ideal situation for the property investor as it eliminates interest rate risk from the deal. However, it does come with some downsides:

- First, breaking out of a fixed rate mortgage prematurely will incur an interest penalty, thereby reducing the return on your property. Always check out how your lender's penalties operate. Remember, in the event of an imminent correction in the property, you might be of a mind to sell quickly in order to take your profit, or avoid losses.
- Secondly, with most fixed rate mortgages you will not be able to accelerate capital repayments without incurring penalties. This means that rental increases cannot be used to chip away at the outstanding debt and shorten the mortgage term. Again, check

your lender's stance on this and what the penalties would be for accelerated repayments.
- Thirdly, depending on conditions, you might be of a mind to refinance the mortgage over a longer term, perhaps due to falling rents, which you may not be able to do on a fixed rate mortgage without paying penalties.

Theoretically, for a bank the profit margin on a **fixed rate mortgage** is the difference between the rate offered to you and fixed rate swaps on the wholesale market. So the next time you are offered a fixed rate and you want to give your lender a shock, start talking swap rates and watch him sputter into his coffee. You can check rates on the swap market over the term of your mortgage by ringing a stockbroker or a competitor bank. By identifying the profit margin, you may be in a position to negotiate a cut in the fixed rate on offer.

Variable rate mortgages move in line with general interest rates, but they allow for accelerated capital repayments and usually there is no exit penalty when you sell the property. Staying variable through thick and thin also means that you are not trying to second-guess the interest rate cycle. You can always fix a variable rate mortgage should you wish to do so, particularly if interest rates fall and fixed rates become more attractive.

Interest-only mortgages

Interest-only mortgages are becoming more common in the Irish market. This means that no capital repayments are made to the lender and instead only the interest is serviced. Traditionally, interest-only mortgages were adopted by professional property developers because they significantly lower the servicing cost of mortgages, but they also come with higher risks. The principle risk is a fall in property prices. The ideal situation, and that which pertains in the traditional mortgage, is to have rental income pitched at a level capable of making capital repayments as well as servicing interests. In the interest-only mortgage this does not happen, consequently any fall in property prices leaves you more exposed. Interest-only mortgages are speculative in nature as they assume that mortgage debt can be cleared by rising property prices. It's an assumption that can prove false because property prices don't always rise, and are capable of falling sharply.

Pension mortgage

Pension mortgages are a variation of the interest-only mortgage. An interest-only mortgage is arranged with a lender and the borrower undertakes to apply part or all of the retirement capital available from pension investments to repay the debt by retirement age. This means that throughout the term of the mortgage interest relief is gained from interest payments to the bank, while indirectly there is also tax relief on capital repayments because contributions to pension schemes are a tax write-off up to certain limits.

The revolutionary changes introduced in the Finance Act 1999 and 2000 allows those investing through personal pensions, PRSAs and AVCs to fully liquidate retirement funds at retirement age, taking the first 25% as tax-free cash and part or all of the remainder, after paying tax, at the marginal rate. This factor has increased the popularity of pension mortgages.

The downside to pension mortgages, however, is that no capital repayment is made to the bank on an ongoing basis. In reality, life has ways of changing things, and delaying a capital repayment to the end by taking a large bite out of your retirement fund increases the risk to the mortgage. When you link mortgage debt to the return on assets in retirement funds you can create an umbilical cord between the performance of equities, which comprise the lion's share of retirement funds, and your debt. This was also the guiding principle in the defunct endowment mortgage market.

If your retirement fund itself also invests in property, you are doubly exposed to a downturn near retirement, which is why retirement funds supporting private property mortgages are best invested in uncorrelated assets that can out-perform the cost of borrowing. But while there is a likelihood that the rate of return on a well-managed retirement fund will out-perform the cost of borrowing over the term, this is not guaranteed.

Which to choose?

To answer this question, much depends on the relative strength of your balance sheet, i.e. are you in a position to choose the more 'risky' interest-only or pension mortgages? For most people, buying certainty is best and making direct capital repayments from an ordinary annuity mortgage makes more sense, even if the interest write-off diminishes over time as more capital repayments are made. The traditional capital repayment mortgage affords you more protection from the downside of any slide in the property market, whereas interest-only mortgages and pension mortgages leave you more exposed.

So now you know – investment property is for you, of course it is, you're Irish, it's firing through your veins, encoded in your DNA and anyway, admit it, you're an addict to the property supplements. The next step is to seize up property opportunities and to learn to tell the good from the bad and, no, it's not just about jumping up and down on the floorboards to check the springiness!

CHAPTER 10

Measuring Property Opportunities

Glossary

- **Unquoted plc:** A public company that's not quoted on the stock market.
- **Prospectus:** A formal statement or document giving all of the available details about the investment as distinct from a sales brochure, which does not.
- **Currency hedge:** An investment, usually in derivatives, designed to reduce the risk of loss arising from currency movements.
- **Flipping:** The practice of buying an asset and selling it off quickly.
- **Drag effect:** The reduction in return caused by costs.
- **Due diligence:** A detailed and careful inspection of an investment opportunity
- **In escrow:** money held by a third party like a solicitor, to be held by him/her pending the fulfilment of certain conditions.

Whichever of the four routes to property investment you take, you will be faced with assessing, or evaluating, value for money before you take the leap. While nobody can accurately predict the future of property markets, which are beyond your control, there is nonetheless much that is within your control. In a nutshell, you can make more money from property **by avoiding bad investments** than you can by investing in real crackers, so it pays to keep your wits about you and to know what to look out for. So, in this chapter we get under the bonnet and analyse the different options available to you.

Measuring geared syndicated property schemes

Just to recap, a geared syndicated property scheme is a collective investment with a group of other investors that uses a combination of investor cash (equity) and borrowings. An increasing number of these schemes are coming on the market from life offices, private banks and stockbroking firms and administered as unquoted plcs or close-ended unit-linked funds. When assessing the prospectus for such a scheme, remember that good **prospectuses** will be well presented and will contain the most important information of all: the financials. A good tip is to **read these backwards**, beginning at the last page, because the 'meat' is in the financials and that information is placed at the end. When reading the financials, here's what to look out for:

- Examine costs very carefully. Begin with upfront costs to see who is getting what, as this will depress the rate of return on the investment regardless of any inbuilt projections by the scheme promoters. Upfront costs will cover stamp duty, bank arrangement fees, scheme arrangement fees and commissions, i.e. the cost of distribution.
- Be careful of schemes where some of these upfront costs are expressed as a percentage of the total amount of money, that is the total accruing from both investors' equity and bank borrowings. Ideally, upfront costs should be linked to the amount of equity being raised. Remember, an upfront cost of 2% on a scheme that is geared two-thirds is effectively a charge of 6% on the amount of equity being raised.
- There is likely to be an annual fund management charge and

once again this should be expressed as a percentage of the equity, rather than the equity plus borrowing.

- Look carefully at the gap between the net rental yield and the cost of borrowing to the scheme. So, for example, if the net rental yield is 6.5% and the cost of borrowing money is 4.5%, there is a healthy gap of 2% pa. This protects the scheme from any potential vacancies and indicates that there is plenty of liquidity within the scheme to ensure it remains self-financing throughout its term.
- Check who is receiving commissions and how much they are receiving. Be particularly careful of schemes marketed by a bank that is also lending to the scheme. In these circumstances the bank may be more motivated by getting a margin on its mortgage than by selecting good property in good locations with strong leases and good tenants.
- Where the scheme is engaged in development, i.e. speculation – buying land, seeking planning permission, and then building – it makes sense that it has an incentive for the managers. An incentive fee will typically be built in where the scheme managers share in a percentage of the profits above a set internal rate of return (IRR). Make sure that the incentive isn't excessive. It is usual to see this set at 10% or 20% of all profits above an IRR of 8% or 10% a year. As a general rule incentives on rental schemes are a bad idea, particularly if the scheme designers are already taking plenty of money in upfront fees.
- Check to see how the property, or portfolio of properties, has come on the market and if the price being paid represents reasonable value. Ideally, there should be a discount to normal prices because the property or portfolio is being shifted easily, without the cost of marketing being incurred by the property owners.

Remember, geared syndicated property schemes may not have the transparency associated with quoted public companies, thereby exposing you to the potential for high charges. This does not mean there aren't very good geared syndicated property schemes available for investment, but make sure you read the fine print before committing because it's a one-way ticket. Remember, your money will remain in an illiquid investment for the full term of the investment.

Measuring property plcs

Unless you are skilled at assessing quoted companies, and particularly property plcs (which require a detailed understanding of the property business), you would be wise to seek the advice of a good stockbroker (see Chapter 13 for advice on stockbrokers). You can pick property plc stock from the stock market (Chapter 13, Equities for the Director Investor, will help), or choose to invest across an Exchange Traded Fund that tracks the fortunes of a mix of companies. Exchange Traded Funds generally have annual management charges of up to 0.5% pa, but you will also have to pay your stockbroker for the service. A set rate of commissions will be quoted, declining with the size of your investment. Commissions will also be payable when you sell.

Measuring open-ended unit-linked funds

Loot! has a chapter dedicated to investing through funds, including unit-linked funds (see Chapter 15). You will be given units in the fund calculated at current asset values for the properties the fund contains. As a middleman between you and the property, the life office has to be paid, including recovering the cost of selling to you, i.e. commissions paid to selling agents. The fund will also have to pay property managers and meet other expenses. In the Irish market you can expect to run across funds that load much of these costs upfront as entry costs, commonly called bid/offer, spreads. As a result, these can be up to 5%. Alternatively, these can be spread over the first number of years in the form of a beefed-up annual fund charge. Should you pull out during this period, the residual charge is levied against you. These are called back-end loaded funds. Both fund types will have annual management charges, typically in the range 0.75% –1.50%.

Where these funds are being invested overseas, cautious investors should check to see if there is a currency hedge to protect you from any decline between the Euro and the currency in the country in which the fund is invested. Currency hedging costs will create a performance drag on the investment, but are nonetheless worthwhile for people who are using these to generate income. Take special care in differentiating between funds that don't borrow and geared funds. In a rising market gearing amplifies your return, but in a falling market geared funds will fare much worse than those that have no borrowings.

Measuring direct investment – what's the best strategy for you?

There is a number of options open to you for the direct investment route, so the thing is to examine and assess each in turn so you can figure what best fits your circumstances.

Extending your own home is the first and most basic strategy to examine. This would involve building a separate access and renting out the extension for student accommodation, or other tenants. This is a tried and tested method of generating rental income in specific locations, e.g. close to colleges, or near an expanding factory, where rental accommodation is at a premium. You will need to evaluate carefully the cost of undertaking the development against the projected rental income you will receive. This approach has the advantage of allowing you to manage your property without leaving your home.

Home hopping is a favoured strategy for some Irish families, particularly where much of the work can be undertaken by the family itself. For this reason it is the first-choice option for skilled tradesmen and builders, who move their families from time-to-time to properties that require development, develop them, sell them on and take a profit. You would need lots of energy and momentum – and possibly Kofi Annan levels of persuasiveness – to carry off this one!

Holiday homes are not investment properties, they are second homes. Nor are they working assets, much like your own home. When you invest in a holiday home, you do so for lifestyle reasons. If you want to have continuous access to your holiday home, then you won't be able to rent it into the market.

In certain circumstances, for example, in France, rental properties can be acquired with **leasebacks,** guaranteeing your rental income for a period of time and usually providing yields of between 4% and 6% before tax. These come with the option of using the property yourself for family holidays for a few weeks of the year. Where guaranteed rental streams are available, bear in mind that any increase in the rental income in the local area will not be passed on to you but instead will be absorbed by the management company. Guarantees are only as strong as the company giving them, so check out how strong it really is and remember, if it goes bust, so does your guarantee.

Take special care around schemes that guarantee the rental income by inflating the acquisition cost. You can only check this by ensuring that the price that you pay is reasonable against similar properties in the area – so it means our favourite pastime again: a little research. There is little point in paying way over the odds for a property only to have the extra premium you've paid returned to you in the form of a so-called guaranteed and taxable rental income. This has been a much-used trick of the unscrupulous for many years.

Flipping properties that have been **bought off plans** as soon as they are constructed is a favourite way of making money in the property market, however, you need to exercise extreme caution. Typically, properties bought off plans can be acquired for 10%–15% less than the projected market price once the development has been built – for a small downpayment. This is pure speculation and is a gamble on rising market prices. It is used by the developer as a way to raise finance, but you could get caught buying a property at a price more than it is worth should prices collapse.

The residential investment property market comprises detached homes, semi-detached, town houses, duplexes and apartments. As a general rule **detached homes** rent for a premium, but you need to look closely at local property conditions to see which of these is likely to provide best value. Take special care of shared area maintenance charges that apply to exclusive developments and apartment blocks, as these create a drag effect on your rental income and depress the net rental yields. Look closely at management contracts to see how they might impinge on you as the owner, what you may be liable for and what controls you have over the setting of future charges.

Look out for properties where **simple makeovers and minor fixes** will allow you to increase rents and market value. There is a host of TV programmes dedicated to this kind of thing, and they show just how much can be done by painting, carpeting, landscaping, upgrading kitchens, converting garages etc.

Commercial property is non-residential, which means investments in property, retail units, industrial units, storage facilities, hotels, hospitals, etc. The characteristics of commercial investment are more detailed and therefore require more skill and much larger investment than residential, making this option unsuitable for inexperienced investors. There can be increased costs with commercial property because when tenants move out and new tenants arrive, expensive improvements are usually required to match the space to the new tenant. Commercial properties are more exposed, both positively and negatively, to under-supply and over-supply in the local property market and are generally affected more quickly by economic downturns. Remember, businesses are quicker to move, slim down and cut costs when times get tough than are families.

Commercial leases also require more detailed and professional evaluation than residential leases, and demand a comprehensive understanding of the contractual obligations between the landlord and the tenants. Loan to values on commercial property are usually tighter than for residential property, in the range 60%–80%, so you'll need a bigger chunk of cash to get going.

Investing in **raw land** subject to planning permission, or in under-developed land, contains substantial risk and reward. You need to be prepared to wait many years for profit and remember, there will be no rental income arising to feed mortgage finance. In Ireland, it is almost impossible to locate new opportunities that have not already been spotted by seasoned property developers, who usually swoop down in their private helicopters to buy up all the land in the path of progress. However, you might be able to identify a property that has additional space and for which a planning application could be made.

Even where you do buy land, remember there may be ongoing local property taxes, particularly overseas, and you will need to cover insurance and maintain the land generally. Loan to values for mortgages also tend to be lower than investment property because of the lack of rental income.

Success in the development market requires detailed and professional homework and a full understanding of all the costs involved. You will be dealing with matters relating to water access, sewage lines, utilities and the local roads. There may also be very substantial levies in the event of a rezoning application being successful as municipal authorities seek to recover the costs of local infrastructural work. Pay particular attention to environmental issues, as well as to the potential for resistance to planning applications from local residents.

Measuring properties outside your local area

When you go outside your local area, there's an awful lot you simply don't know about the new location. To be successful in investing in property, you need to minimise your risks and maximise your rewards. This can only be done by **detailed and methodical research**, the type of thing we don't like to do – we much prefer to hop on a plane and start pitching! But if you don't want to end up with a money-pit and a declining balance sheet, here are some of the things you need to consider:

- Begin with the **economic picture** of the country, region and your specific location. Why, in particular, are the economic drivers likely to create growth and push up both rents and property values? The fundamental equation is always supply and demand. But why is supply restricted and demand likely to grow? There is little point in investing in an area where demand can be met by supply, and perhaps over-supply.
- Is **population growth or decline** predicted and, if so, why? This can happen because of changing demographics, particularly younger people moving into or out of an area. As populations generally are greying and with a net fall, an increased local population in a given area will most likely be due to movements within the country.
- Is there likely to be **job growth** and **rising income levels**? Job growth generally comes hand-in-hand with improving economic circumstances. Look closely at the increases in real wages, in other words, are people earning more relative to inflation? Look for locations with good, well-paying jobs, particularly those based on knowledge industries rather than old industries that could move quickly to cheap labour economies and devastate the local area. Seek an area with diversification of business so that it is not overly reliant on one large employer. Economic history is dotted with ghost towns and a glut of vacant property following the closure of major employers.
- Has there been a significant increase in wages and job quality in the recent past? Look, in particular, for a **recession-resistant local job market** in traditional areas, such as civil servants, hospitals and the education sector, in other words, jobs unlikely to be outsourced.
- Look at **supply and demand** in the **local** property segment. When an economy is improving, particularly new accession countries, families like to move upmarket, out of old buildings and into modern properties with good facilities, but local average wages will restrict the choice to a particular size and quality. Find out what the current fit is for these families, because this is where the growth will be. If you are looking for property to rent to

international business executives and families moving in with foreign companies, bear in mind that they will have children and will need to be near American, British and French schools.

- Look for **entry barriers** into the local market, particularly where there is unlikely to be sprawl. Many Eastern European countries' city centres contain old towns that are often the most desirable residential locations. These come with premium prices, but contain civil and embassy centres for historical reasons. They also have a fixed amount of property stock. If you invest in the suburbs, remember suburbs have a way of growing outwards and an unpopular suburb may remain forever so. A golden rule: just because it's cheap doesn't mean it's a good investment.
- In Eastern European countries pay particular attention to the type of property the **returning migrant workers** will choose in order to benefit from improved domestic economic performance and job availability over the years to come.
- Learn something about the rate of **planning permissions** occurring in the local market. Generally these can be checked out through municipal authorities. This will tell you something about the rate of positive or negative absorption that is likely to occur. Where space is limited and planning is difficult but economic circumstances are improving, property prices are likely to rise. On the other hand, where there are multiple planning permissions being processed and wide parts of the city are being developed, there is a potential over-supply, which would drive down prices and increase competition for rents.
- Many developing countries that were previously under socialist regimes have **environmental issues.** Check these out, particularly the presence of heavy industry, and query any problems that have arisen in the past. Environmental issues will inevitably be brought to the fore as the country matures, standards rise and people become more demanding. Remember, just because you bought something near a river in a city location doesn't mean that's where people will want to live, particularly if there are outstanding environmental issues. Look upstream!
- Particularly in former Soviet and Communist countries ensure

your solicitor checks for any problems with title documents, especially when title is not in the sole name of the seller, or, in some cases, the seller has no rights to the property at all!

- Be careful of buying in areas subject to substantial flash **floods** and extreme weather events. This particularly relates to low-lying areas, which could be severely hit by dam breaches. Remember, just because it hasn't happened in the recent past doesn't mean it won't happen in the future: look at New Orleans.
- Always independently check **local rental levels** and be particularly cautious of a large number of 'To Rent' signs – a sure fire signal of over-supply. Remember, a local letting agent acting as the sale agent will always over-estimate potential rents. Investigate local market occupancy rates. Generally, occupancy rates will be contained in property and trade magazines. If you find declining occupancy rates, that's a sign of a declining market.
- Check to see if **concessions or discounts** are beginning to arise in the local market because of increased competition for tenants from landlords. Concessions can come in a number of guises, for example, payment of utilities, rent-free periods, free car parking space, etc.

Government policy and taxation

It is critical to closely investigate government policy and taxation issues before investing in a property market. Here are some of the things you need to be vigilant about:

- Make sure you understand the **culture.** Are people honest and do they pay their bills on time? Are utility and service companies reliable? Is there corruption in the local planning process? Will the local mayor, or worse, the local mafia, look for a slice of the action? Some countries have a *higher* corruption index than others and this is worth checking before you are seduced by cheap prices and bail in.
- Changes in **Government policy,** or a change in Government,

can have very significant impacts on the property market. As a general rule, left-of-centre Governments tend to err on the side of policies designed to create a greater distribution of wealth. This policy approach isn't always good news for foreign investors. Will large-scale social and affordable housing be built next to your posh suburb as a Government flagship scheme? Is it intended to build a brand new mini-city nearby in a green field site over the next number of years? What are the trophy development policies being promoted by political parties and how might these affect property prices?

Taxation is a vital issue to get right, but remains something of a blind spot for many Irish investors. We all know it's boring and detailed, but it's also a key to success . . . or failure.

- Ideally there should be a **Double Taxation Agreement** between Ireland and the country in which you are investing. This reduces the impact of double taxation, but it isn't always a deal breaker, particularly where a low taxation policy is designed to attract foreign investors in order to develop a country. Some countries don't have Capital Gains Tax, for instance, and taxation on rents can be low so that, when taken in combination with Irish tax, it might be reasonable. Other countries have tax on income, gains and inheritance that would make even an Irish socialist blush.
- Don't over-estimate the attractiveness of countries with low tax or no tax. Remember, you will still be liable to pay Irish tax on the difference.
- Make sure you **fully understand tax on rent, capital gains tax, stamp duty** and especially local **municipal and community charges**.
- Be careful of basing too much of your decision on a favourable tax story because Governments can change the tax system – and pull the rug out from under your feet in the process.
- On the positive side, some Governments are quite far-seeing and proactive in developing and improving the property stock. Look

for Government **development incentives** encouraging employers, both domestic and overseas, to relocate, and seek to position your property in the path of progress.

Looking at leases

If you are buying a property in order to rent it out, again you need to do your homework to ensure a smooth path. A lease is a contract between a Lessee (tenant) and a Lessor (landlord). The contract transfers the right of possession and use of a property to the lessee for a period of time, and for an agreed amount of money. Always, always, always make sure your contract is in writing. These are the other considerations you should keep in mind:

- Remember, where you are buying a property with existing tenants, you are not just buying a property: you are buying a set of leases and each of these needs to be examined closely. Make sure you get a copy of all **lease agreements and additions or modifications** to the lease that have occurred since its original signing. You will be legally obliged to follow the terms and conditions signed by the Lessor and the Lessee.
- Check to ensure the lease agreement **complies with domestic law**. Check the charges for late payments, bounced direct debits and other fees. Make sure that any increase in rent is clearly defined under the terms of the contract. Pay particular attention to the expiry date of the lease and any concessions to the tenants, such as upgrading and installing equipment.
- Beware of tenants inserted into properties specifically to encourage a sale. Study the accounts to see how long the property has had tenants, otherwise you may find your income source has moved on as soon as you take possession.
- Commercial leases are a lot trickier and more complex than simple residential lease agreements. Look for a **summary of the main conditions** of a lease in advance, covering rent roll, tenants, lease length, square footage and concessions. Check for

issues that relate to tenants, such as rights of expansion, restrictions on other tenants, etc.

- Watch out for capped rentals in markets that have strong tenancy rights, like Germany. These will prevent you from raising rents.
- Insist on **financial and bank statements** to confirm that rental income has and is being paid: don't just take the vendor's word for it. Remember, you will be organising bank finance on the availability of a certain net rental income, so you have to make sure it's real.
- Check out your potential tenants thoroughly, particularly their **financial strength**, and know something about their sector. Just because the lease agreement contains a penalty in the event of default doesn't mean you are going to get paid – at least not without going through a legal process that could prove extremely costly, lengthy and, ultimately, futile.
- **Dig for gold**: you may find commercial properties with lease agreements that haven't been fulfilled by tenants due to incompetence, negligence, or laziness on the part of the landlord. These opportunities are gold dust, providing you with the possibility of taking over and driving up rents to match the unfulfilled parts of the lease agreements.

Doing the math

A quick evaluation formula commonly used for **residential property** is the **Gross Rental Yield**. This is the gross rent divided by the gross acquisition cost of the property. So, for example, a gross rent of €6,000 a year on a €100,000 acquisition gives a gross rental yield of 6%. Sometimes this is expressed as the **Gross Rent Multiplier** by dividing the rental figure into the acquisition figure, i.e. in this example, 16.66 times. It can be said that a property is being bought at 16.66 times its gross earnings.

The **commercial property** formula is very similar. The rent plus all other income from the commercial property is divided by the total growth acquisition cost. For example, if a commercial building is being bought for €1m and the total rents plus other income amount to €70,000 per annum, the **Gross Income Yield** is 7% and the **Gross Income Multiplier** is 14.28 times.

Gross rental yields in Irish residential property are currently, at best, 3%, which means that property is being bought at 33 times its earnings.

There are other simple measures available that you can use. The first is to calculate the **Net Rental Yield.** This is the yield you can expect at the outset, i.e. a snapshot of the first year. The formula used for Net Rental Yield is:

Rent expected – (maintenance costs + taxation – interest relief) ÷ total property acquisition costs = Net Rental Yield*
*(*the price, stamp duty and all other fees)*

Ensure you take account of *all* expenses, including common area charges, and allow for a vacancy period; it is unwise to assume that you will have 100% occupancy. Vacancy rates will vary according to local market conditions and are typically lower in city centre locations, perhaps as low as 10% or 5%. Holiday locations vacancy rates, on the other hand, could be 50%, or six months of the year. To give yourself an accurate picture, make sure you reduce your rent expectation by a reasonable vacancy rate. To help you ascertain a reasonable rate, check out the local market. If you are still unsure, then in strong markets it is reasonable to assume a vacancy rate of 8.3%, or one month.

Check the **Price per Square Metre** as this takes the price down into a common unit cost. The cost per square meter you are paying can then be measured against the cost per square metre in the local area for similar type property of similar quality – you can do this by talking to a wide number of real estate agents.

Surveyors use **Replacement Value** to calculate the cost of constructing a similar property. When taken together with the Price per Square Metre, this gives you the basis to compare against other properties. Obviously if the price proposed is below the replacement cost, there is a barrier to entry in the market which will discourage a construction company from building something similar and selling it at your price. Where the replacement value is higher than new buildings in the area, your price may be inflated.

Do be aware that these simple measures, helpful though they might be, do not tell the full story because they have not taken account of:

- The effect of costs and taxation
- Any tax benefits such as allowances or deprecation that may be coming with the property
- The effect of gearing as equity builds up over the years ahead
- Possible capital appreciation

These numbers can be crunched by a professional into a spreadsheet that looks forward over a period of ten years and takes account of your sunk costs at the outset, including stamp duty, location fees, etc., maintenance charges, utility costs, etc. and rental income. These financial models are grist to the mill for professional property scheme analysts. They allow easy adjustment in order to assess how sensitive the return is to changes in costs, rents and appreciation.

Cash Flow Models such as these provide an **Internal Rate of Return,** which is the return from all the cash flows over the period. The reverse side of the coin is a **Net Present Value**, a mathematical technique that compresses the analysis to one capital sum. This is useful when comparing different property investment opportunities.

Unless you have a degree in finance, you may find running this type of number-crunching daunting and difficult. Don't despair! Most accountants and tax advisors are skilled at pushing these numbers through software, so ask them for help.

Negotiating

Negotiating a price is a skill all of its own. The best place to start is to make sure you have built up your knowledge of the local market through methodical and proper research. This will arm you with knowledge of the market, perhaps even equivalent to the vendor's knowledge. Most importantly, don't be a blushing bride: bring your knowledge to the negotiation so that the vendor's expectations are lowered and he doesn't see the negotiation as making a quick killing from an uninformed buyer.

The trick to any negotiation is to try to learn something of the vendor's reasons for selling without giving away too much information about why you want to buy the property. If the seller is sticking rigidly to a premium price, look for ways to get the vendor to pay for improvements or repairs that will improve the value of the building, such as fitting a kitchen with new appliances, new carpets and curtains, etc. Be very careful of an old property requiring repairs and improvements that have been priced by the vendor. Get an independent valuation of these matters from a suitably qualified professional. In particular, where there has been any structural works undertaken to an old property, insist on an independent engineer's report.

Undertaking a due diligence on a property, particularly an old property, is a vital undertaking *before* contracts are exchanged and you have gone beyond the point of no return. If you are paying a booking deposit, make sure that it's in **escrow,** that is, not paid over to the vendor. The deposit should be held by the sales agent until all of the terms of the agreement have been met on both sides.

Check the **financial accounts**, examine rent rolls, look at bank statements, check all tenancy security deposits, look for copies of rental agreements and side contracts. Examine **planning permission** and compliance. Check that all **utility bills** have been fully paid and are up-to-date.

Due diligences can be as simple as a Surveyor's and Engineer's report, or complex if you are dealing with a commercial property with multiple tenants. Visual inspections will usually reveal **surface defects,** such as faulty appliances, old wiring and poor roof conditions. However, there can be **hidden defects,** for example, wet rot, dry rot or pipe corrosion. While you may look for disclosure of these matters, make sure it is also thoroughly investigated by an independent professional.

When you are inspecting the property initially, it is useful to have a **checklist of items** so that you do not become distracted or rushed. Look at the roof and attic, plumbing and electrical systems, air conditioning, landscaping, drainage, doorways, windows, signs of subsidence and violations of planning permission. Pay particular attention to slanted or soft flooring on any level. Check the basement. Watch out for cracks and bear in mind that hairline cracks in recently renovated plasterwork may be a sign that something has been covered up. Be very careful of bulging retaining walls or poor drainage, which are signs of potential subsidence.

If there is evidence of moisture that has not yet been dealt with – the question is, why? Check in particular for bad smells, or evidence of ongoing problems. In foreign locations bear in mind the potential for insect infestations, for example, wood-eating insects are a common problem in some countries. Finally, look for any environmental problems, particularly in commercial properties where certain types of 'dirty' tenants may be sloppy in storing toxic materials, etc.

When you are buying a property in a sun resort, be sure to visit the development at different times of the day to see how the sun strikes your balcony and swimming pool at different times. Don't forget to visit the area at night, too, to ensure it's not a meeting place for vagrants and drug dealers!

Checking your title

The simplest and easiest way of owning a property title is **sole ownership,** which allows you unencumbered discretion to deal with the property as you see fit. **Joint tenancy** is where two or more people hold the property in equal shares and where, typically, the entire value passes automatically to the surviving joint owners on death.

Tenancy in common is the ownership of property where the owners have a stated share of the entire property. This differs from Joint Tenancy because each owner can hold a different percentage and can sell his/her interest at any time.

Property partnerships are business relationships between two or more people who pool their resources together and invest in the property market. On the plus side, good partnerships typically bring together people of common interest and complementary skills, such as a tax advisor, property specialist, architect and developer. Much like any partnership, it is wise to establish a written partnership agreement, particularly to deal effectively with issues such as succession in the event of a partner's death, or a partner's desire to sell to the other partners.

Property is often purchased through a **limited company** that has either been set up for the purpose of acquiring the property, or is already holding the property. A limited company has an independent legal existence, which complicates the tax situation. Remember, when you buy an existing company you inherit any claims against it, so a professional due diligence on the company is a must.

When a company holds a property, it receives the rents and pays the tax. If the company sells the property and makes a profit, it pays tax on profits. These revenues are paid into the company. When monies are paid out of the company in the form of salaries, directors' fees or dividends, tax is paid by the shareholders. When the company is sold, tax is payable on profits. Tax issues surrounding non-trading companies, e.g. investment companies that invest in property, require specialist tax advice. As a general rule, you are better off buying personally than through a limited company structure, although in some foreign countries title transfer is traditionally through a holding company for each property.

Okay, that's a lot for you to digest! But at least you know that property isn't the soft option, but rather needs hard research and thinking. Just in case you're still tempted to stray from the path of investment righteousness, we'll quickly take a look at what you must definitely *not* do when opting for property investment.

CHAPTER II

How *Not* to Invest in Property

Perhaps warnings about property investment seem pointless to you – but there are very good reasons to be careful, even with what is often regarded as a sure-fire winner. For a long time wealth has been created by careful and well-researched investment in property, but the continuous surge in property values, particularly for Irish homes, has created a new breed of investor – an investor who breaks just about every rule in the book.

The rising tide lifting all the boats has created a dangerous sentiment: that investing in property is a one-way ticket to getting rich quickly, that property can go only in one direction and that the good times will last for ever. Lessons to the contrary from history, on both equity and property bubbles, haven't deterred our exuberant new property investor. Historically low interest rates, which are necessary to breathe life into the faltering economies of Germany, France and Italy, have created a goldrush in lending in Ireland. It appears like a penalty kick. Thanks to a low European base rate, money can be borrowed very cheaply, typically at less than 4%, and this can be secured against the massive equity Irish property-owners now enjoy on their homes and other properties. But it is dangerous to assume that just because the banks are lending you money, your investment planning is being rubber-stamped and risks are low. A sharp economic reversal can haul back property prices, drive up unemployment, lead to long vacancy periods and trigger a sharp reversal in property values in poor locations.

Gearing works wonderfully by transferring a rising capital value onto your balance sheet, while the bank merely enjoys its profit margin on the mortgage finance. But the rate of acceleration that gearing brings in an upward-moving market is matched by an equally sharp reversal in a falling property market. The bottomline is: you can't afford to be lackadaisical about property – ever. In spite of this, many people I meet have ideas about property that make my hair stand on end. So I'm going to share some of them with you, then we can look at the moral of each story and you'll take away some very important lessons.

The video shop

Late one evening I visited a local video shop to rent a movie. Another customer approached me and asked if I provided financial consultancy, you know, like, on the spot. He was buying a property in Turkey and wanted to know if I thought this was a good idea – as if picking property were a matter of picking a country. He confirmed he had engaged a Turkish solicitor, so the first question I asked him was if he had checked out the credentials of the solicitor to make sure he was qualified and authorised. I asked how the solicitor had validated that question, an essential factor in avoiding buying a worthless piece of paper that has been sold to a half-a-dozen other people. He didn't know. Next I asked him if there was a Double Taxation Agreement between Ireland and Turkey. He didn't know. Then I asked him what he knew about tax on rents, tax on gains, community taxes, stamp duties and tax on rental income. He didn't know.

What did he know? A few of his friends had bought in Turkey, too, so it seemed a good idea. I asked him if he was aware what would happen if he went to Turkey and he hadn't paid his taxes. He looked at me blankly. I suggested he rent *Midnight Express*.

You should never commit large parts of your balance sheet to anything simply on the basis that your pals are doing it. Pyramid-selling schemes thrive on this false sense of security in numbers.

George in Shanghai

In 2005 George Lee, RTE's ubiquitous Chief Economic Correspondent, paid a visit to China. He provided insightful and enthusiastic reports on the massive development of the Chinese economy, set against the alluring backdrop of vast building projects. I knew it was only a matter of time before the phone started ringing with queries about China. The fact that property warnings had been issued in connection with overvalued Chinese property on the foot of potential exuberant speculation in the Chinese property market wasn't a deterrent. Oh no. The Irish found their way and within a few months another company nobody had ever heard of was marketing Shanghai property on Irish radio. I was asked a lot of questions about it from people eager to invest, and I had just one question to put to them in return: what happens at the end of a long day when you get a phone call from China to tell you that there's a burst pipe in the apartment and the management company is nowhere to be found?

Just because there is a construction boom on the TV doesn't mean that property prices will continue to follow an upward trajectory. What if much of the increase has already happened in values, or if there is a big over-build that triggers falls?

Crazy emails

I had an email from an investor who had bought two apartment units in Christchurch – Christchurch, New Zealand, that is, not Christchurch, Dublin. I emailed back asking him if he had ever been further south than the Canaries. He hadn't. I've had emails asking me about Moldavian property. For the uninitiated, Moldova is a small poor country east of the Ukraine, and has been subject to major political upheaval in recent times. Albania appeared in another hopeful email.

Never buy property in a location you haven't had independently assessed by professionals you trust, or that you have not visited and researched yourself.

The new accessory

Irish investors are picking property destinations, it would appear, based on the latest fashion trends. It's purely speculative, but the blatant risks seem to be subdued by the comfort of fellow travellers. Now I've nothing against the firm that has taken the development risk turning a nice profit on every unit sold, but I suspect that, sometimes, when buying off plans, Irish investors are being ripped off by selling agents with inflated property prices and fairytales about rental income. First it was Spain, then Hungary, then like it spread a virus to Croatia and Turkey, and now it's Bulgaria. The advent of new States to the European Union in 2004 and the potential new additions, like Bulgaria, Romania and, perhaps, Turkey, are taken as proof of one-way bets on property killings.

In terms of investors' preparation for these acquisitions, you will find little evidence of the type of research and methodical approach outlined in *Loot!* Just a lot of gut instinct. Some of these itineraries begin with a short overseas trip. There's a party every night, a sing-song, then a descent into the local property market complete with hangovers and a tour of the available property stock. No wonder Irish investors are greeted with glee: local real estate sales agents just can't believe their luck. Here come the happy-clappy Irish with loads of lolly, a couple of standard questions and no idea about local property and market forces. Irish investors come home with glints in their eyes having compared local property prices against prices back home, even though such comparisons are completely and utterly irrelevant.

When I ask simple questions like, 'Who told you about the rent you can expect?' the answer is invariably, 'the selling agent'. Of course he did! It's an unregulated market and the agent, acting for the vendor, is selling the property at a commission usually significantly higher than commissions in the Irish property market.

Irish investors are regarded as wealthy visitors in poorer countries and easy pickings for profiteering. We did the

same to Americans who came to Ireland in the old days, so why should we expect anything different from people desperate to improve their earnings? Being nice won't defend you – only hard-nosed research can do that.

Property exhibitions

Property exhibitions held in hotels the length and breadth of Ireland have become standing room only events as foreign property sales agents, often twinning up with domestic real estate agents, take in vast numbers of bookings based on properties Irish investors have never set foot in – they have simply bought the photograph and the story. Seasoned property investors who have visited these exhibitions have been appalled to see the queues and the veritable frenzy as Irish investors rotate between tax advisors, solicitors and sales agents.

Just about the worst place you could pay a booking deposit on a foreign property is in an Irish hotel within a large crowd that's had its dander up following a presentation by an overseas agent oozing charm and simplicity. Ask yourself, who is paying? Do I really want to buy into an Irish housing estate in a foreign country? Why aren't these properties selling domestically? Do the prices quoted represent fair value? Is the presentation by the developers, who have put their own capital at risk in the market, or is it given by selling agents paid by commissions and maybe by hidden add-ons to developer prices?

Don't assume development is a doddle

Don't take on development risk too lightly, especially abroad. Here's a few working definitions I received from a developer happy to share his experiences.

ARCHITECT'S ESTIMATE:	The cost of construction in heaven.
MANAGEMENT CONTRACT:	The technique for losing your shirt under perfect control.
COMPLETION DATE:	The point at which liquidated damages begin.
LIQUIDATED DAMAGES:	A penalty for failing to achieve the impossible.
QUANTITY SURVEYORS:	People who go in after the war is lost and bayonet the wounded.
LAWYERS:	People who go in after the Quantity Surveyors and strip the bodies.
SUB-CONTRACTOR:	A gambler,who never gets to shuffle, cut, or deal.
TENDER SUBMISSION:	A poker game in which the losing hand wins.
TENDER SUM:	A wild guess carried out to two decimal places.
SUCCESSFUL TENDERER:	A contractor who is wondering what he left out.

Who is most vulnerable if things go wrong

Irish families with modest financial strength who have literally bet their house on an overseas property purchase based on a single trip abroad, if any at all, are most exposed. They have mortgages secured against Irish homes, some of them on an interest-only basis, and all the while they are pumping money into an overseas property purchase, that property is now standing vacant. That means the second mortgage is being funded out of earned income at home.

Rising interest rates, or any shock to the Irish economy that could lead to unemployment in sectors exposed to the forces of the global economy, have the potential to create very significant hardships as loan repayments have to be met. Unfortunately, it is only when there is no rental income forthcoming, or it's well below expectations, and the subsequent sale of the foreign property yields less than the purchase price that the lesson will be learned. These are very real possibilities.

Methodical, well-researched investment in overseas property, whether in Britain or further away, is a sure-fire way to grow a balance sheet over the long term. But investing in property on an emotional urge, comforted by the vast number of fellow Irish investors doing the same thing, is fraught with risk. The current wave appears no different from multiple experiences in investment history: surging numbers bailing in to the wrong asset at the wrong time, without carefully considering the proposition.

Irish investors with significant balance sheet strength and with gearing of 50% or less can absorb the risks of investing in foreign property and any potential cyclical downturn. The most exposed sector is the recent investor with high gearing on modest balance sheets and working in vulnerable employment sectors, like manufacturing.

Whatever the future may bring, one thing is certain – if many of these Irish overseas property investors do well, it will be by complete luck and not the notion that the Irish have some innate ability to sniff out good property deals. Don't just follow the herd – protect yourself.

CHAPTER 12

How Equities Work – Are You an Equity Investor?

Glossary

- **OEIC:** Open-Ended Investment Company – an investment structure with a variable capital pool that normally invests in a wide range of sub-funds.
- **UCITS:** Undertaking for Collective Investment in Transferable Securities – European legislation governing modern collective investments that operate across the EU.
- **Churning:** Selling and buying assets purely to generate commissions.
- **Dividend:** Payment of income on a share – a method of passing value through to shareholders.
- **Capitalisation:** A measure of company size determined by the shares in issue multiplied by their current share price.
- **Dividend yield:** The ratio between current dividend payments and share price.

If the balance sheets of the biggest businesses on the planet, like food, utilities, financial, industrial, pharmaceutical, technology and telecommunications, don't grow over the decades ahead, we're all stuffed – and it doesn't matter where you have your stash! Investing in growing businesses isn't just about making money, consider the impact on Irish property prices, income and competitiveness from Intel, Dell, Hewlett Packard and Microsoft, from Elan, IAWS, and Kerry. That's why the commonly held belief that investing in shares is dangerous isn't just wrong, it's completely bananas. If it weren't for businesses, we wouldn't have an economy and you could kiss goodbye to your property value!

Investing in equities (shares) is simply a must because it lets you share in the wealth created by businesses for their owners. This comes as growth in the price of your equities and can also come as income payments called dividends. Equities in strongly growing businesses and sectors should out-perform property returns over the long term, albeit at the price of higher volatility or choppiness in values. The debate about property versus equities and which is best is a waste of time. Both have different characteristics and both have roles to play in building your balance sheet and, as largely uncorrelated assets, together they can reduce the overall risk compared to being overly concentrated in one to the exclusion of the other. Of course, you can lose money because equities can fall in value even more so than property, but equities have better recovery ability and you can protect yourself quite easily by not putting all your eggs in one basket and by holding long term.

The irony is that many people who would never knowingly buy shares, mainly because they perceive it to be as risky as betting on a novice chase, are probably already invested in shares through pension schemes and savings policies, most of the assets held by which are in **shares**. So you may already have invested in equities and lived to tell the tale! But if you are anxious about this kind of investment, look at the following criteria.

Equities are definitely not *for you if:*

- You need the money back in the very short term, like within five years.
- You've lots of loot and only a little time left.
- You already suffer from insomnia and nerves from reading media headlines.
- You were defrauded in the past and now you don't even trust the postman.

- You rang the Gardai recently to report a stalker and it turned out to be a mirror in the shower.
- Your favourite cult just declared the world is set to collapse and businesses will be wiped out.

Remember, getting good returns long term isn't predicated on picking the whiz, bang, flash share or sector, it's more about using lots of commonsense, avoiding obvious mistakes and reigning in your emotions – both greed and fear. If you feel you can do that, you should be able to handsomely out-perform inflation long term. So come on in, it's fun and interesting!

Starting out

You don't need to become an expert, but understanding some of the basics is important, especially if you are going to weather the significant downturns that will happen from time to time. The future is likely to bring increasingly larger swings in both directions – up and down – so understanding the game will help you keep your long-term focus while others panic and sell.

There are two basic types of investor: passive and active. So the first thing is to figure out what kind of investor you are. If you want to be a very passive investor, that is someone who doesn't want to delve too deeply into the world of equities, there is a number of basic investment strategies you can follow:

1. *You can go on auto-pilot – index tracking*

Tracking indices means investing across large company indices – a pre-set basket of shares organised according to who is the biggest and providing a natural mix across all sectors from food to pharmaceutical. Nobody is driving: the shares are selected purely according to who is the biggest in the market or sector. The ISEQ 20, for example, tracks the top 20 Irish shares, like AIB, CRH, Bank of Ireland, etc. The big European index is the EuroStoxx 50, which tracks shares like L'Oreal, Deutsche Bank, etc. There's the FTSE 100 in London (commonly called 'the Footsie') and the S&P 500 in the USA.

Index tracking works well, especially in rising markets, but in falling markets don't expect someone to be hitting the brakes. Studies have shown that between 50% and 80% of those who professionally manage large company portfolios (active management) in the European, UK and US markets find it hard to beat the index in a rising market, so why take the risk of picking a lousy pilot! Index tracking appears to work best in large, established markets, such as the US, UK, and Europe, where company information is plentiful. However, tracking is of questionable worth for small stocks and in specialist markets and sectors, such as China, South East Asia, Commodities, Technology, etc. Here human judgment and professional analysis, which are part and parcel of active management, can add a lot of value.

You can buy into large company indices through unit-linked funds available from Irish life offices and through Exchange Traded Funds via stockbrokers. A reasonable variety of actively managed funds is available through Irish life offices, but for real width and depth a much bigger variety is available through OEICs (Open-Ended Investment Companies) from bases in the financial services centres of Luxembourg and Dublin, and also distributed through stockbrokers and certain Investment Intermediaries.

2. You can fancy the turtles – dividend investing

This involves investing in big companies which aren't trying to go too fast and take over the world in their sector, which have strong cash balances and a proven track record in maintaining good dividend payments. Dividend investing is a complementary investment style and takes in companies like financials, utilities and food.

3. You can fancy the hares – growth investing

This means focusing less on dividends in favour of shares that reward investors through share price performance, like Pharmaceuticals, Technology, and Bio-Technology companies. In a strongly rising market this style should out-perform the Turtles, albeit at the cost of increased volatility.

4. You can fancy the cheapies – value investing

This approach looks for shares that are under-priced when set against company profits, potential profits, or assets. Value investing usually won't involve selecting growth shares, whose prices are typically sold at a premium compared to the value of company assets. Unit-linked funds available from certain life offices provide these strategies, as do Open-Ended Investment Companies (OEICs), which comply with European UCITS rules, guaranteeing full accountability and transparency on charges.

5. You can opt for regional investing

Funds also exist that can provide investors with more global exposure, particularly into China and the South East Asia and Pacific regions. These investments are higher risk funds than those that concentrate principally on Pan-European and US large stocks.

6. You can use a stockbroker

Funds aren't the only way you can invest in equities. Alternatively, you can establish a portfolio with a stockbroker and use its discretionary services whereby you delegate active management to the stockbroker. If you choose to delegate this way, watch out that trades made are in your best interest and not churning opportunities, carried out simply to generate commissions for the stockbroker. If you prefer to be more hands-on, other types of stockbrokers will operate on your instructions only and provide you with research and advice as you need it.

What exactly is a 'large company' in investment terms?

We have referred to 'large companies' in our skip through the equity investment options, but you might well be asking what actually constitutes 'large'. Well, there is no accepted worldwide measure on what constitutes a large company. What might be regarded as a large company in a market such as Ireland would be a medium-sized company, at best, in the US. Some guidance is obviously necessary, however, so see below for *Loot!*'s own measures, which can be used as a general rule of thumb for the US and London stock markets. (Note: 'Cap' is short for capitalisation.)

Category by Asset Values

	United States	London
Large Cap.	More than $5bn	More than £3.5bn
Mid Cap.	$500m - $5bn	£350m - £3.5bn
Small Cap.	$50m - $500m	£35m - £350m
Micro Cap.	Less than $50m	Less than £35m

So, which type of investor sounds more like you?

What's the point in taking an aggressive approach to investing in equities if it gives you an ulcer every time the stock market falls? There is no 'right category' of equity investor, there is only the category that fits you best. You are best placed to answer which of the following investor types sounds more like you?

The Passive Investor

The business sections of the media make interesting reading, but you would never subscribe to a specialist finance publication for the purposes of tracking what is happening in detail. You would prefer convenience shopping and like the idea of putting money into well-known brand names and the most popular funds. The Passive Investor represents the biggest market for equities, but that investment is rarely direct. The Passive Investor invests almost exclusively through funds. If shares are held directly, it's usually a small punt, or a by-product of a life office or building society demutualisation.

The Passive Investor makes up his or her own mind, usually on the basis of information presented to them from financial institutions, or by financial advisors. Passive Investors rarely seek and evaluate the information for themselves. They don't regard it as important in their lives. Passive Investors can be extremely successful businesspeople and professionals, who have made lots of money doing what they do best: running their own businesses. They lead busy lives and do not have the time for equities and don't want to invest aggressively in anything they don't fully understand.

The Novice Trader

'Novice' describes the level of experience you have gained so far by investing **directly** in equities. A Novice Trader usually begins with funds, later switching to buying shares directly. When direct investment produces better results than collective investments, the novice investor will allocate more resources towards direct share purchase.

Novice Traders can become highly successful at investing in a small number of stocks with which they have become very familiar. Their experience in a particular industry or service sector helps them to understand which companies are best positioned to outperform. Many Novice Traders will use a 'system' to guide their investment decisions.

The Novice Trader doesn't really want to spend a lot of time and energy in highly active research and trading, preferring to undertake a periodic review and occasionally make some changes to the current mix. A typical portfolio for a novice investor will have most value held in the companies that comprise the very largest in the stock market, with the rest in medium and small companies.

The Active Trader

Funds are definitely not for the Active Trader, who is more akin to a professional fund manager. The Active Trader likes to get stuck in, and typically enjoys reading and learning more about financial matters. The successful Active Trader is keen to make money, and plenty of it, but in a carefully controlled manner whereby he/she seeks to maximise his/her knowledge. The Active Trader is someone who is prepared to put in the necessary time, energy and planning to do the job right. They might concentrate on medium to small companies, energised by the possibility of the explosive value that is possible when the smaller end of the market is less well researched. Their results can greatly exceed those of the large fund industry because the Active Trader has the advantage of being able to manage a much smaller sum of money, and to concentrate on a narrower range of equities. Many Active Traders are members of informal networks that work on the principle of sharing information. The best-known of such networks is TheMotleyFool.com

The **unsuccessful** Active Trader is usually somebody who's not fully informed, or who has made the classic mistake of letting their knowledge catch up with their experience! Learning by making costly mistakes is one sure way of crippling your financial strength. *Loot!* gives a basic grounding in the principles of running your own equity portfolio, but specialist reading is essential to hone your skills.

Other investment options to consider

Investment clubs, the Internet and an investment strategy

Investment clubs are a great idea for the gregarious investor. Clubs help small groups of people to get together and pool their resources. This lets members take a spread of stocks – a position they might not be able to attain on their own. By sharing information club members gain valuable experience from one another and build up a consensus portfolio. Pooling also benefits the group by minimising transaction costs through brokers. And, of course, they can also be great fun, helping you to widen your circle of friends while you make money! Despite the downturn in world stock markets from 2000 to early 2003, the growth in investment clubs has continued. On-line dealing makes it far easier to execute deals and substantially lowers costs. Thanks to the Internet you can now see your portfolio updated daily, which gives you a greater sense of control.

Clubs normally require members to commit to investing a regular sum, taking a medium-term view on performance, and are a great structure to calm the nerves of the excitable with the cool headedness of the more experienced investor. Most investment clubs operate well in a rising market, but in a decline some investment decisions look like errors and blame starts being thrown around. Pretty soon, members stop coming up with ideas for fear of getting it wrong. But help is at hand: growth in clubs has been matched by specialist training companies, for example, 'Invest Like the Best' (www.investlikethebest.com), an Irish firm that teaches members about markets and how to apply best professional practices in clubs.

Ethical investing

Ethical investment means imposing an additional standard or criteria in your portfolio to ensure that the companies in which you buy shares are operating to high social standards. When you are running your own portfolio, you can impose your own restrictions, such as environmental records, race records and commitments to things like worker safety. You can invest in Ethical Funds through life offices and OEICs.

A quick anatomy of equities (shares)

Whatever type of investor you are, understanding the basic anatomy of shares is a first step, so hang in there and let's take it bit by bit.

Why do we invest in equities?

You invest in shares because you expect the share price to increase over time. Share prices increase when the **earning power** of the company increases. When this happens, the company's ability to pay higher **dividends** also increases. You seek not just an increase in the **capital** but also an increase in **income**. Just like buying anything else, you want to buy at cheap prices and sell at top prices. Ratios can help determine whether or not the buying price for a share is cheap (see P/E ratios, page 164).

Assessing an equity

Businesses change, and so does their relative value. This information is captured in the paperwork produced by companies. The three main pieces of paperwork are the **Profit and Loss Account**, the **Balance Sheet** and the **Cash Flow Statement**. These are important documents and must be published quarterly in the US and half-yearly in London. Each one provides a snapshot of the business' performance from a different angle, so you have three angles allowing you to piece together the bigger picture.

While the paperwork shows what has happened in the past, share prices show what is reasonably expected in the future. **Share prices are forward-looking**. As the stock market also looks forward, anything it sees that it doesn't like, either for the economy or for an individual company, will dampen expectations and possibly push down share prices. If these expectations fail to materialise, the share price goes back up again.

What to look for

Investors endeavour to find companies that are **undervalued** relative to their prospects for **growth**. It's not an easy endeavour: opinions on companies' prospects can vary, even when everybody is looking at the same set of figures or ratios. Therefore, investors look both ways. They look for companies whose share price may be **re-rated upwards**, and for companies whose share price may be re-rated **downwards**.

Most people make their money by buying shares and later selling them. Some investors make money by **selling short, also known as shorting**. This is the reverse of normal trading. Selling short means you first sell, then you buy. Shorting works by borrowing shares from someone who holds them, promising to return them later. You then sell the borrowed shares at the current market price – a price you believe is overrated. When it falls, you buy the same number of shares back again for a lot less money because the share price has fallen. This is called **covering your short**.

Market movements

Market-makers are members of a stock exchange who have a duty to make a continuous market for certain types of share. If market-makers sense that there has been a lot of short selling of a particular share, they may put on a **bear squeeze**. This means they push up their quoted prices, forcing the **bears** – that is, those who are short-selling – to buy at a bloated price. When this happens, newspapers will report that prices rose because of **bears covering shorts**. Conversely, when speculators pounce on a company in an attempt to deliberately force its price down, for example, by circulating rumours about the company, it is called a **bear raid**. So a bear squeeze can trap bear raiders! (The vocabulary is one of the best things about all this stuff! You can now impress your friends with nonchalant statements of bears with shorts that need covering!).

When the price of shares is continually rising, it is called a **bull market**; when share prices are falling, it is called a **bear market.**

Assessing value

There is a number of initial, or surface, indicators of potential value that can catch the eye, but knowledgeable traders will dig deeper before investing in a share. One of these initial indicators is the **dividend yield**. Say you bought shares in Mars Trips Limited for 200c, and the company is paying a dividend on its shares of 10c. This 10c as a percentage of the share price is 5%. This is known as a dividend yield and it will change every time there is a change in the share price on the stock exchange. If the share price rises, the dividend yield will fall because the dividends represent a smaller proportion of the share price quoted. Lower dividend yields may be an indication that a company is growing fast. A high yield, on the other hand, may indicate that a company's profits are not going to increase very fast, or that the company represents an above-average risk.

So, how can you tell if the shares in one company in a particular sector are expensive in comparison to another in the same sector? One of the rough measures employed to do just this is **price/earnings ratio**, or **P/E ratio**. P/E ratio tells you something about the distance between the earnings of a company and its current share price, therefore it links earnings to price. The P/E ratio is calculated by dividing the **earnings per share** (EPS) of a company into its share price.

An example is the best way to explain. Let's say that Voxpox Limited has earnings per share of 15c and its share price is being quoted at 180c. It will have a P/E ratio of 12 (i.e. 180 divided by 15). You may hear people say that Voxpox has a P/E ratio of 12, or that its shares are selling at 12 **times earnings**, or that its shares are on a **multiple of** 12. If the P/E is low in comparison to similar-type shares, it may indicate a buying opportunity – subject to more detailed research.

P/E ratios for similar companies in similar industries or service sectors are used by way of comparison. The typical P/E ratio for **utility** stocks, such as water companies, electricity companies, etc., is usually very low, but these are steady stocks that pay good dividends. The P/E ratios for technology companies may be well into double digits. To compare a P/E ratio of a utility against a technology company wouldn't make sense, but to compare the P/E ratios within these sectors against one another is a way of beginning to get an insight.

Share types

Ordinary shares have voting rights and are the most common shares traded. However, you can also own a slice of a company through **preferred shares**. Preferred shares dividends are normally fixed at higher levels than ordinary shares, but normally come without voting rights. Holders are entitled to receive their dividends before ordinary shareholders and if the company is liquidated, preferred shareholders are at the top of the queue.

Unlike normal dividends, the dividends associated with preferred shares are set at the time that the shares are issued and do not increase. This limits the performance of preferred shares, but it also makes them less volatile. Preferred shares often come with a conversion option, in which case they are known as **convertible preferreds**. This means they can be converted to ordinary shares at a pre-set price.

Investment returns versus investor returns

A common cause of head-scratching is the big difference that can arise between the return for the market as a whole over a period of time and the much lower returns experienced by certain types of investor. It's even possible to get high positive investment returns from a market while the investors experience negative investor returns! The reason for this anomaly is easy to figure out though when you consider common investor behaviour. As markets naturally keep moving up and down, many investors buy shares only *after* hearing the market has done well. This means they are buying at the peaks. The cure for this investment ailment is time: the longer you stay in, the more likely you are to experience average investment returns. Once again, the key to success is contained in the golden formula of investing: buying in and staying in through thick and thin is likely to produce better results than over-active trading.

The index family

When you catch broadcasts on stations such as CNN and Sky News, you will frequently hear reference to movement in **stock market indices**. The worldwide market is choc full of indices. You have already made the acquaintance of the **Eurostoxx 50**, which captures the share prices of Europe's fifty largest plcs, the **FTSE 100**, which tracks the biggest 100 plcs in London, and the **S&P 500**, which tracks the big 500 in the USA. The **ISEQ 20** was launched in 2005 by the Irish Stock Exchange and is an Exchange Traded Fund that tracks Ireland's twenty biggest plcs. The **Dow Jones Industrial Average** is comprised of the 'biggies' in the US. It tracks the movement of thirty of the largest companies traded on the New York Stock Exchange. It is often referred to simply as **The Dow Jones**.

For every market there is an index, ranging from broad market indices to indices for special sectors and styles, and the index family is getting bigger all the time.

Preparing for the rollercoaster – a brief history of crashes

Okay, okay, so you're being tempted by equities and here I am putting a halt to your advances! Well, it may seem bad timing to bring up the subject of investment nightmares but, like all things in life, forewarned is forearmed – and you need to be prepared for every eventuality, both practically and psychologically. Those of a nervous disposition – keep the smelling salts handy!

Speculative fever was the cause of the **1929 Wall Street crash**. It pushed the American economy into a slump that lasted throughout the 1930s and also had an effect in London, albeit less severe. Speculative fever was also a driver in the technology bubble of 2000, when all the guff about the 'new economy' was blown away and many companies and investors were found to have grossly overestimated their future earnings potential.

Basically, speculative fever is what happens when share prices on a stock exchange run too far ahead of the **fundamentals**. This happens when prices are pushed up and are not based on a realistic valuation of what earnings are likely to be. Instead, a buying frenzy takes hold and pushes reason roughly aside and the market begins to feed on itself – until the inevitable crash. In the US in the 1920s, the stock market collapse was preceded by speculation in land. Investors were buying land and selling it again the next week. This trading eventually carried across to the stock market, where investors bought shares using their existing stocks as security and taking out loans to buy yet more stock, a practice known as **buying on the margin**. The stock market began to get dangerously top-heavy, like a great inverted pyramid, until it finally, inevitably all came tumbling down, and it wasn't a pretty sight.

In the early **1970s** it was the **oil crisis** that precipitated a stock market crisis, when the world supply of oil was threatened. The shockwaves were felt globally – even the oil-producing nations were affected by the subsequent fallout – as the international stock markets took the view that the value of businesses would be hugely affected by lowered economic activity. In London the broad-based index, the FTA All Share recorded massive losses in 1973 and 1974, but in 1975 bounced back by nearly 140%. Imagine losing your long-term focus at that time and selling out after two lousy years at the end of 1974, missing out on what happened next! That's a very important lesson, indeed.

Here's the pattern of the 1970s and 1980s in London as recorded by the FTA All Share Index – a textbook example of how essential it is to hold your nerve from one sharp fall to the next! Check out what happened following the 1973/1974 oil crisis and leading up to the next famous 'crash' in 1987:

1970	−7.52%
1971	+41.93%
1972	+12.85%
1973	−31.35%
1974	−55.34%
1975	+139.94%
1976	−3.23%
1977	+37.89%
1978	+2.99%
1979	+3.06%
1980	+28.95%
1981	+5.77%
1982	+23.59%
1983	+22.64%
1984	+25.22%
1985	+16.03%
1986	+22.34%
1987	Black Monday!

What about the infamous October 1987 Crash when a long bull market came to a sudden halt on Black Monday, 19 October? In London the situation was exacerbated by severe weather over the previous few days, which caused widespread damage to communications. As a result, on Monday morning the stock exchange barely had a pulse and communications technicians were working round the clock to get things back on line. Over the preceding two weeks Wall Street had seen heavy falls in the Dow Jones Industrial Average.

At close of play on Monday, 19 October the FTA All Share Index was down 10%, while across the Atlantic the Dow Jones was crashing to a huge one-day fall of over 22%. The next day London fell 11.4%. The effects were felt worldwide, but was it a crash?

Well, that depends. Those who had been in the market continuously over a number of years read the events of October 1987 as a correction. Those who had bought into the market at the end of the bull run, driven by speculative fever, were the ones who saw it as a crash. For example, an investor buying in London in July of 1987 would have been looking at losses of over 36% at the worst point, yet an investor in the market for the full year recorded a growth, despite the events in October. Economists were out in force to explain why the arcane mechanisms of economics could account for what had happened, like currency movements, trade imbalances, budget deficits and so on. But what happened was the same as what had happened in 1929: prices had raced away from the **fundamentals**. When the lightbulb came on, the number of people selling hugely exceeded the number of people buying and therefore prices crashed. The same pattern was repeated in the Technology stock collapse in 2000.

When a bull market is in its final phase there is a typical burst in share price movement. This occurred in the first half of 1987 as the number of investors entering the market increased, carrying with them a large number of speculators. After a solid bull market for several years nothing, apparently, could go wrong. This had the effect of pushing the FTA All Share Index up to a peak of 48% in July, but there was no sign from company profits that a 48% increase was justified.

After the correction, when prices stabilised at levels that made sense of the fundamentals (things like company earnings and dividend yields), the market regrouped and moved on. The economic collapse predicted by many never occurred. The 1987 crash also showed that even big stock markets like London can be dramatically affected by **liquidity**, i.e. where the number of sellers greatly exceeds the number of buyers. One thing is certain, though, history will continue to repeat itself. When P/E levels shoot up through the roof, when dividend yields go the opposite direction and when everybody's diving into the market, you're at the end of a bull run.

What influences equities?

Predicting influences on equity values is not a precise science, but you do need to know in what directions the wind can blow, and what it can cause. Share prices, as we've seen, contain the expectation of what companies will be worth in the near future. Therefore anything that affects that expectation will cause share prices to move. Accordingly, the two most important factors are company earnings and interest rates.

Company earnings

Shareholders have a direct stake in the company and its profits, but share prices are quick to adjust to optimistic or pessimistic expectations for the company. Changing forecasts of earnings, whether from factors specific to the company and its sector or to the economy, will affect the current price of the company's shares. For example, you may read a headline about a company issuing a profit warning. This doesn't mean the company is going bust, but that its actual earnings are likely to come well within forecasts – a clear signal that its share price may have been overvalued by the market.

Interest rates

When interest rates rise unexpectedly it has the effect of deteriorating the outlook for growth in earnings because companies and their customers have to pay more money to their lenders. The effect will vary according to the level of borrowing companies have on their books.

The second impact is **opportunity cost**, that is the amount of money investors could get by putting their money in less risky assets, like cash deposits. When rates rise, money already in the equity markets goes back into cash. This affects liquidity by reducing the number of buyers, thus depressing prices. When interest rates fall unexpectedly, the opposite occurs and shares rise.

Technical analyst influences

Analysts look at the historic price pattern of a share. They believe that price movements can be predicted by looking at what has happened in the past. An analyst might decide that he will operate within a certain range, pegging the level below which he won't fall and above which he won't go. When the share hits these glass floors or ceilings, the **technical analyst** makes his move. When large numbers of analysts act on the same information, the effect can wash over the markets. While not choreographed, these movements have the effect of turning the predictions of technical analysts into self-fulfilling prophecies. As soon as the share price falls to the glass floor, they buy back into the market, and sell again once it hits the glass ceiling.

Currency effects

Investing in non-Eurozone equities contains currency risk, which can lead to threats or opportunities. For example, you buy a Japanese share in the Tokyo stock market and it grows at 10% for the year. During that period the yen weakens against the Euro by 20%. You incur a loss of 12%. If the yen strengthened by 20% against the Euro, you'd have made a gain of 32%.

When a currency weakens it has the effect of making exports cheaper, therefore companies can perform better. The opposite is a great worry. An over-strengthened currency increases the price of goods and services going into export markets. This can make companies uncompetitive and have a negative effect on share prices.

Companies, particularly bigger companies, have dual listings on the London and US stock markets in order to attract investors. When a US company is quoted in the London stock market its share price will be denominated in sterling. A UK investor who buys the share using sterling is therefore not incurring any foreign currency **exchange costs**, but this should not be confused with foreign **currency risk**. It is not the currency of denomination that counts, but where the assets of the business are invested and where the cash flows to the company arise.

For example, an Irish investor places money in a unit-linked fund issued by a life insurance company in Dublin. The fund invests in American equities. The investor pays a cheque to the insurance company in Euro and receives valuations in Euro. As a result, the investor feels he is not exposed to foreign currency risk, but he is: he just can't see it. The value of the units in the fund will move directly in line with the share prices of the companies in which the fund invests, plus changes between the Euro and the dollar. This detail isn't reported to the investor, who only sees a unit price expressed in Euro. Don't be blind-sided by the currency on the balance sheet: if the equity is based abroad, you are exposed to currency risk and you must be aware of that.

Technical corrections

The term **technical correction** is used frequently by the financial media. It refers to the period after a short burst of movement in share prices, when the prices suddenly fall into a short trough. This is the impact of **consolidation**, whereby investors decide to sell in order to protect their gains. As soon as prices have fallen into the trough, investors buy back into the market.

Sentiment

Despite all of the computer equipment, the knowledge and training, there is a lot of human nature at play in decision-making. The market does not contain a single network through which all investors talk to one another. Instead it communicates through various channels, such as the media, and through informal grapevines, which still very much dominate trading areas such as London and New York. This set-up creates **mood**, and mood is a transient, untameable thing that can give rise to all kinds of misperceptions and rumours.

The sentiment that investors hate to hear is **uncertainty**. Uncertainty usually means that an equally large number of people believe prices to be overvalued as believe the opposite to be true. When this tilts into negative sentiment, prices fall. When you hear that investors are **nervous**, it doesn't mean that they are swallowing Prozac – it is simply a way of describing the enigma of sentiment within a market.

Rumour

Rumour doesn't always arise accidentally; quite often it is used as a deliberate way of influencing the market in order to make money. The most powerful rumour is **take-over rumour**, particularly when it is specific and has a resonance of truth. For example, a rumour may circulate that the senior management team of Tweedle Dum had two days of discussions with some senior managers from Tweedle Dee with a view to taking over the company. This news, even if unsubstantiated, can have a dramatic impact on prices.

A take-over climate can take root in a market during buoyant times. When a take-over climate pervades, an element of speculative fever is introduced to the market. As a result, rumour pushes up prices well before any take-over actually occurs.

Weight of money

The weight of money movements has a particularly important influence on the global financial markets. Small economies and stock markets are affected by the tidal waves of money sloshing around world markets, lifting stock market prices where there are massive positive inflows, and sharply depressing stock market prices when money is pulled out.

Political influences

Swings from socialist Government to right wing Government can have an effect on stock markets, as can changes in existing Government fiscal policy. A Government may decide, for example, to reduce taxes in order to trigger an economic uplift. This action can boost the stock market. Alternatively, a Government may signal an increase in taxes for the wealthy, triggering fears of a flight of capital. In smaller countries, particularly fledgling democracies, political risk may be very high. Governments and policies change frequently and sometimes decisions can lead to civilian unrest and instability. The more unstable the region, the more unstable are its stock markets.

You can relax now, that's the tour of equities over! However, if you fancy yourself an Active Trader, a whiz prepared to take on and beat the professionals, then we've got more to talk about. Go on, admit it, you'd get a buzz battling for better value amongst the big boys. For you, investing in funds just ain't enough – you're a trader! Go on then, get into the next chapter. If this is not you, skip the next chapter – you're not missing out, you've just got more important things to do than gluing yourself to a PC and share volatility for the rest of your life!

CHAPTER 13

Equities for the Direct Investor

Glossary

- **Bond yield:** The ratio between the income payable by a bond and the cost of buying it.
- **Dow Jones Industrial Average:** New York Stock Exchange index that tracks the prices of 30 of the largest plcs in the USA.
- **Raider:** Generally unwelcome buyer sweeping up the controlling shares of a company.
- **IPO:** Initial Public Offering – the flotation of company on the stock market.
- **Dividend yield:** The ratio between the income paid on a share and the cost of buying it.
- **Index tracking:** A method of investing across all shares comprising an index.

If you can't quite see yourself married to your PC as an Active Trader, then don't give yourself piles reading this chapter – stick to using funds to invest in equities. But for the insomniacs, the technicians and the nerds out there, follow me into the world of the Active Trader.

The paperwork you'll need to read

First, you'll need to understand how to read the information produced by companies. These are called the **accounts**. As we noted earlier, publicly quoted companies must produce accounts half-yearly for the London stock market and quarterly for the US stock markets. The accounts produced are the **Profit and Loss Account, the Balance Sheet and the Cash Flow Statement**. These operate under a set of accounting standards and are produced by **independent auditors**. Publicly quoted companies are required to produce considerably more information than companies not publicly quoted, including the **director's report**, together with detailed **notes to the accounts**.

The accounts normally open with a statement from the **Chairperson**, but the most important statement is the **auditor's report**. It is the job of the auditors to certify that the accounts represent **a true and fair view** of the company's profits. Where the accounts are **qualified** by an auditor, the position can be quite disastrous for a publicly quoted company.

The **Profit and Loss Account** shows the results of a company's trading over the past financial period, measuring it against similar results for the previous financial period.

The **Cash Flow Statement** is simply another angle from which the same figures can be examined. It has become increasingly more important, however. This is because while many businesses can look robust in their Profit and Loss Accounts and Balance Sheets, they can actually have failed because they have messed up their ability to manage their cash flows. **Over time, what a company reports in profits should be reflected in cash flow generated.**

The **Balance Sheet** of a company is just like the balance sheet shown on page 179. It gives a snapshot, at a particular point in time, of the total value of the company's assets and liabilities. Equivalent figures are provided in balance sheets for the previous financial period. The balance sheet is a useful measure in providing an overview of the wealth of a company, but taken in isolation it can be misleading.

Some companies manipulate their financial data – a practice quite within the rules of accounting standards – by methods such as bringing forward some items and delaying others in order to present the balance sheet in a better light. This is called **window-dressing**. The term **creative accounting** is used when figures are skewed excessively, as witnessed for WorldCom, whose ex-CEO Bernie Ebbers was sentenced to twenty-five years in prison upon being found guilty of accounting fraud. Several balance sheets may be produced by a business, but large companies usually have a holding company that produces the ***consolidated*** **balance sheet** for all of its subsidiary companies, each of which will have separate balance sheets.

Careful study of the information produced by companies can give investors helpful insights. An investor's objective is to ascertain whether or not the price quoted for the shares is too high or too low on the basis of the information presented in the accounts. Where careful analysis leads to an opinion that the share price is low, this represents an opportunity to buy. On the other hand, where analysis reveals that the share price is too high, this may be an opportunity to go short.

Most of the information you need to examine converts to **ratios**. Ratios arise when you compare one number against another.

Say hello to Tweedle Dum

Tweedle Dum Plc is a very simple company – all of its figures have come in with nice round sums. This is because Tweedle Dum Plc doesn't exist. Nevertheless, it has produced a **Profit and Loss Account** and a **Balance Sheet** that you can use to understand where these ratios arise and how to calculate them. There is also a **Statement of Cash Flows** for Tommy Turtle Plc so you can see what one looks like, and what to look for in it. (See pages 178–80).

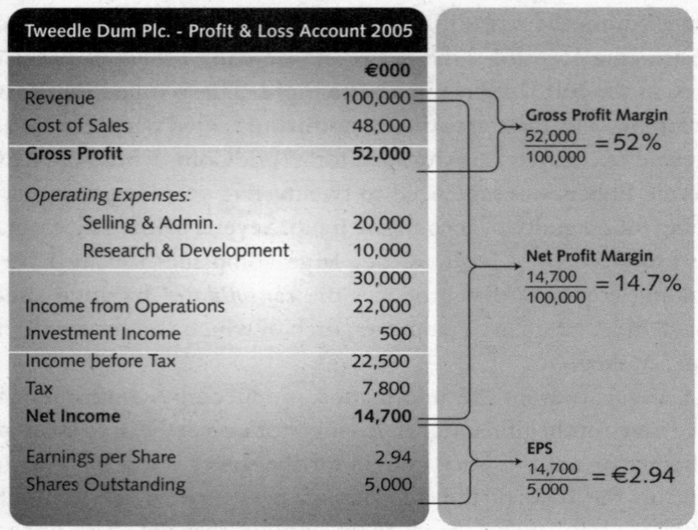

Tweedle Dum Plc. - Profit & Loss Account 2005	
	€000
Revenue	100,000
Cost of Sales	48,000
Gross Profit	**52,000**
Operating Expenses:	
Selling & Admin.	20,000
Research & Development	10,000
	30,000
Income from Operations	22,000
Investment Income	500
Income before Tax	22,500
Tax	7,800
Net Income	**14,700**
Earnings per Share	2.94
Shares Outstanding	5,000

Earnings per share (EPS)

The Profit and Loss Account tells you how much **net income** the company has earned over a particular time period. This net income has been earned by the shareholders. How much is attributed to each shareholder depends on the total number of shares outstanding. In the example of Tweedle Dum, net income was €14.7m, with 5m shares outstanding. The EPS is calculated by dividing the net income by the total number of shares outstanding, giving an **earnings per share** of €2.94.

P/E ratio

The **P/E ratio** is the market's price tag for a share and is calculated by dividing the current share price by the earnings per share over the past twelve months. The P/E ratio is often quoted next to a stock in newspapers. Let's say that Tweedle Dum plc is currently

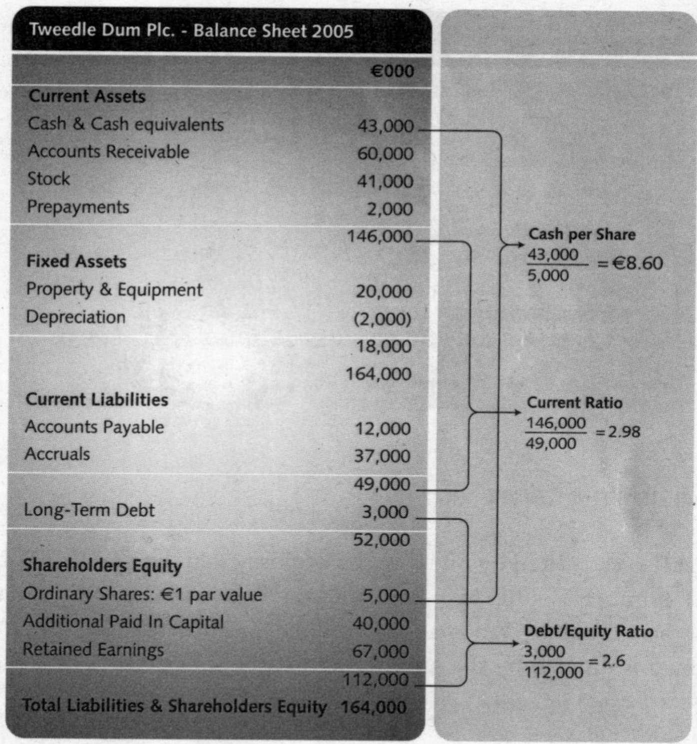

Tweedle Dum Plc. - Balance Sheet 2005

	€000
Current Assets	
Cash & Cash equivalents	43,000
Accounts Receivable	60,000
Stock	41,000
Prepayments	2,000
	146,000
Fixed Assets	
Property & Equipment	20,000
Depreciation	(2,000)
	18,000
	164,000
Current Liabilities	
Accounts Payable	12,000
Accruals	37,000
	49,000
Long-Term Debt	3,000
	52,000
Shareholders Equity	
Ordinary Shares: €1 par value	5,000
Additional Paid In Capital	40,000
Retained Earnings	67,000
	112,000
Total Liabilities & Shareholders Equity	164,000

Cash per Share
$\frac{43,000}{5,000} = €8.60$

Current Ratio
$\frac{146,000}{49,000} = 2.98$

Debt/Equity Ratio
$\frac{3,000}{112,000} = 2.6$

trading at €44.10 per share. The P/E ratio is the share price, €44.10, divided by the EPS, €2.94, which equals 15. Therefore Tweedle Dum stock is said to be trading at 15 times' earnings.

You need to be a little bit careful of P/E ratios because EPS may be based on past earnings, in which case the P/E ratio is called a **trailing P/E ratio**. Technical analysts investigate the potential **future** value of a company and often use the projected earnings per share. This means that the current share price is divided by the **projected** EPS, in which case the result is a **forward** P/E ratio.

Tommy Turtle Plc Statement of Cash Flows	€000 2005	€000 2004
CashFlows from Operating Activities:		
Net Income	15,000	16,000
Adjustment for Depreciation:		
Depreciation	1,800	2,000
Changes in Operating Assets & Liabilities:		
Accounts Receivable	(18,000)	(12,000)
Stock	(12,000)	(8,000)
Accounts Payable	2,000	4,000
Accrued Expenses	3,000	6,000
Net Cash from Operating Expenses	(8,200)	8,000

Net assets per share (NAV)

NAV is calculated by dividing the ordinary shareholders' funds by the number of ordinary shares outstanding. For Tweedle Dum, the shareholders' funds appear on the balance sheet as €112m, which is divided by the 5m shares in existence, giving a NAV of €22.40.

Gross margin and net margin

The gross margin and net margin in the Profit and Loss Account are probably the terms most familiar to those involved in retailing. The **gross margin** is calculated by dividing gross profit by total sales. This is an indication of how much profit is being made at point of sale, which can be ploughed back into the business to pay for its operating costs and expenses. It does not tell us how much of every Euro made at point of sale adds to the bottomline. To calculate Tweedle Dum's gross margin, you divide the gross profit of €52m by total sales of €100m, which gives a gross profit margin of 52%.

In Tweedle Dum's Profit and Loss Account the bottomline is the net income after paying operating expenses and tax. This is €14.7m, producing a **net margin**, when compared to sales, of 14.7%.

The important thing about gross profit margin and net profit margin, just like many other ratios, is how they compare to previous figures.

For the sake of clarity the simplified accounts for Tweedle Dum do not contain the equivalent figures for the previous financial period. In the real world you will be presented with these figures. If you examine the gross profit margin and the net profit margin for the current and past financial year, you will be able to see whether or not margins are being maintained. If they are not, this gives you cause for further investigation.

Dividend Ratios

The **dividend yield**, which acts as an indicator of the current cost of a share relative to the income it produces, is calculated by dividing the gross dividend per share by the share price.

Let's say that Tweedle Dum's shares are trading at €40 and that the directors of Tweedle Dum have decided to pay a dividend of €1.50 per share. This means the yield will be €1.50 divided by €40, producing a dividend yield of 3.75%. Now, let's say a few weeks later the share price has jumped dramatically to €50. Remember, the dividend is still €1.50 per share. The new dividend yield will therefore be lower: €1.50 divided by €50 equals 3.0%. Falling dividend yields normally mean increasing share prices, and vice versa.

Dividend cover is another way of expressing the proportion of profit that the directors decide to pay out as the dividend. For Tweedle Dum the total profit for 2005 is €14.7m. The directors have decided to pay €1.50 per share to the 5m shareholders, so that will cost the company €7.5m. The dividend cover is calculated by dividing the profit by the total cost of paying the dividends: in this case, €14.7m divided by €7.5m. Tweedle Dum is therefore said to have dividend cover of 1.96 times. The dividend cover is a measure of the **safety** of the dividend. The more strongly covered it is, the safer it is and the lower the chance of the company reducing it or dropping it entirely should profits fall. When companies pay dividends, even though they have just made a loss, they do so out of their **reserves**.

The **dividend payout ratio** measures how much of the company's profits are being paid out in dividends. It is calculated by dividing the dividend per share by the earnings per share. The bigger and stronger a company is, the more likely it is that the dividend payout ratio will head towards 50% – meaning that 50% of profits are being paid out as dividends. Where the dividend payout ratio is particularly high, this can be a sign that the **dividend may be cut.**

The **dividend per share** (DPS) is the total amount of money the directors are setting aside to pay dividends divided by the total number of shares – the reverse of the earlier calculation. In our example the directors are setting aside €7.5m and there are five million shares, so the DPS is €1.50.

You must bear in mind the impact of **tax** on dividends. Companies paying dividends are often compelled to **retain** tax, normally at the basic rate for tax-payers and to pay it to the Revenue. The dividend will be paid **net** and will therefore be known as a **net dividend**. To calculate the gross dividend you will need to gross up the net figure by reference to the basic rate of tax.

For example, let's say a net dividend is quoted at €1.40 per share and the basic rate of tax is 20%. This means that €1.40 represents 80% of a higher figure. To arrive at that higher figure, divide €1.40 by 80 and multiply by 100. Here, the gross dividend is €1.75 per share.

Dividend yields, particularly those of the strong stocks used by investors for income purposes, are often compared to bond yields. The most common position is to find that equity yields less than bond yields: this is the natural position for the market. A bond investor will not gain increased income, but an equity investor is looking not just for an increase in the capital value of the share but also an increase in dividend payments to be decided by the directors of the company. It is for this reason that dividend yields are usually lower than bond yields and are said to be trading at a **discount** to bond yields.

Gearing

Gearing is a term used to describe the relationship between money borrowed, i.e. debt, and shareholders' money, i.e. equity. In much the same way as gearing is used to maximise return on property investment, companies use gearing to fuel growth. The level of gearing, or the relationship between debt and equity, is also called the **debt/equity ratio**.

The more debt a company holds, the more is exposed to interest rate risk. When interest rates rise, the company's ability to service debt can begin to hit its business. This does not affect **equity finance**, however, which is also called **risk capital**. A highly geared, or leveraged, company is one that has a large amount of money borrowed in relation to its equity, while a low leveraged company is one that has large equity and little borrowings. The **debt/equity ratio** is calculated by dividing long-term debt by the total level of shareholders' equity.

The current ratio

The current ratio measures the short-term liquidity of a company by comparing its current assets, i.e. cash, stocks/inventories, receivables, etc., against its current liabilities, such as accounts payable, accruals, etc. It is calculated by dividing current assets by current liabilities. As a general rule of thumb, investors look for a relationship between current assets and current liabilities of, at the very least, 2:1.

Return on equity

Return on equity (**ROE**) is a commonly used measure of profitability. It is calculated by dividing the company's **earnings** by the total shareholders' **equity**. In the case of Tweedle Dum for example, this means dividing €14.7m – the net income from the profit and loss account – by the total shareholders' equity, taken from the balance sheet. The calculation is €14.7m earnings divided by €112m equity. This gives 13.13% ROE. For large companies a ROE in excess of 15% is regarded as excellent. For smaller companies ROEs in excess of 20% are typically demanded by investors in order to compensate them for taking the additional risk by not investing in larger companies.

Return on assets

This is another commonly used ratio and it measures the pre-tax *profits* of the company as compared to the *capital* used to run the business. It can sometimes be more useful than return on equity, which tells how the company's earnings relate to the shareholders' money, because it tells how profitable a company is irrespective of financing and ignoring the benefits of a low tax rate. Instead, **return on assets** (**ROA**) measures the return against all monies, including from loans. To arrive at ROA, take the profit before tax and before interest on long-term debt and divide it by the assets employed. The assets employed will be the shareholders' funds, but not including goodwill, plus long-term loans, deferred tax and majority shareholder interests, all of which will be noted on the balance sheet.

Other terms you may come across

Scrip dividends: an opportunity to take more shares in lieu of a dividend payment.

Fixed charge: when this appears in connection with borrowing it indicates that specific assets have been pledged against the borrowing. This is to differentiate it from a **floating charge** where **all** of the assets of the business are assigned against the borrowing.

Unsecured creditors: those transacting business with the company whose lending to the company has not been secured. Typically this means suppliers, who are the last in the queue when a company goes bust. The local tax authorities are also unsecured creditors, but may be given the first position in the unsecured creditors' queue.

Overtrading: refers to a company that may be growing too fast compared to the resources it has to keep the business going.

Rights issue: refers to a decision by a company to sell more shares as a way of raising more capital. This usually depresses share prices because it increases the number of shares in circulation.

Goodwill: often appears in balance sheets and is regarded as an **intangible asset**. It will have its own note in the accounts to tell you how it has been calculated. When a company is taken over, the difference between the acquisition price paid and the net assets of the company is regarded as the premium the buyer pays for the goodwill of the business.

Contingent liabilities: appears where there is, for example, a legal case pending against a company that it could lose and it is entered in the balance sheet as a possible liability that will need to be paid.

Warrants: a way for a company to raise money that does not appear in its balance sheet. Warrant is another name for guarantee. Warrants issued by companies give the holder the right to subscribe, at a certain, fixed price, to the shares of the company at a future date in time. Generally the subscription price will be fixed above the current share price of the shares.

Revaluation reserves: these occur when a company revalues some of its assets and finds that they are worth more than had previously been noted in the accounts. This typically happens in relation to property.

Net tangible asset value: the net asset value, **excluding** goodwill.

Ex-dividend: when you buy a share ex-dividend it means you are not entitled to the current dividend payment. That will go to the selling shareholder.

Cum-dividend: this is the opposite to ex-dividend and means that when you buy the share you will get the payment of the current dividend.

Investment approaches

There is a range of different approaches that can be used for investing directly in equities. Proponents of different systems defend theirs as 'the best' but there is no such thing as a best system. There are simply systems that do or don't work.

Value investing

The investors concentrate on stocks with low price earnings ratios which other investors are avoiding. They purchase these in the hope of making big gains when the stock recovers.

Asset investing

Investors buy shares on the basis that the share price is not a proper reflection of the assets of the company. Such investors look carefully at the asset mix, particularly for things like copyrights, brand values, etc. Asset investors are particularly interested in companies that could become take-over targets, knowing that corporate raiders are looking at the exact same issues as the asset investor.

Cash flow investing

Investors buy stocks that generate a great deal of cash on the basis that these companies are likely to buy back their own stock, or go on an expansion trail.

Aggressively growing company investing

Investors typically concentrate on medium to large companies that are growing aggressively, in spite of their scale. Investing in aggressively growing small companies is a very tricky business when this is the only method of analysis employed. This is because many small companies take off at an accelerated pace and then hit a brick wall when they overtrade.

Market timing

This approach is favoured by analysts using elaborate computer models to determine which way prices are likely to go and attempting to predict when prices are likely to rise and when they are likely to fall. These investors frequently move in and out from a cash position.

Sector rotation investing

Investors move money from one industry to another on the basis of improving or deteriorating economic factors. For example, during a recession an investor may choose to invest in utilities, switching to stocks such as automobile stocks when the recession finishes.

Getting organised

Make sure you use **specialist software** that allows you to track the values of the various shares you have and the decisions that you take. **Quicken** is a good example of a workable piece of software.

If you want to be very active you need to bear in mind that trading costs money, so locate a good international **discount broker** that's giving good value for money and not overcharging for small trades.

Make sure you get on to the **Internet**: it is an inexpensive way of pulling down high quality information.

Get your thinking right

Rule number one: be prepared to invest for the **long term**. A lot of people go into equity markets telling themselves that they are in it for the long term but in reality they are hoping to make a short-term killing and jump out at the first sign of trouble. The single worst possible thing you can do is to make the typical herd mistake of buying in at the top and selling out at the bottom. You should buy stocks systematically, **spreading** your investments **over time**. This reduces the risk of loading all of your bets into a very short period.

You wouldn't go to a house auction without a set price in your mind: stocks are no different. After doing your research, **set a price** at which you will buy a particular stock and stick to it. Having put all of the necessary effort into researching a company, don't just leave it at that after you have bought the stock. Stay on top of it and examine all of the financial information produced by the company. Don't be reluctant to ring the company secretary to get accounts and to ask for further information. That's what the company secretary and his or her office is there for, i.e. to look after shareholders and prospective shareholders. Remember, their job is to serve you.

Finally, **measure your performance** against an appropriate stock market index rather than against how others are doing with their stock portfolios. Your stock portfolio will directly reflect your personality and your research. Just because your portfolio is behind somebody else's does not make their portfolio any better than yours. It just means it's different. Theirs may contain a big lucky strike and may have higher risk, or it could be just around the corner from a big dip. In times of uncertainty, do not ditch your first principles – read them again.

The types of direct investment opportunities available

Cyclical companies

These companies are tied to the ups and downs of an economy, so you can do well by investing in heavy industries like car manufacturers, chemicals, steel companies, etc., if you invest at the right time. Bear in mind that because these are very large companies, they are popular, and demand pushes up their prices. They are likely to be cheap only when they are unpopular. This means that the best time to buy cyclicals is smack in the middle of a recession.

Growth stocks

Buying stocks in companies whose earnings are always growing makes sense. The problem is that their share prices, particularly for the well-known **growth stocks**, have already discounted in the earnings growth. This means that the current share price for most large growth stocks is not cheap. As a general rule the higher the P/E ratio, the greater the enthusiasm already built into the stock price. Looking at a company's low P/E ratio relative to other companies in its sector is a way of isolating a potential cheap growth stock.

Dividends

If you are interested in investing in companies that pay good **dividends** so that you can get strong income cheques in the post, you need to be careful about these companies' level of exposure to interest rate risk. Examine their debt/equity ratio. Dividend cover will also be an important measure. For example, a company that pays good dividends but has low dividend cover and high gearing could get hit by a double whammy in the event of an interest rate rise.

Out of favour stocks

These stocks are located initially by looking for low P/E ratios relative to others in their sector. Remember, a low P/E ratio can often be justified – the company is in trouble. There is a big difference between an out of favour stock and a company in trouble: don't get them mixed up. Some stock prices may be artificially low when measured against earnings because they have become unfashionable and the weight of money has moved against them. This happens to companies at the edge of an index, such as the Dow Jones or Eurostoxx 50.

If the company falls off the index because of the growth in a new entrant, index trackers will sell it, pushing down prices. Companies are also deserted by large investment funds because they are unfashionable. If the investment funds return, the weight of money can have a substantial impact on share prices. You could score an out of favour stock higher if it is clear that the executives have recently bought shareholding in their own company.

Value investing

This means checking the current price against the value of company assets in the hope that its share price will rise at some point in the future and cover the gap. This is particularly so if it is subject to a take-over bid by a raider. A raider may believe it can acquire the company for a cheaper price than the asset level and then engage in asset stripping. To see if a share is selling at less than its break-up value, you need to look at net asset value per share and tangible asset per share.

The **net net working capital** is a measure of how much cash a company could raise if it were liquidated. This is very similar to the current ratio, except you add in long-term debt. It is calculated by taking all of the current assets, i.e. cash, receivables, stock/inventory, securities, etc., and deducting all of the debt owed by the company, i.e. short-term and long-term debt. As a general rule, if the **net net working capital** is greater than 25%, you may have found an undervalued share.

A common experience for very small investors is to take a shareholding in a company that is floating. The process of the demutualisation of large societies in the UK, as well as the privatisation of large state-owned companies, has given many investors an experience they would not otherwise have had. **New issues**, also called **initial public offerings** (IPOs), come with a great deal of hype. Ironically, for mutual societies members' own money or, in the case of a semi-state, the tax-payers' money is used, to sell back to the 'shareholders' their own money – and to spend an exorbitant amount of it in telling them why this is such a good idea!

Quite often the enthusiastic public reaction to a high-profile IPO is followed by a big lift in the share price, confirming the widespread consensus that everybody got it right – but this euphoria is then followed by a fall as more sober assessments take root. One of the best times to buy an IPO is during depressed market conditions rather than during bull markets, when prices tend to be exaggerated. For IPOs the quality of historical performance information is often not as good as publicly quoted companies. This does not mean that IPOs represent poor value, but it does mean you need to ask a number of critical questions:

- What sustainable competitive advantage will the IPO have in comparison to established firms?
- Is the IPO simply a vehicle for company executives to make a

killing on share options if it is a mutual or semi-state or, if it's a private company, is the IPO the big retirement plan?
- What's the likely P/E ratio compared to other companies in the same industry?
- How many shares are going to be issued and will the issue be fully subscribed?
- What is the record of the stockbroker bringing the company to the market and how has it performed in the past?

You are probably better off buying an IPO some months after it has gone public, when the enthusiasm has worn off the share price.

The market movers and shakers

Market-makers have to do just that: make a market. They are compelled to deal in certain types of share. **Broker dealers**, on the other hand, may hold shares on their own books, which they will then sell to clients, but they have no obligation to make the market. Market-makers and broker dealers may also act as **agency brokers**, executing clients' buy and sell orders and charging a commission on each deal.

Investors can buy shares for cash or **on the margin**, which means using borrowed funds. These funds will be lent by the broker, who will charge interest on the loan. The **broker's loan rate** is usually about 1% above the prime rate. If you are playing with borrowed money you can magnify your return, but equally you can magnify your losses. By using this service you buy shares and delay payment for them, selling them later at a higher price and clearing the loan. Things can go disastrously wrong, however. If your stock halves overnight, you may be subject to a **margin call**. This means that you must put up additional collateral to cover your loan or your broker will sell your stock immediately.

Shorting is achieved using the margin account. It is not for the fainthearted or the inexperienced. This does not automatically mean that shorting is not for you. If the sums of money involved do not represent a large proportion of your overall financial strength, it can make sense. But in the hands of the **uninformed** borrowing heavily to invest in equities is a form of gambling.

As a direct investor, you may wish to make your investments via a stockbroker, whom you can then call on for help or advice, as necessary. If this option appeals to you, here's the lowdown on engaging your very own broker.

Dealing with stockbrokers

In Ireland stockbrokers tend to be expensive. This is especially so for the Active Trader, who is likely to find better value from on-line discount international specialists who charge low, flat fees per trade. The level of commission charged by local stockbrokers scales down depending on the deal size, but you can expect commissions to begin from 1.5%–2%. Government stamp duty of 1% is also payable. Remember, when shares are sold, a similar commission is charged again.

Where you give a stockbroker the discretion to actively trade your portfolio, bear in mind the inherent conflict between trading and boosting commission revenues. You should also insist on measuring the return on your portfolio against the index of the market in which the stockbroker has placed your money because you can bypass active trading costs simply by buying the Index as an Exchange Traded Fund, usually at annual costs of less than 0.5%pa.You don't have to give the stockbroker discretion to trade your shares. You can retain that discretion for yourself while taking advice from the stockbroker.

Your shares can be held in paper form, as certificates, or electronically. When you hold your share certificates you can deal through any stockbroker – you remain the legal owner at all times and your dividends are paid directly to you. The downside is that you can't move as quickly as electronic settling.

Your shares can be held electronically in two ways. The first way is through a Crest Personal Member account, which registers you as the owner of the shares and the direct recipient of dividends and gives you the freedom to shop the market for best dealing rates and flat fees among stockbrokers who maintain the service for you. The second way is through a Crest Nominee account, which differs fundamentally because you are not the legal owner of the shares, although you remain the beneficial owner of the shares. In this case, in the event of the liquidation of the stockbroker your investment might be at risk to the liquidator. There is already legal precedent in Ireland where the Courts ruled in favour of the liquidator after the collapse of a Cork stockbroker, marking a fundamental shift in default risk for investors who use nominee services. The stockbroker establishes a nominee company to hold client shares in a single account. You pay flat fees to the stockbroker for maintaining the account, typically up to €100 per year, and you execute all deals through the stockbroker's service and prices.

Discount broking

Modern telecommunications have revolutionised the service available to individual private investors. The **Internet** gives investors access to information that was previously the exclusive preserve of stockbrokers. Before the introduction of the Internet, investors had to pay fat fees to brokers to cover the expense involved in communicating with somebody down on the stock exchange floor, who was following your buying and selling instructions. Changes in technology have now shifted power down line to the small investor, reducing trading costs dramatically.

Following the abolition of fixed commission agreements between stockbroking firms many moons ago, a new generation of stockbrokers has emerged. For the small investor the most valuable of these is the **discount broker**. Discount brokers do not get involved in bringing a company to market, an activity known as an **initial public offering (IPO)**, and may not have research analysts on staff. Normally the only thing that a discount broker does is to execute orders for buying and selling. It does not offer advice.

Discount brokers can be split into two categories: the normal discount brokers, who will carry out instructions but may also provide some research material, news, etc.; and the **deep discount brokerage,** which normally does not provide ancillary services and merely executes instructions.

Building up a relationship with a good discount broker is particularly important if you fancy yourself as an Active Trader. Full service brokers charge transaction fees, typically **averaging 1.5%** of a small investment, with a scaled-down percentage for higher sums. Remember, there is commission at both ends – when you buy and when you sell.

A full service broker is supposed to undertake a detailed fact-find of your position and to know exactly what your targets are. He/she will usually provide you with tons of research and will develop attractive portfolio models to convince you why you should invest in the stocks the full service brokerage believes are best for you. It would be a mistake to believe that colourful presentation of information will lead to out-performance. Whatever you do, ensure that the advice provided to you by a full service brokerage is measured against an appropriate stock market index. If you are paying fat fees to a full service brokerage, it is only performance against the index that can tell you whether or not the service price you paid for was worth it.

Apart from the obvious commission and fee charges of stockbrokers there is also the **spread**. This is a slight difference between the buying price and the selling price. For example, if a stockbroker tells you that a stock price is trading between 'twenty and a half', what he/she means is that anybody who buys the stock will pay €20.50, while someone who sells it will receive only €20. The difference, 0.50c, is the trader's margin.

Giving instructions to your stockbroker

Once you have taken the step of engaging a stockbroker, you need to be confident in your dealings with him/her. There are different types of instruction or order you can give your stockbroker:

Limit order

When you give your broker a limit order you are telling your broker to buy or sell a particular stock at a specific price, or better. For example, if Catch-up Plc is trading in London at stg£7 and you want to buy it at stg£6.50, you can place a purchase limit at stg£6.50. It also works in reverse, that is when you are selling a stock. For example, if you are holding Golden Oldies Plc at €15 per share and you fancy that if it goes to €20 per share you will sell, you can place this selling limit with your broker.

Day order

This is an instruction to your broker to buy or sell a stock at a particular price on a particular day. If the transaction cannot be placed on that particular day, your order does not carry forward.

Stop order

A stop order is used to protect the profit you have gained, or to limit any further losses. The most frequently used is the **stop-loss order**, which tells your broker to sell if the stock hits a specific price. For example, say you bought Peter's Crisps Plc at €20 and they are now trading at €40. You may wish to protect your gain by placing a stop-loss order at €35. When prices fall it's not always very neat, and the nearest market price the broker may be able to get for you could be less than the €35 limit you stipulated. For example, the broker may be only able to do the trade at €33.

Stop orders can also work in reverse, particularly when you are selling short. This is where you provide an instruction to your broker to buy up a share if it falls to a specific price, set by you.

Good-this-month order

Where you provide an order to your broker to buy or to sell a stock at a particular price during a long time period, such as a month, this is known as a **good-this-month order** (GTM).

Good-this-week order

The same thing can be done for a week-long period, in which case it is known as a **good-this-week order**.

Good-till-cancelled order

Where you give an open-ended instruction to your broker to buy or sell a particular stock when it hits a specific price, this is called a **good-till-cancelled order** (GTC). The GTC remains an **open order** until such time as you cancel it.

Employing a system

Many investors, especially more recent converts, see investing as being like a maze they have to negotiate – there are unexpected twists and turns, blind alleys and decoy paths, all tempting you away from your logical orientation that would bring you to the centre and back out again safely. A little help from other quarters is always useful, which is why you'll meet lots of investors who carry a ball of string into the maze so they can chart a course through it – their 'ball of string' is a system.

A system is any methodical process you employ that over-rides emotional decisions. There are numerous systems for investing in shares and each claims success. They work when they remove the natural human urge to come in on a high spot and flee during a fall. There is no such thing as 'the best system'. Good systems encourage the user to adopt a **logical, unemotive and systematic** approach to buying and selling equities. While there are many variations, we are going to examine just one system, to give you an idea of what comprises a decent system – and how it works. The system we're concentrating on is **Dividend investing**.

Dividend investing: a workable system

The largest stocks generally have the lowest volatility in share price. They have become large because they have been successful at building up their businesses for many years. These large stocks pay dividends to investors. It can be difficult to locate a share price that is cheap because the information produced by these companies is very closely scrutinised. Your benchmark is index tracking funds. These track the index by buying all of the stocks on the index and holding them.

You already know that stocks with the lowest **dividend yields** have a strong share price. Conversely, those with higher dividend yields have lower share prices. Dividend investing comes with a number of benefits for the novice investor:

- It will take very little time to do.
- It works on the sound principle of looking for high dividend yields and looks for them at the very top end of the market, where companies are strongest.
- It's simple.

The **Dow-dividend approach** was first described by Michael O'Higgins, a New York money manager, in his book, *Beating the Dow*. It encouraged investors to transact only a handful of times a year. It is not based on any fluke of investment timing, but rather on very sound and simple principles. Since it was first published in 1991 it has been honed by focusing on a narrow band of very large stocks. It was fine-tuned in *The Motley Fool* (by David and

Tom Gardner), a book that is compulsory reading for any equity investor.

The Dow-dividend approach works as follows:

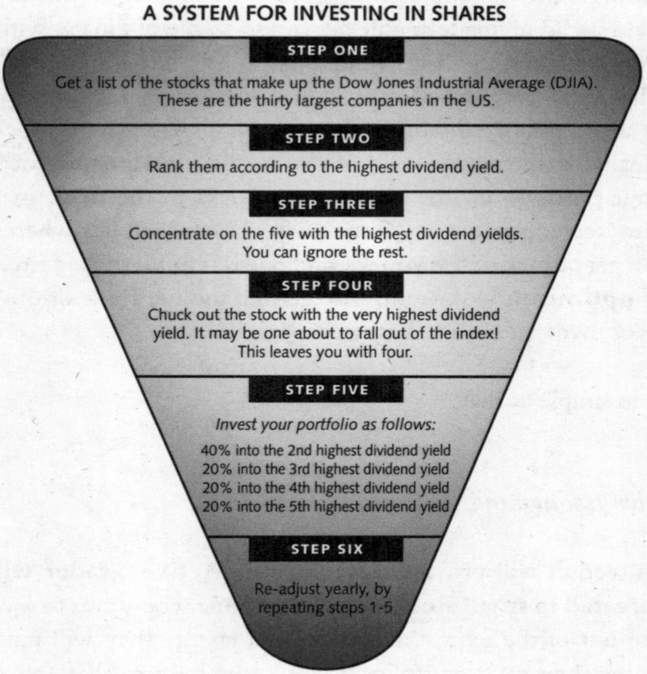

A SYSTEM FOR INVESTING IN SHARES

STEP ONE

Get a list of the stocks that make up the Dow Jones Industrial Average (DJIA). These are the thirty largest companies in the US.

STEP TWO

Rank them according to the highest dividend yield.

STEP THREE

Concentrate on the five with the highest dividend yields. You can ignore the rest.

STEP FOUR

Chuck out the stock with the very highest dividend yield. It may be one about to fall out of the index! This leaves you with four.

STEP FIVE

Invest your portfolio as follows:

40% into the 2nd highest dividend yield
20% into the 3rd highest dividend yield
20% into the 4th highest dividend yield
20% into the 5th highest dividend yield

STEP SIX

Re-adjust yearly, by repeating steps 1-5

Proponents claim the model has been run over continuous time periods of twenty years on the DJIA, producing **double** its normal performance of around 10% pa. Dividend-based investing at the large stock end of the London stock market has claimed similar out performance. So why might it work?

- The model is a systematic way of forcing you to go against your instincts. It gets you to buy the stocks whose share prices have **fallen**.
- It **concentrates** your portfolio on just four stocks. Large collective

investment funds cannot do this: the vast sums of money they have force them into wide-scale diversification. On the other hand, an index tracker has to hold every stock on the index.
- It **removes the risk** of selecting a **laggard** in a narrow portfolio by sweeping out the company with the highest dividend yield and instead giving a double allocation to the company with the second highest dividend yield.
- The system **avoids chopping and changing**, which is typical of active trading and often exacerbated by bad calls on stocks.
- Finally, it meets the need of the **novice** investor by focusing your portfolio on the very largest stocks in the stock market, thus keeping you away from small company stocks where you can get burned unless you research well. It fulfils the requirement of **optimising** your return by getting the most out of the least risky investments, i.e. large companies.

It is as simple as that.

Active trading and small stocks

This section will provide tactics for the **Active Trader who is interested in small stocks**, that is someone who wants to squeeze more out of the extra time, effort and energy they will put into running their own portfolio. If you know by now that you don't want to be an Active Trader, you can skip off and put on the kettle while the rest of us engage in some more brain-teasers!

Why invest in small stocks?

Investing in small stocks, or small caps (capitalisation), as they are known, makes an awful lot of sense if you are looking for exponential growth as compared to the large stocks in markets above you. Large funds cannot reach down to this end of the market because the companies are too small. A routine placement by a large fund could be bigger than the capitalisation of some small stocks. When small stocks become successful, big funds move in to acquire the share, thereby accelerating its price further.

Small stocks can grow quicker than large stocks. Because of the link between earnings and share price, rapidly growing profits can impact the share price of a small company very quickly. Small stocks have an awful lot more room to breathe and, unlike large stocks, are usually in less restrictive and competitive markets. This means their earnings can grow a lot faster until, of course, they in turn become very large companies and are affected by the same factors as large stocks.

Investing in small stocks will be successful only if you undertake careful, planned and systematic research. If you are considering any other approach, such as going with your 'instincts' or on 'tips' from a friend or a broker, don't do it. Stick to the alternative low risk strategies already outlined. Finally, take a look at your lifestyle. If you do not have the time to invest in undertaking the work necessary, stay out of this market. It cannot be done well 'on the hoof'.

I have already mentioned *The Motley Fool* by the Gardner brothers, and it really is essential reading for the small stock investor. The brothers are themselves Active Traders and the book outlines their system for managing small stocks, a modified version of which is given on page 202.

Step One: Distil a Database

You cannot research the entire market. It is simply too large. Cut it down to **a database of about 100 companies** that potentially look interesting. Don't ignore shares in companies that you like and about which you have some understanding.

You're in the market to locate small growth stocks. Over a period of a number of months begin to **cherry-pick** companies whose earnings are being reported greater than they were for the previous financial period. Ignore any company whose earnings have fallen compared to the last period.

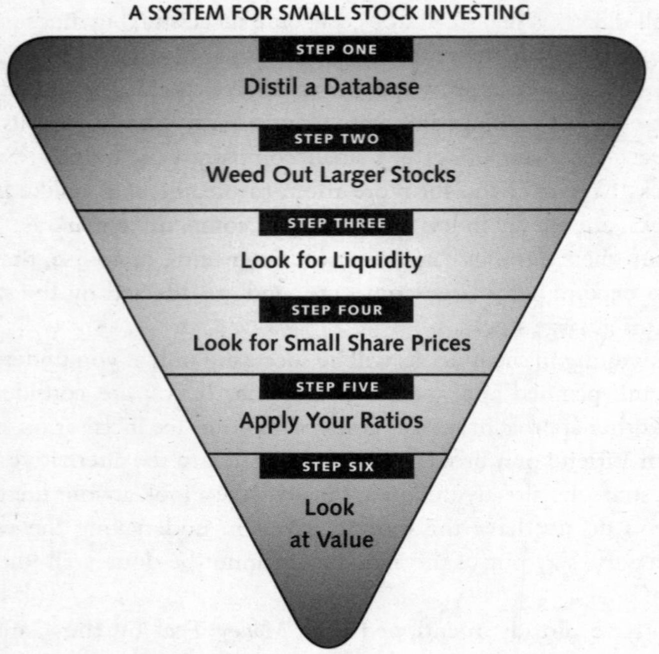

Be prepared to **wait** until you have examined the earnings as they come in. It's not always possible to keep an eye on earnings as they come in each day, so spread the load across members of your investment club, if you have one. Otherwise concentrate on as many days as you can over the period, and you will still end up with a good cherry-picked list.

Step Two: Weed Out Larger Stocks

Weed out companies with **sales volume in excess of €200m**. These are pushing upmarket and institutional buyers will be fishing here.

Step Three: Look For Liquidity

Check for liquidity. This is done by looking at **the volume of shares being traded** in the company. If there is no trading, it is a sign that the stock is illiquid. Too high a volume of trading shows high activity in the stock, making it less likely to be undiscovered.

Step Four: Look For Small Share Prices

'Small' share prices means share prices that are not so tiny they are in the micro-stock end of the market, but not so large that they don't benefit from the effect of increased earnings on share prices. The UK range is probably **between stg£3 and stg£15 per share**, with the equivalent measure in the US standing at **between $5 and $20 a share**.

Step Five: Apply Your Ratios

- **Look for a high net profit margin**, at least 10%. Anything less is too tight. A small increase in operating expenses in a small cap could quickly wipe out a net profit margin of less than 10%. The bigger the net profit margin, the better it looks. A 20% net profit margin might look excessive, but only for larger companies. For smaller companies it may indicate plenty of breathing space in the market in which the company is operating, which is allowing it to enjoy high margins.
- Look for a combination of strong earnings and strong sales growth, ideally in excess of 25% over the most recent financial period.
- Good growth small caps are going to grow a lot faster than bigger companies when they do well. **Check the relative performance** of the share price over the past 12 months by looking at the indicator of **relative strength**. This rates every share on the three main US stock markets in terms of its price movements relative to everybody else. Concentrate on the top 5%. Relative strength indicators will range from 1 to 99. Look for a rating of

at least 95. This means that, relative to all other shares, the share of this company has been in the top 5% of all movers over the past 12 months.

- **Look for plenty of cash** – both from cash and from cash equivalents. Plenty of cash is vital for small companies who do not enjoy the access to the money markets that the large companies have. Remember, a company that has built up plenty of cash is one that has been well managed and is well positioned to take advantage of opportunities for further growth as they arise.
- Ensure that senior executive directors have a strong minority, the bigger the better.
- Check that **cash flows are growing** rather than falling or, worse still, going negative. This will be clear from the cash flow statement. In the statement of cash flows for Turtle Plc (given on page 180), the company went cash flow negative between 2004 and 2005, which indicated that it had failed to manage the timing between paying people, on the one hand, and being paid itself, on the other.
- Check short-term **liquidity** using the **current ratio**. If it's **deteriorating**, watch out.
- Check the **debt/equity** ratio. Avoid long-term debt, which is a heavy load on small stocks.
- Find out if **research and development** has been **maintained** or is improving. If the R & D budget has been raided, a company has been selling its silverware to pay current expenses.
- Ensure that the **number of shares** hasn't changed – a common trick that dilutes value.
- Make sure that **earnings per share (EPS)** is rising. Use your EPS ratio and compare financial periods.
- Check that the amount of **debtors** outstanding as a **percentage of sales is not deteriorating**. This would indicate that the company is not collecting its debts on time, which will hit cash flow.

Step Six: Look At Value

By now you are familiar with various ways of measuring a company, such as:

- ***Net asset value*** – looking at **the bottomline** assets of the company, its current asset strength.
- ***EPS*** (earnings per share) – the direct link between the potential growth earnings of the company and its share price.
- ***Dividend yields.***

All of the above are useful, but for small growth stocks an extra measure is a ratio known as **PEG**, which stands for **price to earnings to growth**. This links the current P/E ratio of the company to its growth rate.

Let's say Liquid Air Plc is trading in London at stg£10, that its P/E ratio is 8 and you have estimated company growth to be 25%. PEG is calculated by dividing its P/E – 8 – by its percentage of earnings growth – 25% – giving a ratio of 0.32. Other things being equal, PEGs less than 1.0 are better. By concentrating on low PEG ratios you are trying to buy 'growth' cheaply. Get the idea?

PEG is a very useful indicator, but it doesn't work all the time, particularly in parts of business where P/E multiples and company growth can be miles apart. It is less valid at the upper end of the market.

When to sell

Some investors like the idea of creating a **cylinder** around a share. This means that they decide to sell if it goes above a certain level, and to buy if it falls below a certain level. You should only sell when the following conditions exist:

- The careful approach you have used, checking ratios, etc., is now beginning to indicate that the share price relative to the company's earnings is beginning to look overpriced.

- You have simultaneously targeted another company to which you can switch.

Passive trading means holding shares through thick and thin for the long run. Active investors hold shares until it is no longer worthwhile holding them. Movements are made only when better opportunities arise.

Active trading and shorting

Detailed research of companies may also give opportunities to 'short' shares, but this is a very high risk activity**. Shorting works if it is done professionally** and is based on careful, planned research. It's a disaster when it works badly. Don't use shorting until you know what you are doing.

- When you are shorting set yourself a **quitting price** (like you would at an auction), such as 20% above the price at which you are shorting, just in case it goes the wrong way.
- The process used for finding undervalued stocks is just as efficient at locating a portfolio: look for high PEGs, well in excess of 1.00.
- Don't get carried away shorting. Limit it. Shorting is about time, and over time stock markets are rising more than they are falling.
- Never short companies that have an explosive potential. A software stock investing in breakthrough technology is an example. If a share price explodes in the wrong direction while you are shorting, you can get very seriously burned. For this reason ensure that you concentrate your shorting on companies that do not have explosive potential.
- Finally, check the trading volumes so that the stock is not subject to a bear raid, i.e. where others are shorting with you. If market-makers sense a stock is being shorted, you could get trapped in a bear squeeze.

Hello. *Hello?* No, you're fine. You've still got a pulse. Now, don't get up too quickly or you'll get dizzy. You've just read an entire chapter on the nitty-gritty of equities . . . and survived. What a feat. You can tell your grandchildren you did it!

PART FOUR

Cash, Bonds, Funds

CHAPTER 14

Cash and Bonds

Glossary

- **LIBID:** London Inter-Bank Bid rate, i.e. wholesale sell interest rate between banks.
- **Liquidity risk:** the risk that an asset may be difficult to turn to cash.
- **Asset-backed:** secured by real assets, like property.
- **IFSC:** International Financial Services Centre.
- **GNP:** Gross National Product. Irish GNP is total value of all materials, goods, foodstuffs and services produced by companies in Ireland in a year.
- **GDP:** Gross Domestic Product. Irish GDP is an estimate of the total value of all materials, goods, foodstuffs and services produced within the borders of the country within a year.
- **Net real interest:** value of interest received after the deduction of Deposit Income Retention Tax and adjusting for inflation, as measured by the Consumer Price Index.
- **Credit rating:** Independent assessment of default risk.
- **Ring-fencing:** separating the assets of investors from the balance sheet of the asset manager.
- **Retail market:** interface between financial institutions and consumers.

- **Wholesale market:** interface between financial institutions.
- **Market value adjusters:** discretionary exit costs applied to premature encashment from certain investments at a time of depressed asset values.

Property and equities get all the sexy headlines and make for the most engaging stories, but Cash and Bonds are the two workhorses at the fulcrum in the investment world and account for about one-third of all assets held by pension funds – especially bonds. That's why learning the basics of how both work and their environment is essential. Let's start with cash.

Why do I need to think about cash assets?

Investing in cash assets or money market instruments doesn't just begin and end with deposit accounts at the local retail bank. Best rates are more usually found from Internet banks and services and from funds. The three most important features are: the **safety** of the product provider, the **interest rate** you get **after tax,** and how that number measures against **current inflation**, i.e. your 'net real interest'. So forget the gross rate, that's for the birds. Deduct tax and inflation.

Let's look at the cash life of John, Sarah and Jenny.

John is the inert customer the big banks just love. He typically stores about €40,000 in cash deposit at the local branch. Ah sure, interest rates are so low it seems just too much hassle to bother with checking out the market or pressurising the bank to pay more. He gets paid 1%, but deduct DIRT and that's now 0.8% and then deduct inflation, say 2.5%, and John's habit is losing him money at a rate of 1.7% pa.

Sarah, his sister, heard about an on-line and on-demand deposit account that pays 3.25% and that's linked directly to movements in the European Central Bank rate rather than to the whims of the bank's senior managers. After DIRT that's 2.6% net and, after deducting inflation, by the end of the year Sarah's money should have held value in real terms.

Sarah's best friend, Jenny, who has a strong income with plenty left over each month, goes one step further. She aligns her mortgage with a bank account that offsets the daily balance against her mortgage, which means she gets a mortgage rate of return on her cash – and doesn't pay DIRT!

So you see, there is something to learn about cash management after all! You betcha! Just consider this startling little piece of information:

A thirty-year-old guy netting 40k yearly and rising at 3%pa will have managed about €5.4million in cash flow by his mid-eighties.

I would hazard a guess that you've never looked at it quite in that light before! It's a bit breathtaking, isn't it? That's a lot of cash in nominal terms, and it backs up the lesson you need to learn here: getting into a lifelong good cash management habit makes a bunch of sense. Then there is opportunity cost – remember, every €100 you leave behind for the bank's own benefit because you chose low deposit rates is €100 permanently lost that you could have had working for you in equities or in property! Ever thought of that?

Good cash planning

Cash is the blood flow that pumps in and out of your financial heart. Managing your cash flows as an individual is just as important as doing it for a business. Businesses sink because of an inability to manage cash flows. People, on the other hand, run up credit card debt and overdrafts and sometimes this leads to other bad things, like bankruptcy, marriage break-up, etc. The threats posed by cash flow are legion. Financial regulators worldwide expend vast resources to ensure that banks, stockbrokers, etc., are always solvent, with enough in reserve to deal with the unexpected. Financial Directors of limited companies do exactly the same thing – and so should you.

Having nothing in cash is just as foolhardy as keeping way too much of the stuff. A reserve in cash of at least 3–6 months' lifestyle costs, or up to 12–24 months' lifestyle costs if you're retired, is a good lifelong investment planning habit. It's good because it does a number of important things for you:

- It means you always have ready cash to meet unplanned expenses, like hopping on a plane to catch Ireland playing in a crunch European decider in Germany or the Czech Republic.
- You don't have to resort to debt to bridge shortfalls in your income after periods of higher than normal spending.
- You can use the reserve to pre-save for those summer holiday costs rather than paying them back as debt after you come home.
- If you're suddenly out of a job, you've enough to run the show for at least three to six months, without selling assets, while you get back on your feet.
- You're forced to consider higher growth assets each time your reserve limit is exceeded.

Don't forget the Taxman – because he sure as hell won't forget you!

If you're a sole trader or a partner, it makes sense to set up a separate **Tax Reserve** deposit account so that you don't get into the bad habit of spending the Government's money to finance your lifestyle and are then forced to borrow each year to pay your annual tax bill. This imposes the discipline that automatically comes with the PAYE system and eliminates the worry of not being able to pay your taxes. There's nothing wrong with running into an overdraft periodically to pay taxes, for example, because of seasonal variations in cash flows that will be bridged by near-term improvements, or because you have invested in working assets over the year. However, spending tax money to pay for having a good time is completely nuts.

Here's how you should envisage your cash flow in relation to tax payments and investment:

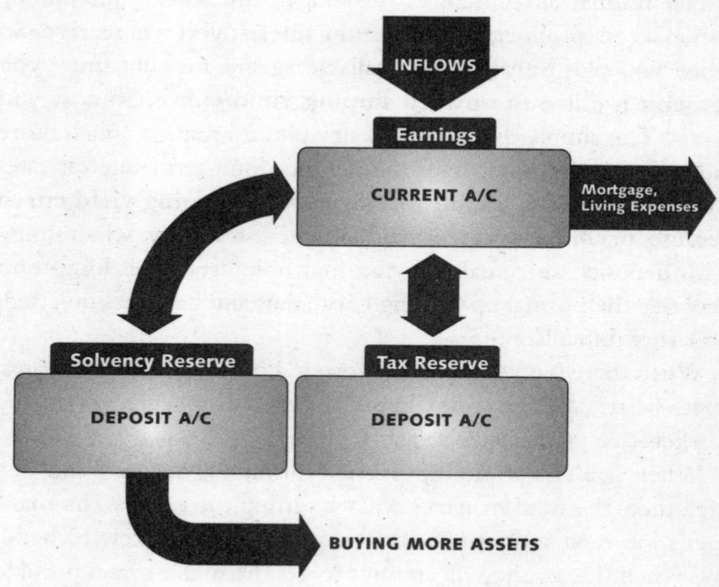

Capital and interest

The difference between cash products and equity products is that your money grows in cash products only by the reinvestment of the interest you earn. If you take out all the interest, your capital will remain notionally the same over time, **but it loses value against inflation**. With equities the 'interest' is the dividend paid, but the capital value of equities can also grow, as can the dividends. That's why investors favour investing in large, blue chip stocks, betting that dividends will increase, as will their underlying capital.

With property the 'interest' is the rent that investors hope to grow over time, along with the value of the property.

Surfing the curve

Under normal circumstances the longer you leave your money tied in a cash product, the greater the interest you will receive. So when you plot interest rates available against lock-up time, you get what is called an **upward sloping yield curve**. So now you know! This simply shows that money plus more time equals more interest. On the other hand, sometimes long-term interest rates are expected to fall, leading to a **downward sloping yield curve** because, of course, you will yield less interest. Finally, when short-term deposits are actually paying higher interest than long-term deposits, the normal up-sloping curve flips and becomes inverted. Not very difficult, is it?

When there is no difference between short- and long-term rates, guess what? We get a **flat** line – a very rare occurrence in the markets (see graphs page 217).

When you've got money invested through a 'Secure Fund' at a life office, the fund manager will be surfing the curve. The manager's job is to anticipate which way the curve is likely to bend, and when. He or she will attempt to get the highest rates possible and to hold them for as long as possible, keeping a nose ahead of the curve shape. The same approach holds true for you as a deposit account saver.

Be careful of advertising

You will see ads that quote interest rates, typically offering lower rates for money to which you have instant access and a little higher if you are prepared to tie it up for 3 months, 6 months, 12 months and so on. Be very careful of institutional advertising. Watch the **term of deposit**. If you are being paid interest over, say, 3 months

6 Tribune

H

TH

ey had

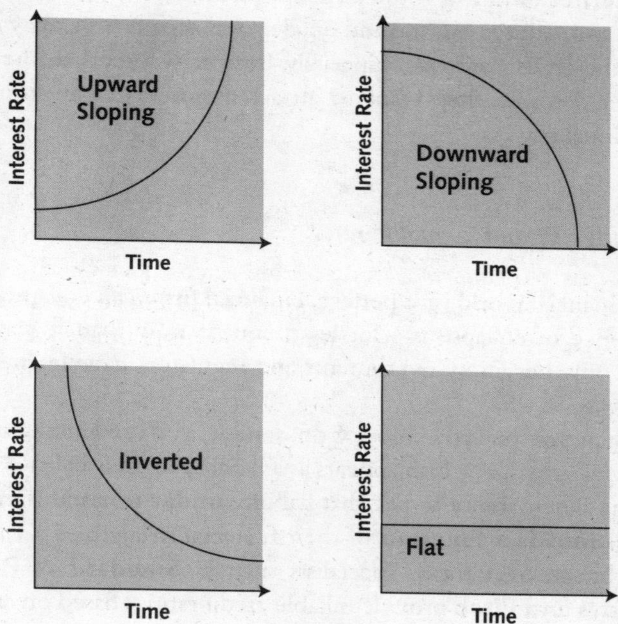

and you wanted to compare it against another product that will pay you a different level of interest over, say, 9 months, how do you compare them? The best thing to do is to translate them to what they would look like if you were being paid annually. Known as the **Compound Annual Rate (CAR)** it is compulsory in advertising, but it often appears as a small footnote below the headline rate advertised.

The competition to manage your cash is growing. Long gone are the days when the old bank brands were the only option. **Credit unions**, for example, are run for the benefit of their members and not for profit. They usually charge lower service fees, allow you to put in smaller sums and pay you more, financing returns from lending money and investments. Credit Unions do not have the same financial strength as banks, however, but your deposits are protected, in part, by an independent depositor protection scheme.

Internet banking is the new option and is a boon for depositors. Look out for on-line and on-demand accounts that pay more than the ECB base rate, especially from newcomers to the Irish market, because they want to attract customers away from the traditional players.

Default risk and available rates

The financial world isn't perfect. Financial firms can collapse. The incidence of collapse is a lot less frequent now than it was, but that's only because Governments and regulators have learned the hard way.

When you put your money on deposit, you are lending it to a financial firm. Your cash appears as a liability in their balance sheet to you. Their ability to pay that liability **under normal banking conditions is a function** of their financial strength. This ability can change over time. Specialists such as **Standard & Poors, Moodys and Fitch** provide reliable credit ratings based on careful examination of the strength of financial firms. **Remember, no retail bank has enough cash to pay out all depositors at once.**

Financial firms with higher credit ratings pay less to depositors than firms with lower credit ratings. Those with lower ratings need to give higher rates in order to attract business from firms with better ratings. When a firm goes bust, depositor protection schemes can provide a safety net. These schemes exist in Europe and the US. In most cases when you place money on deposit it becomes part of the balance sheet of the financial firm. If the firm goes wallop and your money has not been 'ring-fenced' by a trustee arrangement (which keeps it separate from the balance sheet of the financial firm), you can run into trouble. One comforting thought is that as part of an EU (European Union) directive, a minimum compensation level equal to €20,000 or 90% of your deposit, whichever is less, must be available to all Member State citizens.

The various types of cash deposit accounts

Interest-bearing current accounts

A current account comes with a chequebook, electronic access and usually an overdraft limit. But the idea that banks would pay interest on these accounts when balances are positive is only a recent development in Europe. Interest-bearing checking accounts were introduced in the US in the mid-1970s. In Ireland these are a very recent development and rates are still quite uncompetitive, but more competition in the banking market should eventually improve offerings, especially as Bank of Scotland Ireland develops its branch network (the former ESB shops) and Danske Bank (formerly NIB) muscle in to the retail market.

Current account – mortgages

Another recent development in the Irish market has been the introduction of current account mortgages. These are interest bearing current accounts set up to run parallel to your capital repayment mortgage and are available from a small number of lenders. Due to the uncompetitive nature of this segment of the mortgage market, variable rates tend to be marginally higher than the bargain-basement rates available from the mortgage market in general, but this should change with more new entrants and stiffer competition.

These accounts work well when you have surplus cash flows each month in comparison to your outgoings. On a daily basis your current account balance is used as an offset to your mortgage while you make normal direct mortgage repayments. This has the effect of beginning the cannibalisation of your capital repayment mortgage and potentially shortening its term. The current account mortgage is ideally suited to borrowers who reckon on high surpluses of money arising each month from income payments in excess of monthly spending. It is of little or no benefit to borrowers who just about make ends meet each month.

The (passbook) deposit account

These are the old-style, traditional deposit accounts used by past generations who queued up – during opening hours that suited banks – and had the ins and outs of their accounts written in their passbook. The account is liable to a tax of 20%, which is deducted on interest at source and called DIRT (Deposit Income Retention Tax).

Changes in lifestyle and technology, plus rising consumer expectations, has meant banks are steadily replacing the passbook in order to keep up with the number of transactions per customer in the modern world. Nonetheless, the deposit savings account remains the most common type of account in Ireland and marking up transactions on the passbook is still the favoured way of keeping track of money for many older savers. Alongside the standard passbook, you can now also get a regular statement from the bank and can monitor your account on-line.

Banks sometimes like to differentiate their products with buzzwords like 'investment account'. This is just an advertising gimmick. These are just ordinary deposit accounts, with higher rates of interest. The reason for this largesse, however, is because you have to leave in your money for a longer period of time. Some banks insist that you have no access to your money during the fixed-term period, such as 3 months, 6 months, etc. Others allow discretionary access, which means that they will let you have access to all or part of your money, but they retain the right to make a discretionary reduction in the interest rate promised to you at the start.

Unit-linked cash funds

Commonly referred to as 'secure' funds, these are open-ended, unit-linked, whole-of-life policies issued by life companies where the underlying investment is in deposit accounts and short-term money market instruments on the wholesale market. After allowing for management charges, the return from secure funds may not match the best on-line and on-demand deposit rates, however they do provide a useful safe haven for monies held within life insurance companies in other funds. These are gross roll-up funds, which means no DIRT is deducted at source. Instead, tax is paid at a rate of 23% on the profit element of any withdrawal.

So that's the basics of cash, now we need to know how the money market operates, who calls the rates and what kind of things affect rates. Read on!

Don't get complacent about your cash

Banks are in business to make a profit, whether they borrow money off you in the form of a deposit, or lend you money in the form of a loan. They make profit on the difference between what they pay their depositors and what they charge their borrowers. Despite the cosy relationship you believe you may have with your bank, never forget that you represent an opportunity to make a profit. **Many banks manage their cash flow to maximise it at the expense of the uninformed customer**. It's up to you to decide whether that's going to be a large profit or a small profit.

Banks regularly advertise the best rates they offer for **new customers**: it may not be the rate you're getting. Banks may roll over your deposit account at less competitive rates than it would offer if you were to renegotiate terms. Banks also make money by delaying paying the best rates. To do all this successfully, banks rely on customer **inertia**, knowing that most customers won't act when paid less than the most competitive rate. Customers often simply do not know and do not check. Being vigilant safeguards you against being paid less than the best rates available and can add thousands of Euro to your cash **over your lifetime**.

Cash and the wholesale money markets

The **European Central Bank (ECB)**, which is based in Frankfurt, was established to deal with the European currency, the Euro, and is independent of European Governments and the EU Parliament in Brussels. Central Banks in member countries, such as the Republic of Ireland, have ceded certain powers to the European Central Bank. The ECB is the 'lender of last resort' to the banking system. By deciding the terms at which it is prepared to lend to banks, the ECB can have a direct influence on the level of interest rates in the Eurozone economy. The ECB's core objective is to help manage inflation within the Eurozone. The Federal Reserve bank in the USA concerns itself with inflation and economic growth.

Rates of interest will reflect the pressures of supply and demand in the money market for short-term funds. Professional investors are always trying to guess the shape of the future curve. By correctly guessing which way it will bend, they can make moves in advance and make more money than they would otherwise have made.

Banks take in most of their money from individual depositors in the retail market. Remember, these are loans from individuals to banks and they have to be repaid, while interest is paid in the meantime. Banks also borrow money from companies, from other financial institutions and from others, like local Government bodies, who have surpluses of cash they wish to put to work. When they borrow money from these sources it is called the wholesale market, in order to distinguish it from the retail market. Rates payable in the wholesale market are higher than those payable in the retail market.

The wholesale market is important to banks, particularly if they have a temporary shortage of money. Through the money market they can locate other banks that have a surplus of money. This allows banks that are short to borrow funds, and banks that have surpluses to lend funds.

Certificates of Deposit

Certificates of Deposit (CDs) are issued by banks and other financial institutions, and come with an interest rate locked in for a specific period of time. If encashed early, penalties are incurred. Variations include CDs that allow you to set your own maturity date, and the issuer then quotes a customised yield for that maturity date. The Certificates are **tradeable** on the stock market. While in the US they are available to individual investors, in Ireland the CD market is still limited to institutional investors only.

Bills of Exchange

Bills of Exchange are a short-term IOU. They are widely used to provide credit and to finance trade. An example is the best way to explain Bills of Exchange. Let's say Big Ben Limited sells €20m of product to Little Jean Limited. Little Jean Limited now owes Big Ben Limited €20m but, on normal commercial terms, does not have to pay the bill for, say, 6 months. The financial controller of Big Ben Limited has run into a few cash flow problems, however, so he decides that he doesn't want to wait 6 months and he looks around for ideas. There, at the top of the pile, is an invoice that has to be paid within 6 months by Little Jean Limited. Little Jean Limited is not going to pay the €20m until the 6-month period is up, but neither is it going to pay interest in the meantime. The financial controller of Big Ben Limited would like to get somebody interested in taking over the collection of the invoice, but to do this he must be prepared to offer a discount on the €20m due. He sells this into the market at a discount to its face value and the discount is expressed as an annual rate of interest.

Banks operate in the market by 'accepting' a bill, in which case it's putting its name on the bill. It then becomes a **'bank bill'**. This means that the bank is now the guarantor of the payment.

Commercial paper

Commercial paper is another type of IOU used for short-term purposes. Big companies issue commercial paper as a way of raising money. They do this by going to a specialist bank and indicating how much money they wish to raise by issuing commercial paper. Market demand for the company's commercial paper will influence the rate at which its face value is sold at a discount. It is the discount that provides the rate of interest by guaranteeing the investor a higher future value than the amount for which the commercial paper has been acquired.

Swaps

The wholesale money market contains a variety of swaps. Remember as a child you used to swap your toys for somebody else's? Your swapping pal probably lived next door – but what if he or she lived in a different part of the world? That would make swapping very difficult – unless, of course, a market existed to operate the swap. A swap option is a contract in which the parties to the contract agree to exchange liabilities on outstanding variable rate and fixed rate debts. The swap markets therefore provide opportunities for both debt management and for trading.

What are the interest rate indicators?

There are different rates of interest for Interbank Deposits, Certificates of Deposits etc., but the most common rate used in the broad financial media is now set by the European Central Bank and is called **EURIBOR** (**European Inter-bank Offer Rate**). Euribor rates will be different for overnight money, 7-day money, 1-month money, 3-month money, etc., according to the shape of the curve at any given time. In the UK the interbank rate is called **'LIBOR'** (London Inter-bank Offer Rate).

Foreign currency movements and what influences them

The swings and roundabouts in foreign exchange markets, or **'FOREX'**, make money markets look tame by comparison. Waves of money moving in and out of countries can have a dramatic impact on local economies. These movements can, for example, impact on the value of pension funds, many of which have high holdings in international investments. In small open economies, such as the Republic of Ireland, over 50% of pension assets are invested overseas.

The creation of a single European **currency has greatly lessened** the impact of foreign currency movements within Europe, however the Euro itself will vary against sterling, the dollar and the yen. The dollar dominates world trade, accounting for an estimated 70% of it. The relative value of a currency depends on the number of buyers and sellers in a market. Values are monitored closely by Central Banks, which frequently intervene to strengthen or weaken a currency. This doesn't always go strictly according to plan, however. Past history is reddened with the blushes of Central Banks that exhausted their foreign exchange reserves trying to prop up their currency when the markets had clearly already decided it was overpriced and were selling it.

When an economy is working successfully and is increasing its earnings the value of its currency will generally be strong. Some countries have a positive balance in their current account, which means they are exporting more than they are importing. Other countries have deficits each year, which means they are importing more than they are exporting.

A Central Bank may decide to make its currency more attractive to international investors by increasing its interest rates. It needs to be careful when doing this because such increases can have a knock-on effect in the economy. To benefit from the increase, international investors then have to buy into the currency. This increases demand and can in turn strengthen the currency. Of course, it's not all one-way traffic. When international investors believe that a currency is overvalued they will sell it, in which case there are more sellers than buyers and the currency falls in price.

Currencies are priced off one another and expressed as **exchange rates**, which are published regularly. The main traded currencies are the dollar, yen, and Euro. For commercial investors, **trade weighted indices** are used as a way of measuring the strength of a currency. These are indices that capture a basket of currencies comprised of the main trading countries with which a country does business. When one currency rises in relation to other currencies, the cost of selling its goods in international markets becomes more expensive. It is only when its currency weakens that its goods become cheap enough to gain back market share.

The waves of money moving around the world can be split into two categories. First there are the normal inflows and outflows, which can be termed **'current account flows'**. These reflect the balance of trade between a country and those outside it. The second area of flow can be called **'capital account flows'**. This refers to money moving in as long-term investment for infrastructural projects and the like. Large capital inflows can have the effect of strengthening a currency.

In order to protect themselves from volatility, businesses can **hedge** their currency risk. In the **'spot'** market, currencies are bought and sold for **instant** delivery, usually within two days. In the **'forward'** market currencies are bought and sold for delivery in the **future**. Exchange rate prices will be quoted in the media based on spot prices and future prices (where delivery will be typically over 1 month, 3 months, and 1 year). The difference between the spot price and the forward price is called the **'interest rate differential'**.

So much for cash! Now then, what's the story with the other big paper asset, bonds, and what does it mean for you?

The world of bonds

When we use the word 'bond' in everyday lingo we are usually referring to family ties, or a thing guys do playing team sports, or a 007 character in the movies. But bonds have a far bigger role to play in modern life and an antiquity that stretches back at least to Sumerian times, to the ancient city of UR, which was located about 100 miles north of the Persian Gulf! Recovered Sumerian artefacts include tablets to help calculate loan rates which is precisely what a bond is – a loan, but instead of borrowing the money, you lend it!

Bonds are vital tools in modern investment and a well-managed bond portfolio can provide very attractive returns, when you adjust for their lower risk, compared to property and equities. Most Irish investors experience bond markets indirectly through pension funds and directly through An Post, which distributes Irish Government bonds in little bundles – Certificates, Instalment Savings, etc.

You may already have fond memories of excellent bond yields: back in the bad old days, shorn of cash and needing to borrow more money, the Government offered very attractive and tax-free interest rates through An Post offers – remember those? They were loans you lent the Irish Government! These days, the rates available are deliberately set at uncompetitive levels against bank interest rates because bumper tax revenues mean the Government no longer needs to borrow in this way.

When property or equities are in a bull phase, powering ahead and stealing all the headlines, boring old bonds are almost forgotten. In times of economic uncertainty, however, Government bonds, especially Eurobonds, are suddenly handsome and highly attractive again, even to the most aggressive investor.

Low inflation and low interest rates generally make for a good environment for bonds, but when interest rates are increased to relatively high levels it can have a harsh effect. In 1993, when there was a fear worldwide that 1994 would bring high inflation, interest rates were pegged up. There was no inflation spike, but the **expectation** alone drove down the value of resale bonds, for example, when measured against UK inflation, the return on long-term British Government bonds was −14.53%.

The inflation burst triggered by the oil crisis in the early 1970s was a torrid time for bond returns, affecting 20-year averages right up to the mid-1980s, but the much lower inflation environment since then has provided a steadier environment for Government bonds, which have the capacity under these conditions to outperform cash deposits by 1% –2% pa. Higher risk bonds, such as corporate bonds, can do even better.

Whether or not you fancy bonds, the market will affect you. Up to one-third of pension fund assets are held in bonds. If, later in life, you buy a pension income, you will be interacting with the bond market. If you buy shares in a company that raises debt and increases its gearing by issuing its own corporate bond the value of your shares will be affected. If there is a worldwide drop in confidence and in economic activity that leads to a time of uncertainty, property prices and shares could fall and bond values push forward as waves of money seek safe havens. For you, the investor, this means that understanding some of the basics of the bond market is a must.

The anatomy of a bond

Bonds are IOUs. The investor – usually an institutional investor, like a life office fund manager – lends the money to the bond issuer, such as a Government, in return for which the investor receives an IOU in the form of a bond and now becomes the **bondholder**. The investor can trade in these IOUs, or hold them to maturity and get back the original investment, having enjoyed the stream of income payments from the issuer in the interim. Bonds can also be used as a way of raising finance by issuers such as **municipal authorities** and **local Governments**. These bodies issue municipal bonds.

Bonds have three main features: the **yield** the investor will get to maturity; the possibility of a **gain** the investor will have made by buying the bond at less than its face value; the possibility of selling the bond before maturity for a profit. The longer the maturity of a bond, the more its price will react to the ups and downs of interest rates. A **long** bond that is locked into high interest rates relative to current interest rates for long periods such as 20 years is of greater value to a bondholder than a short bond with a similar interest rate.

Fixed interest bonds pay a fixed rate of interest to the bondholder over the specified term. This rate doesn't change. What does change is what the market will pay for the bond. This decision is heavily influenced by interest rates among other economic indicators. If interest rates paid for money in the cash markets fall to less than the rate available on a bond, the price for which that bond can be sold will rise. Conversely, if interest on deposits rises above the rate on the bond, then the resale value of the bond falls. There is one sure way to avoid this risk, and that is to hold the bond to maturity. In the real world, however, investors may find it difficult to hold bonds to maturity because they need cash, or they see an opportunity to profit from selling the bond and simply can't resist.

Bonds are issued from a variety of sources. Remember the bond is an IOU, so the ability to repay it is directly related to the repayment strength of the bond issuer. The safest bonds are those issued by strong sovereign Governments, like Eurobonds and US Treasuries. At the other end of the scale are corporate bonds issued by companies with weak balance sheets and countries with poor financial and economic security. Very large and strong companies that issue corporate bonds may attract a higher credit rating than those issued by small countries.

During the American Civil War the rebel Confederate Government in Richmond issued Confederate Government bonds in addition to printing Confederate money. Whenever the Confederacy needed more money, it simply printed more paper. Inevitably, Confederate Government bonds came to be worth less than the paper upon which they were written. The resale value of a long bond is more sensitive to variations in interest rates than bonds of shorter duration. Normally, in a time of falling interest rates a bond manager will go long, favouring longer duration bonds. When interest rates rise, however, short bonds are likely to be preferred.

Resale Price Volatility

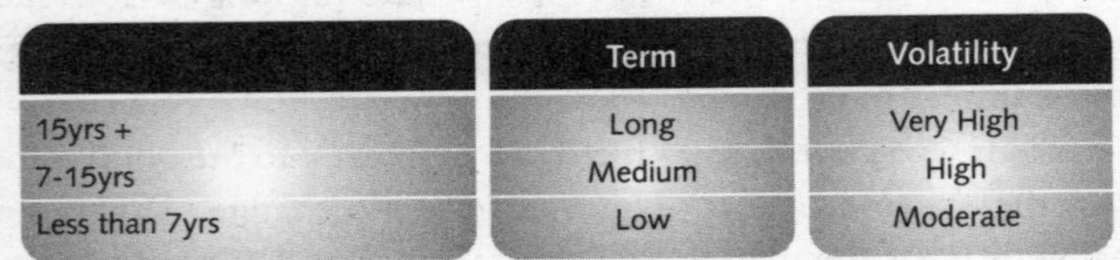

	Term	Volatility
15yrs +	Long	Very High
7-15yrs	Medium	High
Less than 7yrs	Low	Moderate

Of course, it would be folly to invest in bonds purely on the basis of yields without looking at the potential risk that the bond issuer might default – that's why the credit rating of the bond issuer is crucial as it provides a measure of the relative creditworthiness of competing bond offers. Credit rating agencies such as Standard & Poors, Moodys and Fitch score bonds into **investment grade** and **speculative grade**. The better the grade, the lower the interest the bond issuer will pay to bondholders. (See chart on p. 231).

Doing bond sums

A bond will have a **name** and a **face value**: this is how it looked at birth. Let's say that the Atlantis Government is a major western economy whose currency is in pounds. It issues an Atlantean Government bond it calls 'Atlantean Treasury 8%, 09/09'. This means that the Atlantis Government will pay £8 on every £100 of nominal stock issued at launch in September 2000. The 8% is called the **coupon rate**. At its launch an investor places £100,000 in the bond issue.

A couple of years later interest rates available in Atlantis are higher than 8%, dropping the tradeable value of the bond from £100 of nominal stock to £90. Through the market process a new

Credit Rating for Bonds

Grade		Standard & Poors	Moodys
INVESTMENT *Grade*	Highest Score	AAA	Aaa
		AA+	Aa1
	Very Strong	**AA**	**Aa2**
		AA-	Aa3
		A+	A1
		A	A2
		A-	A3
		BBB+	Baa1
	Adequate	**BBB**	**Baa2**
		BBB-	Baa3
SPECULATIVE *Grade*		BB+	Ba1
	Least Speculative	**BB**	**Ba2**
		BB-	Ba3
		B+	B1
	Speculative Major Risk Large Uncertainty	**B**	**B2**
		B-	B3
		CCC	Caa
	In Default	**CC,D**	**CaC**

investor arrives and offers to buy the Atlantean bond from the current holder. The sale is agreed and £90,000 changes hands.

The new holder pays £90,000, for which he receives an income from the Atlantean Government of £8,000 pa. (Remember, the coupon is 8% on £100,000 face value.) You don't have to be a genius to figure out that the interest yield is £8,000 ÷ £90,000 which is 8.89%. This is also called the **income yield**, or the **flat yield**, or the **running yield**.

You've probably already spotted a hidden gain: not only is the new investor getting a yield of 8.89% pa to September 2009 but if he hangs on to the stock, the Atlantis Government will pay him stg£100,000 at maturity. Since he has acquired the stock seven years from its maturity in September 2009 for £90,000, he stands to gain an extra £10,000 over seven years. This is an extra yield.

So what happens if you have to pay more than the face value because interest rates have fallen, making the sale value of bonds rise? Simple. You follow the same procedure, except you will find that the 'hidden figure', the gain to redemption, is not in fact a gain to redemption at all, but a loss to redemption. In other words, it is negative. So, when you add the interest yield to a negative figure, you get a lower one.

Nasty surprises

Some bonds come with two dates on which, or in between which, the bond can be **redeemed** by the issuer. Take, for example, Atlantis Government bond 9.5%, 2006–2010: this means the Atlantis Government can redeem the bond from you as early as 2006, or can wait until as late as 2010. Issuers will move to protect their position, so don't be surprised if the bond is redeemed at a point that suits the issuer, and not you.

Other bonds come with an explicit **call**. This can be well before the maturity date and allows the issuer to exercise its call option on that date. Calculating the **redemption yield to call** is very important as it is quite possible that the call option will be exercised. To calculate it, the above steps are repeated, but move the redemption date forward to the call date.

When bonds are issued they come with thick legal documents called the **indenture**. This sets out the guaranteed minimum number of years during which the bond cannot be redeemed. This is the **call-protection period**. Once that period passes, anything can happen. When the issuer redeems bonds prematurely, it usually pays a moderate premium over the face value.

Not all bonds have fixed maturity dates, however. The infamous British Government 'war loan' is the best-known of open-ended Government stock. Open-ended stock is undated, or is irredeemable.

The effect of supply and demand

Movement in interest rates, or expected movement in interest rates, is not the only thing that can affect the value of bonds. Bonds can also be affected by the law of supply and demand, a law from which nothing is immune. When there is a greater number of sellers than buyers, this pushes down prices, but, conversely, if there is a greater number of buyers than sellers, the demand pressure will push up prices. These types of pressure are more significant in smaller markets, such as small countries, or sub-markets in big countries where there are small numbers of buyers and sellers. The municipal bond market and the lower end of the corporate bond market are examples.

Stock protected from interest rates and inflation

Some types of bond are protected from inflation, or interest rates. In 1994, for example, the UK Government issued a new type of Government bond, called a **floating rate gilt**. It proved to be very popular. This gilt paid a rate slightly below LIBID, an interest rate indicator.

Index-linked stocks are stocks that track geared consumer price indices. These are a very good hedge against inflation because when inflation becomes a threat, the income paid and the value at which the bond will be redeemed are moved in line with a consumer price index, therefore the bond holds its real value when all around are losing theirs.

Governments also issue short-term Government gilts with a **conversion** option. The conversion option allows investors to move to longer dated gilts on fixed terms at fixed dates.

Types of bond you can invest in

Corporate bonds

Just like municipal authorities and Governments, corporate entities also like to borrow money for long periods at fixed rates of interest. They do so by issuing corporate bonds. While Governments can raise funds through the tax system as and when they need to, companies have no such well to draw on. Their ability to pay bondholders is dependent on their strength. For the investor, this means that a company's credit rating is crucial when examining the **corporate bond** market. A corporate bond issued by a multi-billion-Euro international company that has been in business for 100 years is likely to be stronger than a bond issued by a new company. A relatively small company is forced to offer a higher return in order to compete for funds in the bond market.

Investors interested in very long-term bonds will probably feel a lot more comfortable with a Government bond, believing that a Government will continue to be there in, say, 25 years. It is only the very strongest, longest established companies that are able to compete in the long-term bond market. The rest have to settle for the shorter-term market. In the market for Government bonds there are always plenty of buyers and sellers. Not so in the corporate bond market. This extra liquidity risk has to be compensated in the yield paid to investors. Bonds issued by Governments are often used as a yardstick against which to measure the yield from a corporate bond. Even a very strong corporate bond is likely to offer 0.5% pa extra yield in its efforts to attract investors.

As corporate bonds pay higher yields than Government bonds, the market is particularly important to investors who require higher income than that generated by Government bonds of the same maturity. Just like municipal bonds, ensure that you have carefully examined your protection against early redemption calls. It is not uncommon for corporate bonds to be 'called' just after a sharp interest rate fall, allowing financial controllers to pay back bond-holders using lower cost finance.

Corporate bonds are subject to the same market influences as Government bonds when interest rates rise and fall, but one other major force also has an impact on them. This is the **market perception** of the fortunes of the company that issued the bond. If the perception is that the company is deteriorating in strength, its credit rating may be cut, which will automatically decrease the value of its corporate bond stock. It will also increase the yield it will have to pay in any new issues.

Corporate bonds can be secured against a specific asset, or mix of assets, owned by the company, so in the event of a default the bond is asset-backed. In the event of default, **unsecured** corporate bondholders will have to get in the queue to compete with other creditors for repayment. Restrictive covenants are imposed by investors to ensure that a company issuing a corporate bond operates within set parameters, which are dictated by ratios between profits and interest charges. Secured corporate bonds will pay lower yields than bonds that are unsecured.

Convertible bonds

Convertible bonds are essentially part-bond and part-equity and are issued by corporations. They offer regular fixed income, usually at a lower yield than ordinary bonds available from the same source. They work as **part-equity** because they allow the holder to redeem the bond for a **shareholding** in the company. The convertible bond will contain a conversion price, that is the price at which the bond can change to ordinary shareholding.

The true value of a convertible bond can only be properly assessed by close examination of the underlying stock. When the market believes the underlying company is good value, this pushes up the sale price of the convertible bond and vice versa. Convertible bonds offer a guaranteed income, on the one hand, and the opportunity for capital appreciation, on the other, at a level linked to the fortunes of the company. At base, though, this bond type is more akin to equity investment than traditional bond investment.

Zero-coupon bonds

Zero-coupon bonds, or **'zeros'**, pay no interest at all during their lifespan. The investor's return is purely in the gain to redemption. For example, let's say the Atlantis Government issues a zero-coupon bond for 10 years. Instead of paying an annual income to the bondholder, it agrees to pay £100 in 10 years' time for every £40 given to it in the form of a loan through the zero-coupon bond. This means that the future value is £100 for every £40 invested, now over a period of 10 years: a yield of 9.6% pa.

'Strips' is the term used to describe the unbundling of a bond into separate packages comprising rights to interest payments and rights to the repayment of the principal. These packages are then sold off separately. The principal strip carries the right to the repayment of capital at maturity and is, in effect, a zero-coupon bond. If the bond has, say, a run of 10 years and pays income half-yearly, then the interest payments can be bundled into 20 strips and sold separately.

International bonds

The risk associated with international bonds is linked to the strength of the issuing Government and the impact of currency movements. UK Government bonds will carry lower risk than bonds issued, for example, by Russia, but both contain foreign exchange rate risk to Irish investors from fluctuations between Euro/Sterling and Euro/Rouble.

Investors can make considerable gains from currency movements when the value of their currency weakens against that of the bond after the purchase has been made. This increases the value of interest payments from the bond in the investor's currency, and positions them for substantial gains on sale or at maturity. Foreign currency is, of course, a double-edged sword. If the currency of the bond weakens against the investor's currency, the opposite happens and value is lost.

Junk bonds

Junk bonds exploded onto the US market in **the 1980s** when they were marketed as **'high yield'** bonds and quickly became all the rage. Junk bonds are issued by weaker companies with Standard & Poors ratings of less than BBB, which means their bonds are less than investment grade. This does not always mean that the underlying company is a poor one, however. It's always possible that the issuer is an unknown that's on its way up. Junk bonds come with much higher yields for the very simple reason that they carry significantly larger default risk than investment grade bonds.

Many companies defaulted on their junk bonds in the late 1980s and investors lost their money. The modern market is more mature, however, and has yields set at more realistic levels than the big numbers used to fuel the embryonic junk bond market.

Collateralised Debt Obligations (CDOs)

Replacing the junk bond market as a more recent development of higher income-producing assets is the market for second-hand loans. The Collateralised Debt Obligations (CDO) market provides opportunities to invest in pools of thousands of debt-type securities (e.g. mortgages) which have been packaged for sale to investors. The CDO market allows banks and mortgage companies to sell on their debt portfolio into a secondary market, freeing up the capital lent to householders to buy homes, to car owners to change to the latest Cadillac and even to shoppers using credit cards to pay for Christmas! The bank gets capital that it can lend out all over again, and the investor, usually a fund, gets an asset that pays income – the loan repayments of the end borrowers. CDOs will come with a variety of income and risk levels, depending on the nature of the pool of debt packaged for sale, and ranging from secured mortgages to unsecured credit card debt.

So that's the basic lie of the land in the bond territory. It might be all new to you – Irish people have never been particularly bond-minded, unlike their German counterparts, for example – but bonds are worth your attention as a potential investment opportunity and a means of diversifying your portfolio. If you're tempted, here's some extra tips you'll need about investing in this area.

Investing in bond funds

Bond markets, particularly in Europe, are really only designed for large institutional investors who buy and sell in huge volumes. Trading in smaller lots is a lot more costly and a lot more difficult, requiring more time on the investor's part because the number of trades is greater. If you want diversification in your bond portfolio, then funds are a good idea because they hold a large number of bonds of different maturities and varieties and professional fund managers will have access to research on areas of the market that are difficult for individuals to research. Funds can be **distributing**, which means they pay out the income earned each year, after management fees – a handy option for retirees – or they can be **accumulating**, which means the income is reinvested within the fund on your behalf.

Sometimes referred to as Fixed Income funds in the local Irish market, bond funds are on offer from life offices, although the range is narrower and limited mainly to Eurobonds. This situation is likely to change, however, as more corporate bonds funds become available. For the most part your exposure to bonds is likely to be hidden within the mixed asset portfolios of so-called 'balanced' or 'managed funds', but a wide range of specialist funds spanning corporate bonds and international bonds is available from the OEIC's market, the main trading centres for which are the Dublin and Luxembourg IFSC and from Exchange Traded Funds.

Before investing, always examine the investment policy of a bond fund to determine the risk levels involved. Is the fund investing in major Government bonds, such as within the Euro-zone, the UK, US, etc., or is it specialising in, for example, emerging market debt comprising bonds issued by countries such as Russia, Brazil, Argentina, etc.? The potential return from these funds will be much higher, but so is the risk. Also, check if the investment policy includes corporate bonds and ensure you understand the creditworthiness range within which the fund manager will operate. The fund policy might be to restrict trade in corporate bonds to the AA–AAA range, or the fund might invest in B-rated bonds, which are of poorer investment grade. You need to know where the money is going, and what that means for you.

CHAPTER 15

Investing Through Funds

Glossary

- **Unit-linked fund:** A collective investment (pooled) fund administered in units that attach to life insurance policies.
- **Beauty queen fund:** The latest fashion fund with the best performance data that gets all the promotional spend.
- **Balanced/managed fund:** A fund comprising a mix of major assets, that is shares, property, bonds and cash deposits.
- **Fund assets:** The underlying assets in which the fund invests.
- **Units:** A method of assigning the value held by an investor in the underlying assets of a fund.
- **Unit trust:** A trust that pools investors' money in assets and that uses unit accounting to administer value.
- **Investment trust:** A publicly quoted, non-trading company with a fixed number of shares.

Unless you fancy yourself as an Active Trader or a property tycoon, you will invest in assets through some kind of fund. The important thing to remember is not to lose yourself in the torrent of jargon, hype and drivel that seems to go hand-in-glove with the fund industry and to stay firmly focused on three things:

- What assets am I investing in through the fund and how are these likely to behave?
- Why are the fund assets a good fit to my balance sheet and ambitions?
- Am I getting value for money and are all the costs reasonable?

Have you noticed how *Loot!* keeps referring to investing **through** funds rather than *in* funds, which is the common terminology? That's a very deliberate choice of wording, aimed at helping you keep your eye on what really matters: **the underlying assets of the fund**. The fund itself is just a piece of bookkeeping or administration of a collective investment by a wide number of investors – nothing more, nothing less. The fund is the means by which you invest; the assets in which the fund puts your money is your investment. That is the thing you need to keep foremost in your mind: the fund is a vehicle; the assets are the investment.

The most popular types of asset administration in Ireland are unit-linked funds. These are administered by life offices, which continue to exercise a stranglehold on the Irish market. These are issued as policies to investors for lump sums (single premiums) or regular sums (recurring premiums, or savings policies). They are also used to administer pension schemes, which we'll examine in the next chapter.

Elsewhere there is a huge range of funds available, from Open-Ended Investment Companies (OEICs), Unit Trusts and Investment Trusts. The investment choice available from the European fund industry varies in line with the wide diversity of assets available, from Cash to China, from Gold Mining to Government Bonds. Once you've a good understanding of the likely behaviour of the assets held by a fund, it's much easier to understand what's happening to your money.

Why invest through funds?

- Funds allow you to delegate the responsibility for the management of the assets to professional investment managers, rather than undertaking the work yourself. If you deliver babies for a living, for example, that's a big benefit because haring off to deal with tenants, or gluing yourself on your PC to read the Nasdaq isn't possible!
- You get the benefit of immediate diversification because a fund will typically spread your money across a very large number of assets. For example, a fund that invests in large capitalisation companies may hold fifty or sixty different stocks, giving a modest sum a spread it could not otherwise achieve.
- You can make tactical moves within fund families without triggering Irish Capital Gains Tax, which means you can buy and sell in markets like Europe, the UK, etc. and in asset classes like Bonds, Equities and Commodities. That's a big advantage, especially if you want out of a market fast because you see trouble brewing. Consider how long it might take to get out of a bad buy-to-let in Manchester compared to switching from a UK property fund, which would take one email!
- You can defer tax for as long as you like because under the current Irish tax system funds are regarded as gross roll-up investments. This avoids tax payments each year on, for example, rents or dividends when assets are held directly and eliminates tax paperwork. Tax is paid on profits only when cash is physically withdrawn and then at a common rate of 23%. This is an advantage to investors who would otherwise be taxed at the top rate of 42% for income on direct assets.
- You can make partial withdrawals from and additions to the assets held by open-ended funds. That option is not always available with direct assets, like property.

What are the downsides to funds?

The funds industry is **marketing-led**, a fancy way of saying that a lot of new product design and advertising is contrived to milk current fashion trends. This leads to some pitfalls, of which you need to be aware.

- Fund marketing sells hope, not advice. The easiest time for financial firms to sell investment in funds is when there has been a long and consistent past performance in which you can wrap the message and hook the fashion-led investor. This kind of investor likes the safe feeling he/she gets when huge numbers of investors are all doing the same thing. The asset class being sold like this, whether property or equities, invariably disappoints because it's close to the end of its current upward cycle and expectations have been exaggerated for a big finale. This leads to a sell-off at the bottom of the cycle and then the hordes spin off again towards the next great hope now grandly displayed in the front window of the fund industry! It's a cliché, but it works: don't believe the hype.
- Funds, especially balanced funds, tend towards the mediocrity of the centre-ground rather than taking maverick positions that could lead to better asset performance, and are much more influenced by how other funds are performing. Managers often become more concerned with ensuring that their performance data is never too far out of kilter with their competitors in the sector. They are keenly aware that the private investor is largely focused on short-term data and will sell a 'no1' fund at the first sign of slippage, even if the maverick position sets the fund on a much better track.
- Generally, the larger the fund, the more difficult, and increasingly more difficult, it is to get top performance compared to smaller, more mobile funds. Small beauty queen funds become fashionable and then suffer from huge inflows of money in short periods of time. This destroys the ability of the fund manager to repeat top performance.

- Costs, especially high costs, create significant drag on asset performances. In fund investments, part of your money is paid out to salespeople as commissions and to product providers as set-up expenses. Each year there will be a fund management charge, collected daily, and you may also pay fees to sell out of the fund. In addition, there can be further and undisclosed expenses paid out of fund assets which are not captured in the annual fund charge. These costs are deducted regardless of whether the assets are managed well or not – a frequent source of complaints by grumpy investors. The alternatives are pricing models that pay handsome incentives for performance above pre-set levels.

Which fund is best?

Historically, the most common choice of Irish investors have been funds that invest in a mix of assets – equities, bonds, cash and property – promising to move around the mix as and when circumstances change. Also called **managed funds**, or **balanced funds**, they are distinguished by their equity content, which is the dominant asset held and is usually in the range 40%–80%. The lowest equity versions are called Cautiously Managed Funds, mid-equity versions are called Managed Funds, and high equity versions are variously called Performance, Growth, Dynamic or Aggressive Managed Funds. No, there's no end to the inventiveness of the marketing gurus when it comes to thinking up catchy names for the latest fashion fund!

Although dismissed by active investors as big, sluggish and boring brutes, the common-or-garden variety balanced fund, with its mix of assets, has been widely sold to passive investors. balanced funds mightn't sparkle in a strongly growing market, but their lower volatility is a comfort to investors during strongly falling markets when their cash and bond holdings can help put on some braking pressure. The risk and reward trade-off from Balanced funds hasn't been enough to convince informed and discerning investors, which explains the huge growth in fund range width in recent times and the decline in popularity of the old staple diet – the managed fund.

As with all aspects of investment, there is no 'best one'; ideally you should have a portfolio of funds that invests in an uncorrelated mix of assets. You don't get away that easy! It requires a bit of legwork to sort through the options available and see which funds fit best with your budget, your resources and your expectations. The brief descriptions given above should help you to eliminate the least likely, at any rate. Then you can take it from there.

Picking horses for courses

Instead of lumping all of your money into balanced funds, you could pick horses for courses and decide on the asset mix you want for your balance sheet. So what kinds of questions should you raise with your fund manager?

- Do you have access to past performance data against the index of the market in which the fund is investing, or is it just the cosy peer group averages normally favoured by Irish life offices? Where peer group data is all that's available, don't look for no.1 positions – instead look for top quartile positions on a reasonably consistent basis over the long term. Does the fund have an independent rating from an international fund-rating specialist – how many stars has it been awarded?
- What makes the asset manager think his/her fund had got an edge in managing assets in the sector? This will usually come down to personnel, track record and the systems used by the team to select and manage the assets.
- Does the fund manager have the resources to do the job it is claiming it does? For example, how could a relatively small domestic firm deliver top-class results for the management of faraway assets, like China stocks? Assess what you are being told against commonsense.
- Has the past top performance of the fund been built on the

shoulders of one star manager rather than on the team? Has he or she now left? Is the firm a likely take-over target, causing disruption to its asset management arm?

- What are the fund's objectives and risks? This will be contained in the **prospectus,** if available, or, for life office funds, in a technical fact sheet. OEICs in Europe provide fund data that complies with international standards of transparency, so look for fund performance reports against indices and risk measures that report on fund volatility. Life office funds are much more opaque. The quality of the important data varies widely because no standard presentation is enforced and it's often drowned in marketing blurb and selective performance information.
- Is the fund investing only with investors' cash, or is it borrowing money to invest as well? If so, it will be known as a leveraged, or geared, fund. Borrowing money together with your cash has the potential to produce explosive returns, but also carries higher risk.
- What are the fund charges? How will these drag the investment returns? Do the costs represent reasonable value for money? Remember, there's nothing in the world that can't be made a little cheaper – and just a little worse – so expect to pay more for assets that need intensive management. For example, a fund that invests in small caps, or in emerging markets, will require a fund manager to investigate companies on the ground closely. This costs more money than investing in large caps, which make up the FTSE or S&P 500, much of the research for which can be done from a desk. Property development doesn't come cheaply either, so expect to read about beefy upfront fees, lending margins to the fund and incentives that reward managers with a share of profits for property development funds.

What will it cost?

Annual management charges will typically range up to 0.5% for cash funds, 1% pa for Government bond funds, 1.25% pa for balanced and large cap equity funds, and between 1.5% and 2% pa for specialist funds, like those that invest in India, Eastern Europe and South America, or in corporate bonds, Traded Currencies and other alternative asset classes. Remember, it's about getting value for money. Investing purely on the basis of the lowest price isn't something you'd do when buying a home, so don't do it with your fund choices either – although it's important to avoid getting fleeced as well.

The annual fund charges displayed by life offices are not required to capture the full operating costs of fund assets. Known as the Total Expense Ratio, this complete figure is displayed as a matter of practice with OEICs. Exchange Traded Funds quoted on stock markets provide a variety of different ways to invest in indices at prices typically cheaper than those available through life office funds.

When you consider that the long-term average yearly rate of return for mainstream property and equities is probably 6% to 10% before costs, and even less for bonds and cash, it throws seemingly innocuous-looking fund costs into harsh relief. So make sure you get the cheapest possible price for top quality asset management. For example, say you invested €20,000 in 'Fatty' Fund, which experienced 10% pa gross yield in asset growth over ten years, but you paid 5% to get in and 1.75% pa in fund charges. Before paying exit tax you'll have made a profit of €21,979 and got your capital back. Selling to you first day and then servicing your account while paying for asset management obviously costs money, and the total effect of 'Fatty' Fund charges was to reduce the gross yield of 10% by 2.3%pa – in other words, your return was 7.7% pa.

But let's say you also invested €20,000 in 'Cheapie' Fund, which also got a gross yield on assets of 10% pa, but where entry costs were slimmer at just 1% and the annual fund charge was 1% pa.

The profit before exit tax on Cheapie Fund is €26,873 and the drag affect of its lower charges is 1.11% pa. The cash difference in profit before exit tax between 'Fatty' and 'Cheapie' is €4,894. 'Cheapie's' lower charges earned you over 22% more in profit before exit tax over ten years.

How funds charge you

The fund industry is never short of novel ways to charge you and you'll be unsurprised to learn that a variety of different models are used:

Front-end loaded funds

These require you to pay a **fee upfront**, when you first invest. Usually there is no ongoing fee for reinvested dividends or encashments, which means you can withdraw your money at any time without charge. The fund will have an annual management fee levied on assets, however. Typically the upfront costs are up to 5% while the annual management charge will depend on the type of assets managed.

Front-end loaded funds may offer **breakpoints,** or discounts, for large investment sums. The breakpoints are usually staggered. Typically there are no discounts for small sums, up to €30,000 or so. Good discounts usually begin after €50,000 and the front-end load is usually removed completely for investments of substantial sums, such as €1m or more.

Back-end loaded funds

These are increasingly favoured by Irish life offices and work in reverse to front-end loaded funds by **investing 100% of your money upfront**. This can be enhanced further for larger investment. Back-end loaded funds will charge an annual management fee on the value of your assets in the fund. This is likely to be beefed out during the first few years to finance the commissions the fund paid out upfront but didn't deduct from your investment. During these early years, if you fully or partially encash, you will incur back-end charges of up to 8%. The back-end charge declines over time, usually over five years. You may also be allowed to withdraw a certain percentage each year without incurring the back-end charge.

Level-loaded funds

These don't charge a front-end load or a back-end load, instead they charge an annual management fee on your assets in the fund. This fee is open-ended and normally does not decline over time.

No load funds

No load funds have no upfront charge or closed-end charge. They are sold directly, usually over the phone, and because they bypass much of the distribution costs built into face-to-face advice, they take a different approach. In time 'no loads' may become a popular feature of the Irish market, at present they are very popular in the US market, particularly for the informed investor who does not require advice. In the US a product provider of a no load fund is precluded from giving any advice to investors, and can only describe the fund's investment policy, track record, etc. It is up to investors to decide whether or not the no load fund is appropriate for them. No load funds will charge a **management fee**, ranging as low as 0.2% to as high as 2% depending on the asset class and the size of the fund.

Switching costs

These can be applied where you transfer from one fund to another within the fund family. These fees are usually small, although older style products may charge a percentage of the amount transferred.

Right, so far, so good – I hope! We've covered the basics of funds, so you've now got a grasp of what they are, the terminology and the impact on your wallet. Now it's time to issue a weather warning: heavy weather and rough seas ahead! We're heading into the choppy currents of fund types, and there's lots more lingo to be negotiated. We'll steer clear of the flotsam and jetsam, but it's going to take guts and stamina nonetheless!

Unitisation – a pricing model

Funds use a system to track the value of the underlying assets by expressing them as a **unit price**. Most funds are **open-ended**, that is when there is a net increase in investors, more units are created and vice versa. So, when you invest in a unitised fund, instead of receiving security certificates associated with the underlying assets, you receive fund units. The number of units you receive will depend on the price of the units and the entry charges.

When a unitised fund opens for business, units will begin at a notional level of 100. Let's say an investor goes in on the first day with €1,000 and gets 1,000 units. Several years later the unit price is quoted at €4: this indicates that the value of the 1,000 units is now €4,000. A new investor will now face a unit price of 400, so €1,000 will acquire 250 units.

Life offices' unit-linked funds favour dual pricing, which quotes one price for buying units – the Offer price – and one for selling units – the Bid price – with a spread between them of 5%. To do your head in even further, they counteract the 5% difference with extra allocations to investment for larger sums.

So, let's say you tell the salesperson over the counter you have just €10,000 to invest. You buy at the Offer price but if you sold immediately, you'd sell at the Bid price, 5% lower, and lose €500. Now you change your story and tell the salesperson you really have €100,000. Suddenly you're offered coffee, a reclining chair and an extra allocation to investment of 4%. Now 104% of your money is allocated at the Offer price but if you sold immediately, you'd sell at the Bid price, 5% lower, losing €1,200 or 1.2% of your money. A complicated fuss, isn't it?

Single unit pricing, which is favoured by OEICs, removes the confusion of bid/offer spreads completely. There is one unit price and that's it. The single unit price moves directly in line with the underlying net asset value of the fund. It means that entry costs are expressed as a much clearer charge.

Open- and closed-ended funds

Most unit trusts, and unit-linked funds, are **open-ended**. This means they can continue to take in more new money by issuing more units or shares.

Closed-ended funds issue a limited number of shares or units. The price at which an investor buys often varies against the net asset value (NAV), driven by the laws of supply and demand. When demand is low, the shares or units may be selling at a discount to NAV, making it attractive for new investment. When demand is high, the share may be trading at a premium and the investor has to pay extra in order to get in. Close-ended funds administered by life offices are also used for geared syndicated property investment, closing to new investors once the equity quota has been reached, which, combined with borrowings, will allow the fund to acquire the properties it has been established to own. Unquoted plcs can also be used for the same objective, giving investors shares rather than units.

Unit-linked funds

Unit-linked funds dominate the market in Ireland and are issued by life insurance companies. When investments are made as a lump sum, a **single premium whole-of-life policy** is issued. Investments can also be made periodically by premiums on a regular basis, typically monthly. A **unit-linked savings policy** is issued for monthly premium investment. A **unit-linked bond** is often used to describe investments in single premium whole-of-life policies.

Open-Ended Investment Companies (OEICs)

An OEIC is **a company with variable capital**. Instead of having a fixed number of shares, it continually issues more shares to meet investor demand. The company provides a large range of sub-funds for investors and investors can move freely from one fund to another, with the value of their shares reflecting their movements. It is for this reason that OEICs are an umbrella investment. OEICs are regarded as gross roll-up investments under the Irish tax system, so you can move across markets and sectors under the umbrella of the OEIC without triggering a tax event. (You can also do this within unit-linked fund ranges from life offices, but the choice and sophistication of such funds tends to be much narrower). The most popular centres for distributing OEICs in Europe are Dublin and Luxembourg. Most OEICs sold in Europe come under the European UCITS directive. This stands for Undertaking in Collective Investment in Transferable Securities. The UCITS directive imposed a number of standards: the shares of the OEICs must be quoted at net asset value (NAV); each fund must be subject to independent audit; and the assets held by each fund must not be held by the fund manager managing the assets for the OEICs, but rather by a custodian, typically a bank, acting on behalf of the shareholders. To ensure liquidity, products under the UCITS directive may not invest in property.

Unit trusts

A unit trust is a trust with trust status and appointed trustees. It appoints a professional fund manager to manage the assets held by the trust, and uses the unitised system to value holdings.

The charging structure of unit trusts varies from front-end loads to spread loads to back-end loads. The unit pricing system is on a dual price basis, with bid/offer spreads of 5% typically.

Investment trusts

'Investment trust' is a misnomer. It confuses an investment trust with a unit trust. A unit trust is a real trust, whereas an investment trust is a publicly quoted company of a fixed size. The investment trust company is not a trading company, it buys shares in other companies and securities. Investment trusts are closed-ended investment, with shares selling at a premium, or at a discount, depending on whether the market sees them as attractive or not.

Investment trusts do not operate a unitised system. Instead, investors buy shares in the company in the same way as they buy shares in any other company. Buying shares at a discount to NAV or premium to NAV distinguishes investment trusts from unit trusts in the financial media.

Split-level trusts separate the shares of the company into two types of share: **income shares** and **capital shares**. Income shares are entitled to all of the income created by the assets, while capital shares are entitled to all of the gains from the assets. **Geared investment trusts** attempt to increase performance by borrowing money, which, together with shareholders' money, is used to buy an enlarged amount of assets.

Hedge funds

The hedge fund industry has grown exponentially in line with the growth in demand from the worldwide High Net Worth market. Hedge funds come in many varieties, from the hugely complex funds that trade in special arbitrage positions and currencies to the simple funds that combine investor funds with borrowings to take geared positions in certain types of equity. Many hedged funds are characterised by the use of derivatives to hedge positions like options that put floors under specific shares so that the downside potential is limited – at a cost to the fund.

Hedge fund analysis and advice is a specialist field that is outside the scope of *Loot*! Many of the more exotic hedge fund propositions are a mismatch to passive investors. As a general rule, you should not invest in anything you cannot understand, including derivatives that challenge even the most gifted mathematicians!

Guaranteed equity deposit accounts (GEDAs)

Commonly misnamed 'tracker bonds', GEDAs are a popular sale in Ireland and attract savers who are lured by the promises of guarantees and in search of higher returns than cash deposits at a time of low interest rates. The GEDA is engineered by combining derivatives with short-term fixed interest products, such as cash deposits and bonds. The result allows the product provider to market the message that people can invest lump sums for periods typically up to six years with their capital guaranteed, yet share in stock market growth – an appealing message after shocks in equity markets.

The capital guarantee in a GEDA, or 'tracker', is created by putting the vast bulk of money in deposit. For example, say six years rates are 4% pa. Just under 80% of money goes on deposit, or into other money market instruments and short-dated bonds. This is guaranteed to clock back up to 100% over six years. Typically, between 3% and 8% is deducted by the product provider to pay themselves and to finance sales commissions, usually in the range 2%–4%. GEDAs are also illiquid and generally can't be encashed until maturity, except at the cost of substantial penalties.

What's left over buys financial bets on stock market indices, or on certain shares known as derivatives. But since the bulk of money is on deposit to secure guarantees, the scope of GEDAs is restricted, especially when interest rates are low. For example, say the derivative is based on the S&P 500, which grows 40% over the six-year term, equivalent to 5.76% pa, but the GEDA restricts your growth to 60% of the index performance, which means your return is restricted to 3.45% pa.

Guaranteed Income Bonds (**GIBs**) are a variation on the same theme, but instead of investing in equity-based derivatives, the focus is on bond-based derivatives. The yields on GIBs can be artificially inflated by basing the investment on lower grade bonds. Careful reading of GIB prospectuses is required to determine what is actually guaranteed. Usually that's only the income payments, leaving a threat to the capital value at maturity.

GEDAs and GIBs rarely have guaranteed values during the investment term and the investor is locked in for the period. Product providers will pay interim encashment values, but these are usually at their discretion and will be punitive if market conditions are negative at the time of encashment.

With-profit endowments

Endowment investments do not use the unitised system, although people frequently misuse the term 'endowment' to describe unit-linked policies. The endowment policy does provide the policyholder with a **future cash guarantee**, but only at the **maturity date** of the policy. These dates can vary from 5 years to as long as 30 years. Typically the guarantee for single premium policies was equal to a compound rate of return of between 1% and 2% pa, although this has now declined to zero due to lower equity returns. The guarantee is called the **guaranteed sum assured**. Each year the guaranteed sum assured is increased to a higher guarantee by the distribution of a **bonus**. This bonus is called a **reversionary bonus**. When the policy matures a **Final Bonus** may be added if there is undistributed extra money, but these are in sharp decline due to lower equity exposure brought on by pressure from the UK financial regulator following an actuarial scandal in the UK that nearly put paid to its oldest mutual society, The Equitable Life. Founded on Thursday, 16 September 1762 at a meeting in the White Lion Tavern in Cornhill in the City of London, it closed for new business on 8 December 2000, leaving more than one million policyholders uncertain about their future.

Policyholders often think that the future guarantee at maturity is the running value. This is incorrect. The ongoing **surrender value** of the policy is discretionary, and special exit costs known as **Market Value Adjusters** can be levied at a time of poor market conditions to prevent premature encashment being subsidised by long-term investors.

The with-profit fund contains a mix of equities, gilts, cash and property. The objective of the actuary is to smoothen out the ups and downs of the asset values of the with-profit fund, and instead declare a steady annual bonus. The actuary will want the bonuses maintained at a steady level, regardless of whether the assets have fallen, or risen.

Unitised with-profit funds use a bookkeeping method introduced by life offices to prevent the build-up of liabilities on their balance sheets from selling traditional with-profit policies. By ceasing to sell traditional with-profit policies a life office no longer has to reserve as much to meet the liabilities created by the rising guarantees. Policyholders no longer get a future cash guarantee backed by assets held by the insurance company. Instead they are given units in a unitised fund. The unitised fund sits outside of the with-profit fund as a large investor in it, just like a huge policyholder.

The with-profit fund then distributes large volumes of money to the unitised with-profit fund each year. In turn, the policyholders' units increase in value, but the insurance company reserves the right to attach discretionary charges to the policy units at any point. Each year the insurance company guarantees the growth in units – but not in cash terms. Since the units can be subject to discretionary charges, the guarantee is not absolute and can be reversed at any point by the insurance company. Unitised with-profit policies, just like most products that smooth out the ups and downs of asset volatility, can also apply Market Value Adjusters.

Annuities

When a life office covenants to provide a series of regular payments to a policyholder in return for a lump sum, it's called an annuity. The most common is the pension annuity that is paid for life and is based on the average expected life length of the policyholder, or **annuitant**. Life expectancy will be calculated by reference to **mortality tables** and prevailing bond yields – the asset life offices use to back their pension payment exposures. Where someone's life expectancy is **impaired**, the rate of payment may be higher due to mortality-reducing factors, such as Parkinson's or Alzheimer's diseases.

Where the payment is paid for a period of time it is known as a **temporary annuity**. These annuities are called **purchased life annuities** and investors buy them voluntarily with lump sums of money that they hold.

Annuity rates depend on whether the payment is flat, or increasing, or whether it is related to one life or joint lives. A typical joint life annuity passes two-thirds of the income payment to a spouse surviving the death of the main annuitant. At a time of low interest rates, escalating annuities are particularly expensive and can take nearly a decade to catch up with a flat annuity.

Annuities are regarded as part-repayments of capital. This means that, depending on the age of the annuitant, a large proportion of the payment will be non-taxable. The taxable element will be subject to income tax. Pension annuities are fully taxable, even though they also contain repayments of capital, because the contributions to the pension funds from which pension annuities are derived attracted tax relief.

Deferred annuities are policies taken out with insurance companies and purchased either by single premium lump sums of money, or by recurring premiums, typically monthly. The annuity is deferred, which means the policy builds up a capital value but that value is distributed to the policyholder in the form of a series of income payments at a future date. These income payments can be temporary, or for life.

Insist on your rights to disclosure

In response to a Competition Authority finding that the Irish life industry was operating practices offensive to competition law and diluting price competition, the Irish Government introduced **hard disclosure** of commissions and expenses on new sales after 1 February 2001. This demands the disclosure, in cash terms, at point of sale and in a statutory format, of all commissions and expenses associated with investing in life and pension funds. It is designed to report the drag effect of total charges based on certain assumptions about asset growth. Insist on your rights to statutory disclosure at point of sale and examine closely the salesperson's remuneration.

Unfortunately, you're not always protected by hard disclosure. It doesn't cover company-sponsored pension schemes or increased investment in life products, which predate the new laws. Take special care when topping up old policies sold to you before 2001. These can hide extraordinarily high upfront costs that will be deducted from your new premiums, especially in their first year.

Remember, you don't invest in funds, you invest through funds, which are nothing more and nothing less than a means of administrating pooled investments. Keep your eye on the ball at all times: the important factors are the assets, their behaviour and fit to you. And don't forget those charges, watch those like a hawk. Now, with your knowledge nearly complete grab a bottle of Lucozade because you'll need all the glucose you can to stay awake for *Loot*'s final chapter – Investing Through Retirement Funds.

CHAPTER 16

Investing Through Retirement Funds

Glossary

- **ARF:** Approved Retirement Fund – a continuing investment type for retirement capital after retirement age as an alternative to buying an annuity.
- **Pension:** A taxable income for life.
- **AVC:** Tax-relievable Additional Voluntary Contribution which employees can put into a retirement fund to run in parallel with membership of an employer-sponsored pension scheme.
- **FRS17:** International accounting standard that requires deficits or surpluses in company pension schemes to be reported in the main accounts of the company.
- **Retirement capital:** The total amount of money you accumulate in pension funds by retirement.

If there's a financial word more boring on the planet, I haven't found one more effective than the word 'pension'. In audiences everywhere, mention of the mere word induces a pension coma as chins droop to chests, eyelids struggle and once-alert listeners collectively give up the will to live. It's not a pretty sight, I can tell you!

It doesn't help that generations of pensions consultants, industry regulators and civil servants responsible for constant tinkering with pension rules have made a complete pig's breakfast of it. This is

Frankensteinian tinkering we're talking about here! Each new and frightening layer of turgid rules has given pensions a terrifying visage. They look like a creature that started out in human form, but has been bent so hideously out of shape by fresh work each year that nobody can actually remember what it once looked like – or is meant to look like. Remember the yolk Hollywood devised to chase Ripley around the spaceship? Well, that's where we're at with the Irish pension system – indecipherable, scary and utterly alien. Not surprising then that I frequently hear entrenched public scepticism about investing through retirement funds and catch-cries like, 'property is better' – people are just terrified of the thing that is pensions! But what about getting a tax write-off *and* investing in your favourite asset, like property. Billions of Euro in Government tax relief lies uncollected because of lack of clarity about the effectiveness of the modern retirement fund model. Let's see if we can change that, shall we, and get you your share.

The good news – Charlie took away the word 'pension'

Until quite recently you had to surrender most of the money you accumulated in private pension funds for a taxable pension income for life. It was a bummer watching all that lovely dosh disappearing down the plughole of the life industry for incomes that were getting worse as interest rates fell in the run up to the introduction of the Euro. Then out of the blue, in the Finance Act 1999 and Finance Act 2000, then Minister for Finance, Charlie McCreevy TD, took the word 'pension' out of most pension plans, instead creating an open-ended investment model where the assets you accumulate in retirement funds can be held for the rest of your life. *Eureka!* An option at last – an alternative to taking a one-way ticket and buying a pension.

Under the new regime, you can take a quarter of your accumulated capital in the form of tax-free cash at retirement and continue to hold the remainder in an open-ended investment known as an **Approved Retirement Fund (ARF)**, draw downs of cash from which are subject to tax at your marginal rate. There is an anti-accumulation income tax charge set to apply to asset values in ARFs each year, commencing at 1% and rising to 3% of assets, but withdrawals taken can be used as an offset. You can accumulate up to a cool €5 million in ARFs, above which tax will be charged at your marginal rate and you can take a quarter of the pot, €1.25 million, in succulent tax-free loot.

In essence, Charlie's ARFs created a brand new investment model, changing 'pension' into 'retirement' fund and shifting it to the top of the long-term investment agenda for most investors. These revolutionary changes have not yet been made available for employees in employer-sponsored pensions schemes, even though under present rules accumulated capital from these schemes can be moved into the new model when an employee leaves and provided service with the employer is less than fifteen years. In practice, the flexibilities introduced by the Minister are likely to become available in this sector over the years ahead.

Unfortunately, the Irish pensions market is in a shambles, with multiple product choices and a complex series of rules that is a hangover from the pension's legislation of the past, which was predicated on the *passé* notion that employees would stay with one employer for life. The market is badly in need of radical simplification to improve the retirement fund take-up rate and win more public trust. Unhappily, there's little sign of any such radical reform, just more rules and threats to make investment compulsory – a real vote-winner! Roughly about one million workers haven't saved a sausage through retirement funds. That's a shocking figure. If you are already investing in assets through a retirement fund – however small – congratulate yourself on your forward thinking and aim to build on it. If you haven't even thought about retirement funds, you really, really need to take a good, hard look at your finances and start planning long term. If it all seems a little overwhelming, well, here's where you take the plunge: brace yourself for a mind-bending trip through Irish pension rules that would leave even Uri Geller breathless!

Attractive lure for low rate tax-payer's SSIA

There is a once-off incentive for **low rate tax-payers** whose earned income doesn't exceed €50,000 in the tax year before their SSIA maturity, and where no part of their income is taxed at the higher rate of 42%. Those who meet these criteria can transfer up to €7,500 of their SSIA maturity into either a PRSA, Personal Pension or AVC (see page 263) and benefit from up to €2,500 of Government credit, in other words, a matching contribution of €1 for every €3. That's better than getting income tax relief at 20% (plus PRSI and health levy relief), and is equivalent to a once-off relief of 33%. There's also the kicker that the exit tax on SSIA profits of 23% will not apply to the amount transferred to the retirement fund in this way. While restricted to low rate tax-payers, the incentive provides a great opportunity to start a retirement pot of up to €10,000 and follow it up with monthly contributions thereafter. If you don't have any pension plans in place, this is a very good idea to get you started with a decent lump sum.

This incentive is irrelevant to top rate tax-payers, who can switch the SSIA maturity into retirement funds and gain tax relief at the 42% marginal rate and relief from PRSI and health levies.

What can you invest in a pension?

The first thing I'm often asked is: 'How much should I invest?' The answer is dead simple – as much as you possibly can, right up to your limit for tax relief, but without destroying your lifestyle or moving your daughter's wedding reception to Abrakebabra!

If you are **self-employed,** you are entitled to write off up to 40% of your **net relevant earnings** each year against income tax, PRSI and health levies. Net relevant earnings is a figure close to your net profits and the tax relief is subject to a cap of the first €254,000 of those earnings. Your annual tax write-off allowance depends on your age: it is 15% for those up to the age of 29; 20%

between 30 to 39; 25% between 40 to 49; 30% between 50 to 54; 35% between 55 to 59; and 40% above 60 years of age. Self-employed investors have a choice of investing either through personal pensions or through the more recent **Personal Retirement Savings Accounts (PRSAs),** introduced largely to encourage those in non-pensionable employment to take up retirement fund investment.

Proprietary directors of limited companies are entitled to make contributions into retirement funds capable of building up a fund value that in turn could notionally produce an income of two-thirds of €250,000 pa. This is subject to a cap on the value of retirement capital, which can be accumulated to €5m, above which marginal rate income tax charge applies.

If you are an **employee in non-pensionable** employment, in other words, an employee with a firm that does not have a staff pension scheme open to you, under law your employer is required to allow a salary deduction arrangement for you so that your contributions can be made into a PRSA *before* you get paid! The tax relief limits are the same as those for the self-employed, but are based on total taxable remuneration, that is salary plus bonuses and the taxable value of any benefits-in-kind. While income tax relief is the same as with the self-employed, PRSI and health levy relief is different. PRSI and health levy (Class A) for employees is 6% of the first €46,600 of PAYE earnings and 2% above. For the self-employed (Class S) it's 5% on all taxable profit.

Employees in employer-sponsored pension schemes, whether contributing or not, are entitled to invest in a parallel investment account known as an **Additional Voluntary Contribution (AVC).** The maximum level of contribution for tax relief purposes is the same as for those in non-pensionable employment putting money into PRSAs, less any contribution being made by the employee to the employer-sponsored pension scheme. Employer-sponsored pension schemes come in two very different varieties: the **Defined Contribution (DC)** scheme and the **Defined Benefit (DB)** scheme.

In **DC schemes** benefits at retirement age will be a direct function of the total capital accumulated on behalf of an employee through a combination of contributions and asset growth. There is no guarantee or promise to deliver a predetermined result. Group Company Pension Policies issued by life offices are commonly used to administer these DC schemes but not exclusively, so sometimes administration is handled independently of life offices. Individual Company Pension policies are the primary administration tool used for company schemes with one member – in large firms it's usually executives who would prefer their arrangements to be kept separate from the main group, while in small firms it's employees.

In **DB schemes** benefits are linked directly to the years of service accumulated 'on the clock' by retirement age. In the private sector the typical formula clocks up a guaranteed pension income based on replacement of final salary at a rate of 1.66% (or 1/60) per year of service, subject to a maximum of 67% (or 2/3) of final salary. This in turn is dependent on 10 years of service by normal retirement age, with a reduced sliding scale for fewer years' service. Tax-free cash is available, but is restricted to 150% of final salary and is dependent on accumulating 20 years of service by retirement. Where this is exercised, the maximum pension income payable is reduced.

In the public sector the formula is typically based on replacing 1.25% (1/80) per year of service, subject to a maximum pension payable of 50% of final salary. For service of less than 10 years there is a reducing scale. In addition, a tax-free cash lump sum of 150% of final salary is paid subject to 20 years of service accumulated by retirement age.

DB schemes – sometimes called **Occupational Pensions**, or **Superannuation Pensions** – remove investment risk from the shoulders of the investor and pass it to the employer. It is the employer's responsibility to ensure that fund assets are capable of meeting the liabilities created by the guarantees in the scheme. Regular actuarial assessment and reports determine the scale of surpluses or deficits in private sector schemes. In the public sector the liability is covered by the tax-payer and paid out of current tax revenues.

Retirement funds: why investing is a priority

First, the tax model for retirement funds is highly attractive, creating a long-term deferral of tax payments. Contributions to the fund can be written off against income tax. For the top rate (42%) tax-payer this means getting over €170 worth of value for every net €100 invested. The equivalent value for the low rate tax-payer is about €125 for every €100 invested. Contributions also avoid PRSI and health levies.

Secondly, the wide range of fund choices available in the modern market provides investors with an array of asset choice, including equities, bonds, cash deposits and property, as well as geared investment in syndicated property schemes. A common choice is to invest in a balanced fund with a mix of the four main asset classes.

Thirdly, retirement funds are tax-exempt under Irish law. This means that income can be generated within the fund from interest, rents and dividends without paying income tax, and gains can be made on trading assets without triggering CGT. It is only when cash is physically created out of the fund at retirement age that tax becomes payable at your marginal rate of tax.

Whichever way you look at it, it is a highly attractive model under which to accumulate assets, the only downside being that your assets are, of course, tied up until retirement age, typically between ages 60 and 75.

Don't be put off by the complexity of the market, its segments and rules: you should invest as much as you possibly can to benefit from maximum tax relief. In practice, although tax relief allowances can be generous, how much you will invest each year will be restricted by your cash flow. Those in paid employment have a reasonable degree of certainty about how much they can commit to retirement fund investment, but the self-employed and proprietary directors are typically unsure until financial accounts are prepared at the end of the tax year.

Proprietary directors of limited companies are in a unique

situation to boost contributions into retirement funds so that they have the capacity to replace up to 67% of final remuneration. The maximum fund that can be accumulated is capped at €5 million, above which top rate tax is applied. Final remuneration is defined as the average real remuneration over any three consecutive years within 10 years of retirement age. The maximum rate of funding is usually a significant multiple of that which is available to the self-employed. This is one of the advantages of having a limited company structure around a trading business.

This feature is of particular advantage to owner directors of trading companies that are making excess profits that would otherwise be subject to Corporation Tax. Particularly for older investors, where time frames to retirement age are short, the annual contribution could be a multiple of annual salary. Professional advice is recommended on these matters.

Understanding product jargon

Personal pensions

Commonly called personal pensions in Ireland, these are **retirement annuity policies** issued by domestic life offices and created by a single premium or recurring premiums.

PRSAs

Portable Retirement Savings Accounts, or PRSAs, are very similar to personal pensions and can be issued by any qualified PRSA provider. In practice, few firms other than life offices are keen on PRSAs because the product is aimed at the low paid and non-pensionable part of the economy where distribution costs are high and take-up rates are poor. In order to prevent rip-off charges, the regulator, the Pensions Board, introduced a pricing benchmark called a **'Standard' PRSA**. To comply, the product must not bite off more than 5% of every contribution and the fund management charge must not exceed 1% pa. Where the effect of charges is higher than the 'Standard' model, a special declaration needs to be signed by the investor.

AVCs

Additional Voluntary Contributions, or AVC plans, are typically issued as unit-linked pension policies, but not always so. Pension firms can administer them separately on behalf of the Trustees of the main employer-sponsored pension scheme. Even though you may be a member of an employer-sponsored pension scheme, you do not automatically qualify to take out an AVC, especially where your years of service in the occupational pension scheme are likely to lead you to the maximum pension ceiling. The purpose of AVCs is to plug the gap between what would be potentially payable out of an employer-sponsored pension scheme and the maximum allowed under pension legislation. It's important to take advice before commencing an AVC. Do not take up an AVC if you are a member of a Defined Benefit scheme, whether in the public or private sector, which lets you buy a higher, guaranteed future pension directly from the scheme. Taking up this option is likely to be a far more efficient use of your money than investing in an AVC.

Leaving an employer-sponsored pension scheme

When an employee leaves an employer-sponsored pension scheme, they may be offered a transfer value into a new employer scheme or into a retirement bond. As a general rule, transfer values should not be taken from occupational (DB) schemes. Instead the scheme member should opt for the payment of a deferred pension at retirement age. Typically, transfer values price against the exiting member, providing a capital sum that is unlikely to replicate the lost pension guarantee at retirement age, except by taking a high degree of investment risk.

Retirement bonds are used to hold transfer values from employer-sponsored (DC) pension schemes as opposed to the alternative, which is to leave your assets behind to percolate away as an ex-employee by continuing as a scheme member until retirement age or transferring your money to a new employer-sponsored pension scheme. The advantage of a retirement bond is that it transfers the assets from the old scheme into a single premium retirement bond policy issued by a life office, with all of the prevailing fund choices available. A new employer-sponsored scheme is likely to offer similar fund choice for the transfer value.

Small self-administered pension schemes (SSAPs)

Also called Self-Administered Retirement Trusts (SARTs), these are used by proprietary directors to set up DIY pension arrangements. Strict rules surround the operation of these schemes, especially in relation to borrowing, to self-investment and to over-concentration in illiquid assets, like shares in private companies. Schemes can only be established by Pensioneer Trustees authorised by the Revenue Commissioners, and have strict reporting obligations both to Revenue and to the Pensions Board. A Trust documentation sets up a scheme and annual financial accounts are part of reporting requirements.

The advantage of SSAPs is that they allow a proprietary director to by-pass the choices normally available from pension polices administered by domestic life offices. Whether this results in higher returns long term is determined by the hands-on approach taken by the proprietary director in investing in alternative investment strategies, or more focused investment. Proprietary directors with particular skills in investment in, for example, equities or property, may do well, but it is not guaranteed.

In practice, there has been significant over-selling and over-hyping of SSAPs, based on the misconception that these schemes are a gateway into geared investment in property. Many schemes remain in underperforming assets and cash deposits for the very simple reason that the investor lacks either the time or the skill to drive the investment.

Strict rules related to borrowing effectively prevent direct investment in geared property. These rules disallow the use of interest-only mortgages and restrict capital repayment mortgages to terms no longer than 15 years. In addition, scheme assets other than the rental from the property may not be used to service borrowings, potentially triggering the forced liquidation of the property in the event of a default in tenant rents. SSAPs are also prevented from taking anything but nominal shareholding in small limited companies and unit trusts, in order to prevent these structures from being used to overly concentrate SSAP assets.

Generally, setting up a SSAP costs between €3,000 and €5,000, plus VAT. Administrating SSAPs also requires fees, which are best paid on an annual flat fee per time basis. Proprietary directors should not use Pensioneer Trustees and Administrators who charge for administration on the basis of a percentage of assets. This should only be used to pay for asset management or good advice – definitely not for administration.

What should proprietary directors do?

Proprietary directors should not establish a SSAP unless significant amounts of transfers from their limited companies or existing retirement funds can be taken, so that scale can be built that will result in the type of economies that make SSAPs an efficient investment. Neither should a SSAP be undertaken unless it is clear that added value can be created by alternative investment strategies. This is easier said than done.

The alternative for proprietary directors is to use unit-linked executive pension policies – ideally set up on nil initial commission terms to minimise entry costs – and to spread investment across a range of funds using different asset managers. In this way administration reporting, etc., is delegated to the more efficient administration units of life offices, which allows you to benefit from centralised economies of scale and reduces the drag effect of charges. This is particularly suitable for low to modest annual contributions from limited companies.

Investment strategies

Investing in retirement funds is no different from investing in any other fund and the rate of asset performance over the long term will be determined by which assets you choose through the various fund choices available.

Life offices dominate the market for Personal pensions, PRSAs and AVCs. These investments are issued as pension policies, holding units in unit-linked funds, the workings of which were covered in the last chapter. Proprietary directors of limited companies have traditionally chosen to invest through pension policies, but they can also choose to take a DIY approach by establishing **Small Self-Administered Pension Schemes**, or opting for a type of pension policy that can be self-directed through life offices.

Investment choice is not in the hands of members of occupational pensions (DB) schemes. The asset mix will be determined by the Trustees of the scheme on the advice of investment managers and consulting actuaries. These schemes usually contain a mix of assets, much like a balanced fund. Investors in these schemes need only concern themselves with the health of the scheme and whether or not assets held by the scheme are meeting accruing liabilities. This can be determined from the annual set of financial accounts produced on these schemes and from periodic actuarial reports.

Due to the recent downturn, which principally affected equity values, this being the main asset used by these schemes, many occupational pension schemes are running large deficits that can only be bridged by extraordinary bounce-back in asset values, or a very significant increase in annual funding from employers in the private sector.

In recent times the availability of DB schemes has diminished because a new accounting standard, known as FRS17, has placed the deficit or surplus of the schemes into the heart of the main balance sheet and profit and loss of the company. Those in public sector schemes need only concern themselves with the ability of the Government to continue to pay pensions, which will be a function of prevailing tax revenues. If you are in a DB scheme and are offered the option to buy back years of service, jump at it – these benefits are almost impossible to match through private investment elsewhere.

On retirement, should I buy a pension or invest in an ARF?

On retirement, if you surrender the vast bulk of your retirement capital to purchase a pension income (annuity), it's a one-way ticket and can't be reversed. Pension rates are determined by the average age of mortality, which is extending all the time and depressing pension rates, as well as by the rate of return on long Eurobonds. Historically low interest rates and extending life expectancies have very significantly depressed pension rates, increasing the popularity of Approved Retirement Funds as the alternative choice at retirement age.

The choice between pension annuities and ARFs is not black and white, however. Pension annuities pass investment risk directly to the annuity provider, typically a life office, which has particular advantages during times of uncertainty. If you are at retirement age and considering both options, you would do well to seek professional financial advice to ensure you make the right decision.

Increased pension annuity rates may be available where there is a significantly reduced life expectancy as a consequence of ill-health. Known as **Impaired Life Annuities,** these require medical underwriting to assess the reduced mortality of the investor. While this will bring certainty of income at higher rates than normal pension annuities, Impaired Life Annuities are no panacea and choosing the ARF option may be more appropriate. Again, it would be advisable to get professional help to assess your particular situation.

ARFs can be issued by any qualifying ARF provider. At present the market is dominated by life office offerings, but more and more specialist intermediaries, private banks and stockbrokers have acquired ARF licences, stimulating competition and choice.

The advantage of an ARF is that you can choose when and how much you wish to draw down from your ARF, incurring tax at your marginal rate. To encourage minimum withdrawals of at least 3% of assets, an annual tax at the investor's marginal tax rate is to be applied to a notional withdrawal of 3% on ARFs, which make no distribution. This is an anti-accumulation tax rule, in place from 2006, scaling up from 1% of assets to 3%. The marginal rate of tax will also apply to all asset values above €5 million, a ceiling that will be indexed as the years roll by.

When, by retirement age, an investor has pension income elsewhere, including the Old Age Pension, that amounts to less than €12,700 pa, the first €63,500 of retirement capital must be placed into an Approved Minimum Retirement Fund (AMRF), which is an ARF with a special restriction. Growth can be withdrawn each year from an AMRF, but the capital value must not fall below €63,500 until at least age 75. This provision is in place to prevent those with very low amounts of retirement capital in ARFs from blowing it prematurely. Unlike the United States, which also has continuing investment after retirement age and where there are very strict rules with regards to how much can be drawn down, no such rules apply in Ireland. This makes the ARF model both attractive and dangerous.

Special care needs to be taken when choosing between ARFs, particularly where there is high volatility in assets, to avoid accelerated capital erosion when fixed rates of withdrawal are taken at a time of depressed asset values. ARF investors can choose at any stage to surrender ARF capital in return for a pension annuity, a choice that is likely to become more common as rates improve due to advanced years.

What happens if I die before retirement?

If you have invested in personal pensions or PRSAs, the current value of the fund can be payable into your Estate tax-free. For employer-sponsored schemes and SSAPs the maximum payout is restricted to an amount no more than four times remuneration plus a return of contributions paid by the member. Any balance in scheme assets above this level can be used to purchase a spouse's pension, restricted to a maximum of no more than 44.44% of current salary. There is also provision to pay out dependants' pensions at no more than 22.2% of current salary until dependants reach adulthood.

What happens when I die after retirement?

Assets held in **ARFs** may be transferred to a spouse tax-free, but on the ultimate distribution to children, income tax will be paid on the value of the ARF in the final year and any residual balance will not be subject to Capital Acquisitions Tax.

A **single life pension annuity**, whether level or escalating in payment, will cease on the death of the annuity holder (annuitant), or when a maximum number of annual pension payments have been made, usually no more than 5 or 10 following retirement age. Where a **joint life pension annuity** is chosen, the pension will transfer to the other annuitant, usually a spouse, at rates of between 50% and 67%.

Can I take my money before retirement age?

Tax relief is given on pension contributions for one reason, and that is to encourage the build-up of retirement capital and the provision of pension income by retirement age. Rules are strict with regards to access to assets before this time, however special provisions apply to retirement due to ill-health. If this happens, the current value of holdings in personal pensions and PRSAs may be available.

Members of occupational pension schemes may be entitled to pension payments at a scale equal to the pension they would have earned had they remained in employment until retirement age. This is the maximum benefit, but scheme rules may limit it further.

Other rules

There is a bunch of other arcane rules relating to things like the transferability of assets across different types of pension scheme and what happens if you break the ceilings. But, to be honest, it would take up a complete tome to list and explain them all. It would also run the risk of flat-lining even the most analytical reader! You should refer any detailed questions to a qualified pension advisor.

You will see now why pension rules in Ireland are such a mess, but this should not deter you from maximising the amount of assets that can be accumulated by utilising your annual allowances fully, choosing good investments and doing things well. If you find the whole thing too confusing – which almost seems to be the intent of the rules – sniff out a good pensions consultant to guide you; refer to Chapter 8, 'Choosing a Good Investment Advisor'. But no more excuses! Use the tax relief to your maximum advantage to build a retirement asset shelter as close to that cool €5 million as you can get! If you're starting today from zero, just look at all the space you have!

Here are three retirement fund stories, but there are tons of other examples. These will illustrate some of what we've been talking about:

Case study 1

Deirdre is a teacher in a national school, but a late arrival to the profession. By the time she reaches the retirement age of the occupational scheme she holds, she will have accumulated 30 years' service, resulting in a pension of 37.5% of final salary and a tax-free cash lump sum of 112·5% of final salary at age 65.'If only I could get the max,' Deirdre thinks, 'that 40 years of service brings: a pension of 50% of final salary and tax-free cash of 150%.' Deirdre first explores any possibility of buying the extra years of service from the scheme directly. Failing this, she takes out an AVC, putting in as much as she can while getting tax relief. When she reaches age 65, the superannuation scheme will pay her pension of 37·5% of salary and tax-free cash of 112·5% of final salary. Deirdre can then use her AVC to first top up the tax-free cash to 150% of final salary and buy a top-up pension with what's left over. Alternatively, the remainder can continue as investment through an ARF.

Case study 2

Joan, Deirdre's friend, works with a small local firm that doesn't have an employer sponsored pension scheme. Joan hears about Deirdre's new long-term focus and decides she, too, wants into this tax-efficient model of building assets. Joan has the choice of investing through a personal pension, or through a PRSA. The maximum tax-relievable contribution is based on her age. As she's 39, it's 20% of her remuneration, but on her next birthday, when she turns 40, she can up it to 25% of her remuneration. At retirement age, Joan will have the same options Deirdre has with her AVC. Joan can choose to take her benefits at any stage between age 60 and 75.

Case study 3

Of equal age, Michael and Felicity are fellow shareholder directors of their limited company. The company is beginning to make surplus money – more than enough to pay them good wages and

> fund expansion. They've never had a pension scheme before, so they decide to set up a scheme into which company transfers can be made at very high levels each year and written off as a trading expense. Their remuneration from the company is €200,000 each and they've both got fifteen years to go before retirement age.
>
> Under pension legislation they're entitled to fund towards 67% of their earnings of €200,000, which is the earnings cap for a pensionable salary. That's a pension of a little over €134,000 a year each. The calculation comes back from their advisor: the funding rate for each can begin at 100% of current earnings. Had they invested, like Joan, into personal pensions or a PRSA, they would have been restricted to 25% of €254,000 or €63,500 until reaching age 50. They now have the choice of investing in assets through a Self-Administered Retirement Trust, or through executive pension policies from life offices. At retirement age they'll have the same option of either buying a pension or continuing on with ARFs after taking a tax-free cash lump sum of 25% of the fund, subject to a limit of €1.25 million in real money terms today. Any surplus over €5 million in real money terms today, before taking the tax-free cash, will be taxed at 42%.

That's quite enough of all that! Next time you watch Ripley being chased around the spaceship, remember: she wins. Although the powers-that-be have made pension rules as alien as possible, it's still a fantastic way to accumulate assets in a long-term retirement shelter, so you can win, too. If you're a member of a superannuation scheme, especially in the public sector where unions stand guard over future benefits, get down on your hands and knees and say a prayer for your good fortune – because outside it's every man, woman and alien for themself!

Conclusion

Loot! can't catch the fish for you, but you now have a fishing rod and you should know how to fish! If you've learned the key points outlined here, then the world of investment planning should look at lot clearer and you can now venture into the market with a new vision of what's on offer and what might suit you best.

Just consider the jump in your understanding from start to finish. You now know the basics about the major asset classes, how they might behave and reward you. You know how to approach investment property and what to ask, and you have the tools to unravel the once-mystifying world of shares. Would you ever have thought it? Hey, and wasn't it easier than you expected? After all, you can now talk turkey (or fish) and hold your own with financial salespeople and advisors. They'll quickly discern you know the territory and the lingo, so watch charges fall and mediocre investments fly back into the briefcase to be replaced by better value offerings.

And what about our starting point: the SSIA? Don't be surprised if you've changed your mind about blowing your SSIA money. With a bit of luck, that change of mind will be coupled with a new tolerance to take investment risk and chase after higher returns now that you have a long-term view that takes you beyond short-term events and restricted products. You never know, to the surprise of your friends you might yet become engrossed by business stories and economic debates – scanning the finance pages with the same fervour you used to devote yourself to the sports, health and social columns. That's good, because money and how it works drives just about everything – including newspapers!

Thanks for reading *Loot!* Good luck with the money-making and money-saving – I hope you do plenty of both!

Eilie